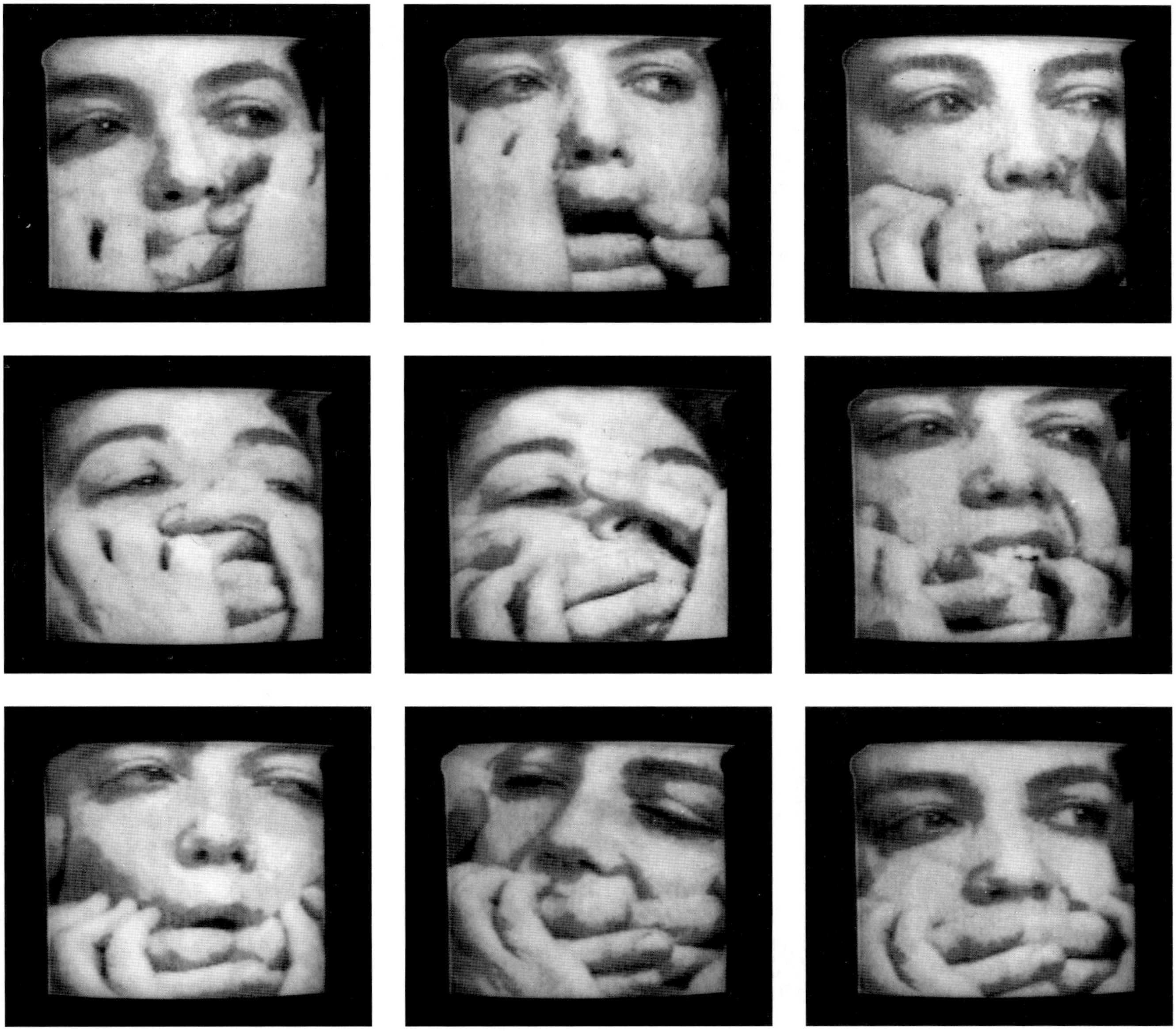

In memory of Edward W. Said (1935–2003)

Mona Hatoum

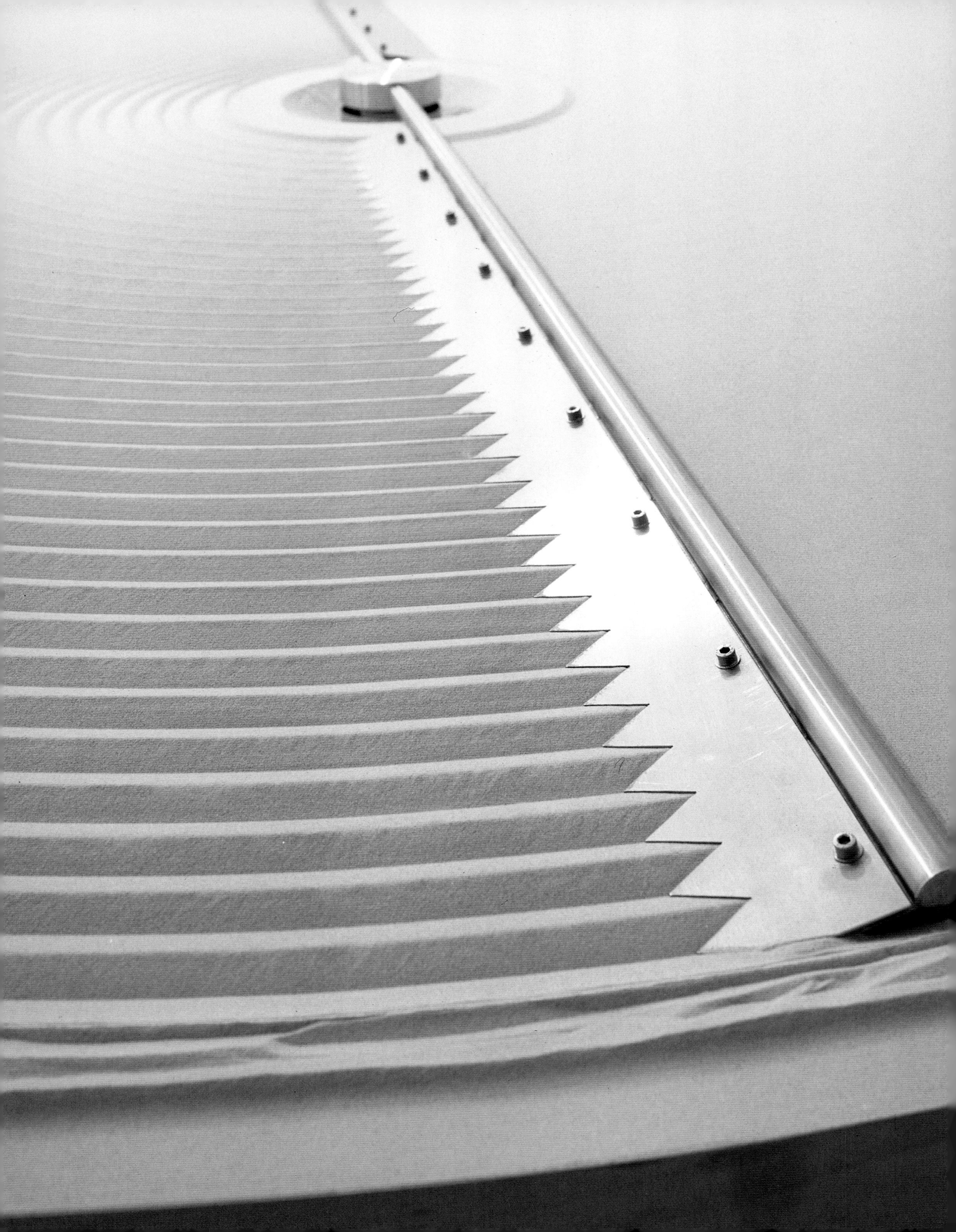

Mona Hatoum

Hamburger Kunsthalle
Kunstmuseum Bonn
Magasin 3 Stockholm Konsthall

Hatje Cantz Publishers

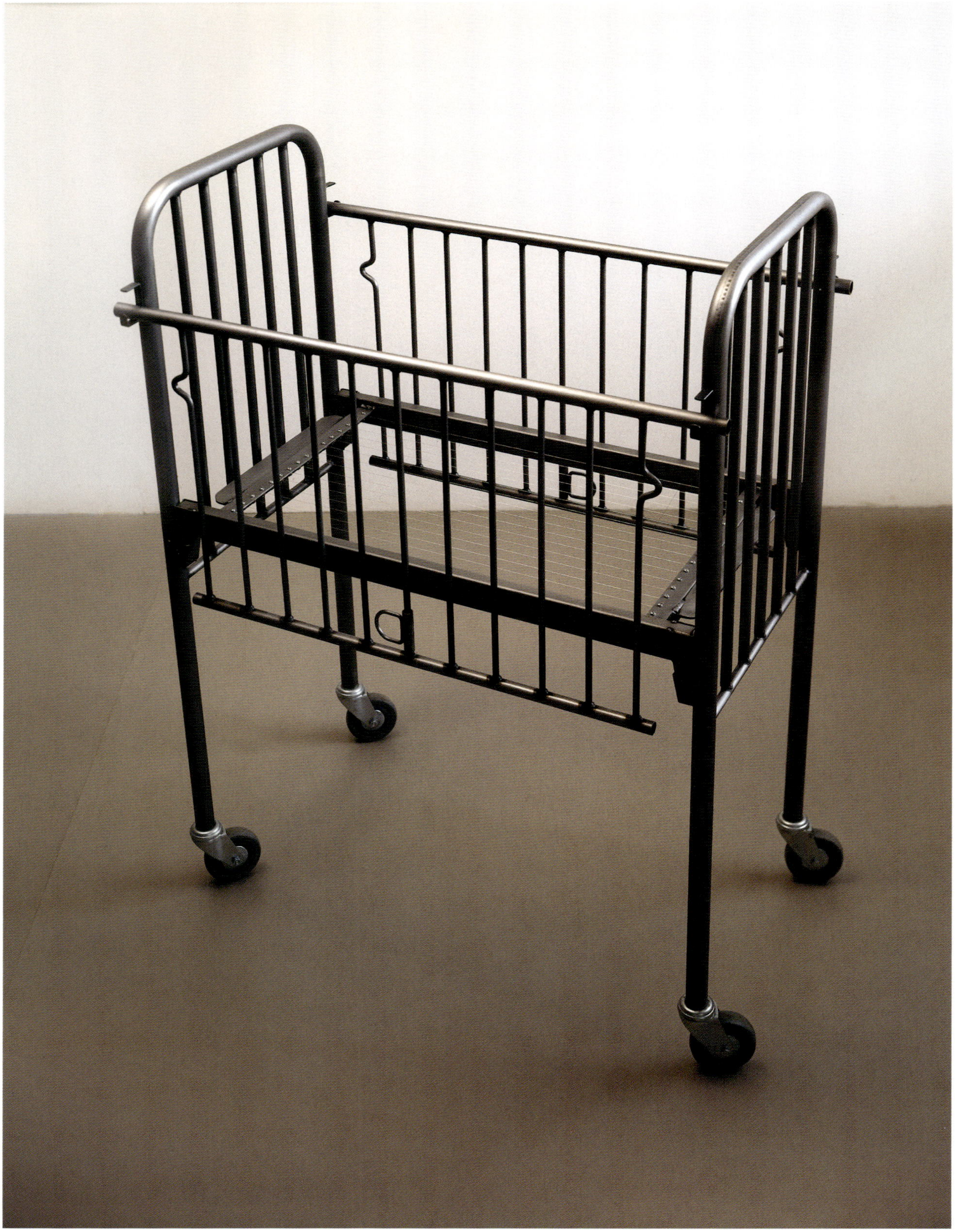

Incommunicado · 1993

Contents

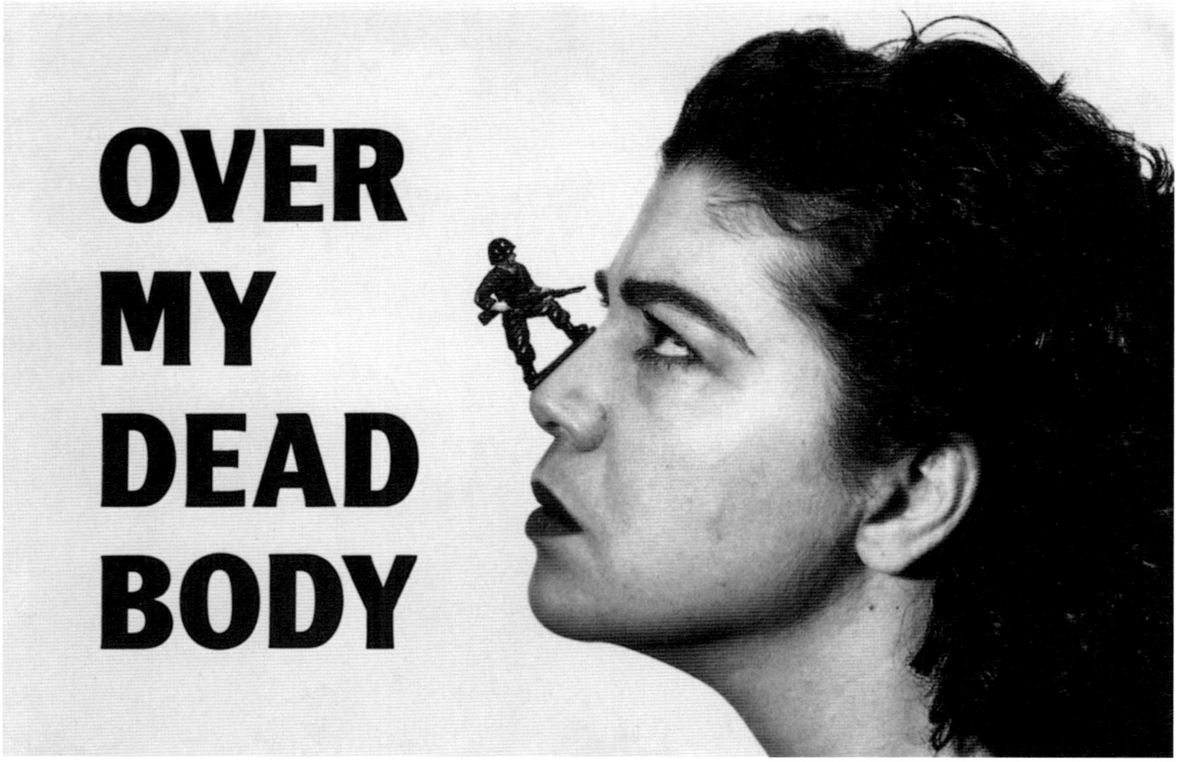

 Over My Dead Body · 1988

Foreword

Life on the move, away from her home country, has made Mona Hatoum sensitive to matters pertaining to power relationships and questions of identity. She was born in Lebanon in 1952, the daughter of Palestinian parents, and has been living in London since 1975. In her sculpture, video, and installation work she repeatedly addresses the vulnerability of the individual in relation to the violence inherent in institutional power structures. Her primary point of reference is the human body, sometimes using her own body – not only in her performances, but also in her video works and installations.

The relationship between artwork and viewer is constantly the subject of reflection in Hatoum's œuvre. This theme is already present in her early performances, which are the focus of particular attention in this publication. Hatoum's performances, especially between 1980 and 1988, exhibit a wide repertory of ideas and forms which act as a precursor to her later sculptures and installations. We gradually follow the direction of the path from the ephemeral aspect of the performance work to video and permanent installations. This book is the first to offer a comprehensive catalogue of her performance work.

Since the early nineties, Hatoum has been producing large installations which succeed in arousing in the viewer contradictory feelings of attraction and repulsion, fear and fascination. *Light Sentence, Corps étranger, Quarters, Home* and *Homebound* are some of her most ambitious installations and are included in this exhibition. These key works combine performative and interactive approaches of her early years with a formal language that derives its vocabulary from Minimalist sculpture and Conceptual Art, which at the same time is charged with personal and political content.

Mona Hatoum commits herself totally and literally to her art. Her choice of particular materials is arrived at in relation to the content, and the range of materials she uses appears to be completely inexhaustible: steel and plastic, textiles and soap, electricity and magnetism, found household utensils and disposable items, glass and rubber ... Hatoum thus fashions an artistic language in which familiar everyday commodities are transformed into strange and threatening devices. This survey exhibition of Hatoum's work takes this diversity into account.

The impetus behind this exhibition at the Hamburger Kunsthalle was provided by an unusual enrichment of the collection: In 2002, the F. und W. Stiftung für zeitgenössische Kunst in der Hamburger Kunsthalle responded to the desire to acquire the video installation *Deep Throat* for the Galerie der Gegenwart. The Kunstmuseum Bonn had also been planning for some time to organise an exhibition of Mona Hatoum's work. Magasin 3 Stockholm Konsthall had been a long-time follower of Mona Hatoum's work and began acquiring her artwork for its collection in the early nineties. The common interest in her work presented an opportunity for these institutions to collaborate on this major survey exhibition. For each of the three venues Hatoum will be creating a new site-specific work.

We would like to thank the national and international lenders for their generous support of this exhibition: Ingvild Goetz and Rainald Schumacher of the Sammlung Goetz, Munich; Prof. Dr. Dr. Thomas Olbricht and Wolfgang Schoppmann of the Sammlung Olbricht, Essen; Miuccia Prada and Astrid Welter, Milan; Alfred Pacquement and Christine van Assche of the Centre Georges Pompidou, Paris; Claude Allemand-Cosneau of the Fonds National d'Art Contemporain, Puteaux; Jay Jopling and Alexandra Bradley of Jay Jopling / White Cube, London; Carolyn Alexander and Theodore Bonin of Alexander and Bonin, New York; Pontus Bonnier, Stockholm; Jan Widlund, Stockholm; Lars Nittve and Margareta Helleberg of Moderna Museet, Stockholm. We would also like to extend our thanks to Claes Nordenhake and Bettina Pehrsson of Galerie Nordenhake Stockholm/Berlin. Thanks also to Gerry Collins and Kira van Lil for their support and assistance.

Organising the exhibition in Hamburg would not have been possible without the financial support of Kathryn Board and Dr. Elke Ritt of the British Council.

Research for the catalogue has been generously supported by the ZEIT-Stiftung Ebelin und Gerd Bucerius, Hamburg.

The Kunstmuseum Bonn is very grateful for the support from Kunststiftung NRW.

Magasin 3 Stockholm Konsthall wishes to express its gratitude to Robert Weil and Proventus AB.

We would also like to thank *die tageszeitung, taz nord*, the media partner for the Hamburg venue.

The new installation Mona Hatoum created for the Hamburger Kunsthalle Dome was supported by Videotronic Nord, to whom we thank Hans-Jürgen Pott and Marcus Plüschau.

Since April 2003, Mona Hatoum has been working in Berlin as a recipient of a DAAD scholarship. Thanks are due to the Berliner Künstlerprogramm/DAAD, in particular Friedrich Meschede, for their support.

We owe it above all to the artist that the first large-scale solo exhibition in Germany and Sweden is also the most comprehensive survey of her work to date. Mona Hatoum has not only generously lent several works for the exhibition, but also invested a lot of time and effort into it. She has produced new works and dedicatedly provided her assistance in documenting the sequence of events and background of the early performances. Without her dedication and her attention to detail, this exhibition would not have been possible.

Uwe M. Schneede
Christoph Heinrich
Hamburger Kunsthalle

Dieter Ronte
Volker Adolphs
Kunstmuseum Bonn

David Neuman
Richard Julin
Magasin 3 Stockholm Konsthall

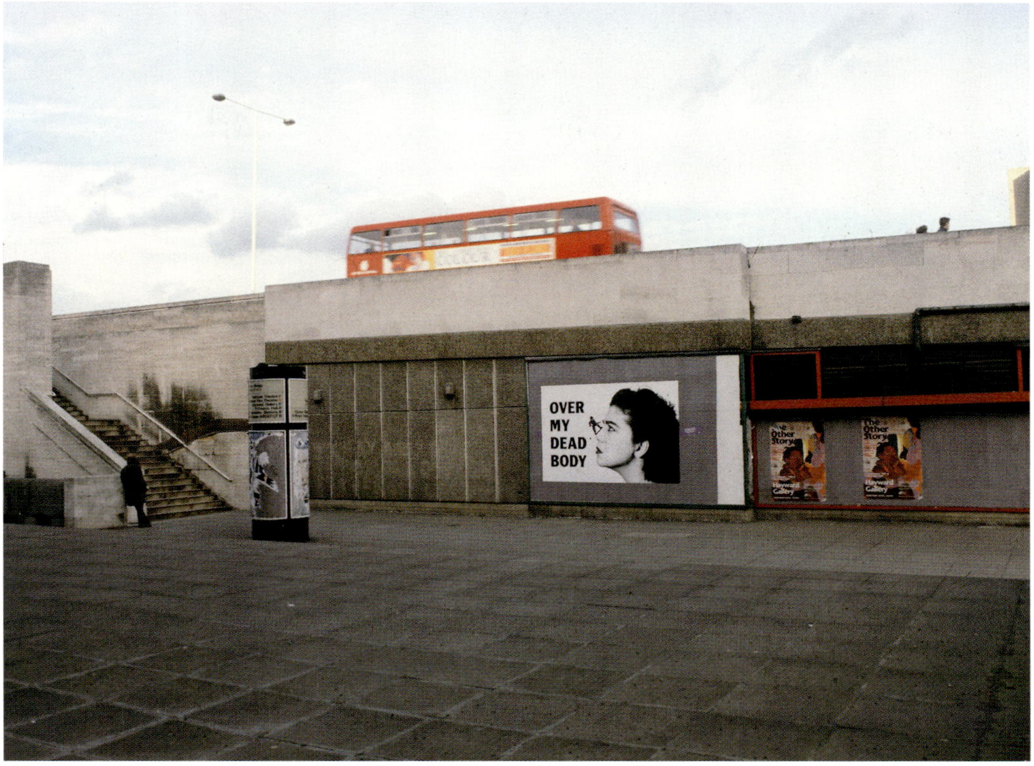

Over My Dead Body · 1988

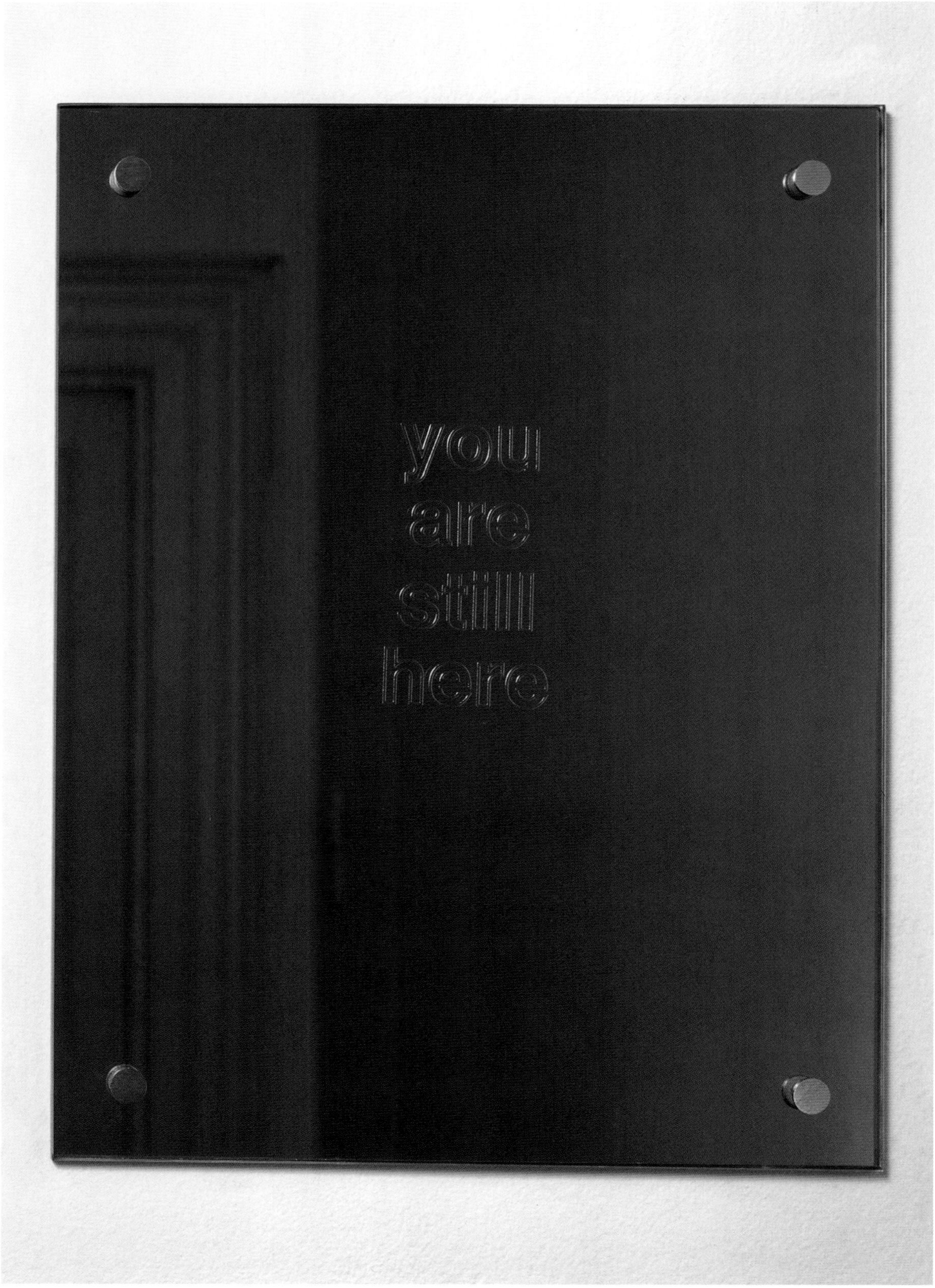

You are still here · 1994

Ursula Panhans-Bühler

Being Involved

You are still here (1994) is inscribed on a mirror, the letters outlined by subtle contours in which the light of the lettering breaks. *You* means 'us' – the visitors to the exhibition, both plural and singular, for the size of the mirror is that of a portrait photograph. There is something perplexing about this device; the moment we look at the writing, we are no longer looking at ourselves, and as soon as we look at ourselves, the letters appear on our face but are not read. Most perplexing of all is how surprised we are by the way the reflection seems, momentarily, to take on a life of its own when we look at the writing. We do not observe the gaze of the reflection directly. We become aware of it only in retrospect, with a sense of unease that translates into the following question: how much of the dramatically divided self have we left behind in that world beyond the mirror, where, as in Alice's famous excursion *Through the Looking Glass*, nothing is quite as it seems.

fig. p. 14 In a 1984 video, *Changing Parts*, Mona Hatoum alternates black and white photographs of an old bathroom, atmospheric details over which the camera slowly pans, with shots fig. pp. 93–95 from her 1982 performance *Under Siege*. It is a desperately extreme performance in which the artist struggles for seven hours to free herself from a container with semi-transparent polythene sheeting, repeatedly slipping and falling on the muddy clay that covers the floor. In the video, we find ourselves drawn inexorably towards the limits, even though this is now 'canned' footage. The screen seems to materialise through the opaque skin of the container and the dramatic tension between inside and outside appears increasingly direct. Between ourselves as onlookers and the young woman struggling to free herself – pressing her shoulders, cheeks and hands against the membrane of the polythene sheet, 'dressed' only in the slimy clay that cakes the film – the barrier suddenly becomes permeable. The fictional, in the form of the projection on the screen, and the material, in the form of the physical membrane, seem to change places in a perplexing alternation between wish and reality until we are no longer certain what or who belongs on which side, or even how.

In the late eighties, Hatoum abandoned performances as politically too direct and turned her attention instead to installations and objects, taking up some of the earlier ideas from her student days at the Slade School of Art in London. From now on, she put her trust in the kind of interactivity that lets the spectator become involved in the aesthetic experience without the presence of the artist herself as performer making her the focus of attention.

Her work, however, was no less radical for all that. Her installation *The Light at the End* fig. p. 15 at The Showroom in London in 1989 had a quite literal potential to shock: six vertical lines of light at the end of an ever narrowing, darkened room turned out to be unguarded electric heating bars mounted on a gate-like metal structure with bars. It posed not only a physical risk to visitors, but also an artistic

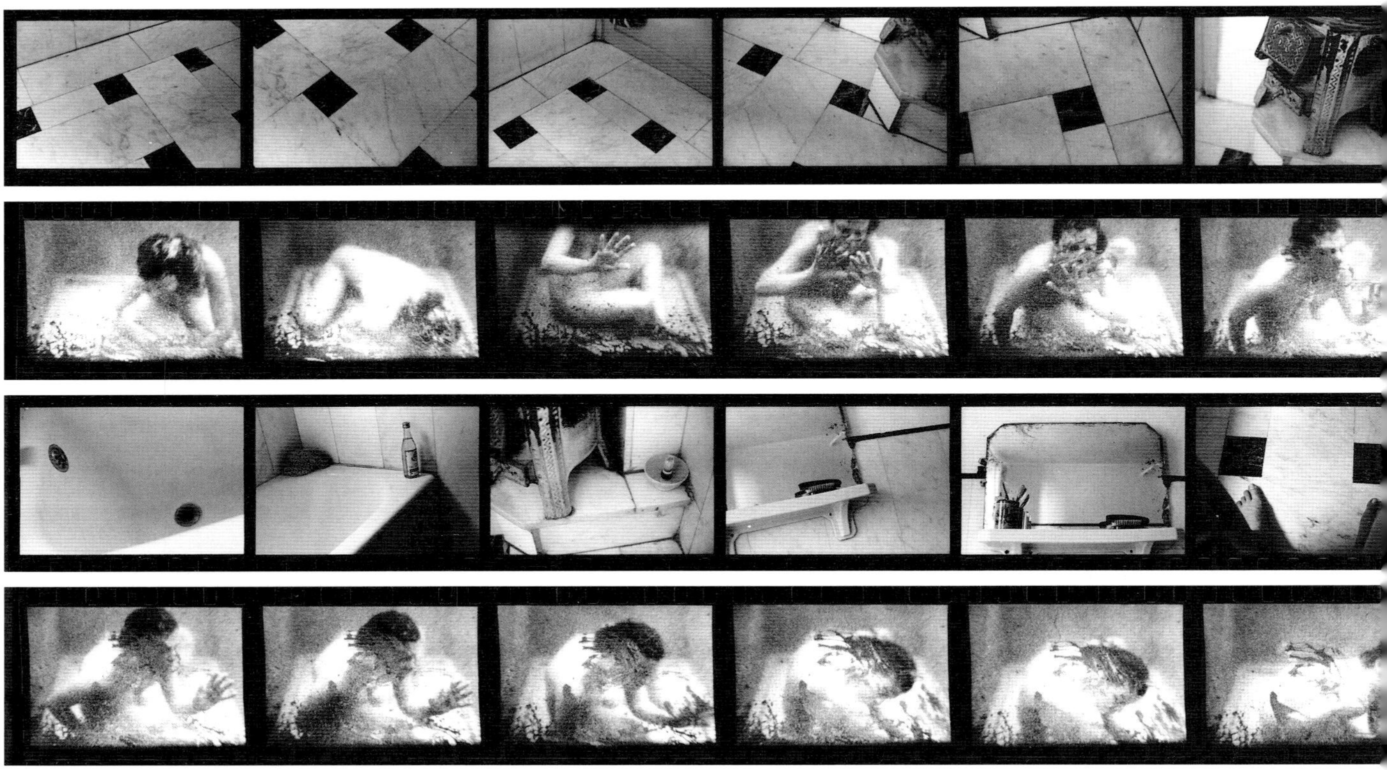

risk to Hatoum, for the interest it generated threatened to turn her into a secular Saint Laurence of today, her creativity doomed to martyrdom on an aesthetically perfect virtual grill. For a while, in spite of having made a culturally electrifying point about desire, she suddenly found galleries and museums showing an interest only in this particular work, or clamouring for something similar.

So it was some time before she was invited fig. pp. 16–17 to present her 1992 *Light Sentence* at Cardiff's Chapter gallery. Whereas, in *The Light at the End*, the electric glow actually involves the spectator physically, this time a single bare light bulb silently grasps at the shadow of any visitor daring to enter the U-shaped installation of office lockers (ordered readymade from a mail-order catalogue) piled six high, with casually opened doors. The light bulb that slowly descends and rises on its cable sets the shadows of the wire-mesh lockers in motion on the floor and walls in anamorphic distortion; as it reaches the floor and tips to one side, the shadows begin to tremble. On entering the strange, serial domicile, the visitor is drawn inexorably into this nocturnal *danse macabre* and, unable to resist the urge to try inhabiting the dizzyingly menacing atmosphere, loses all sense of balance in the moving sea of gridded shadows.

The wire-mesh lockers cast bizarrely three-dimensional shadows that dominate the room with their trompe l'œil effect, while the spectator caught in their midst becomes a flat silhouette, a shadow that does not even fit in at full length because of the discrepancy of scale between the room and those who enter it. The spectator's shadow, split over several

Changing Parts · 1984

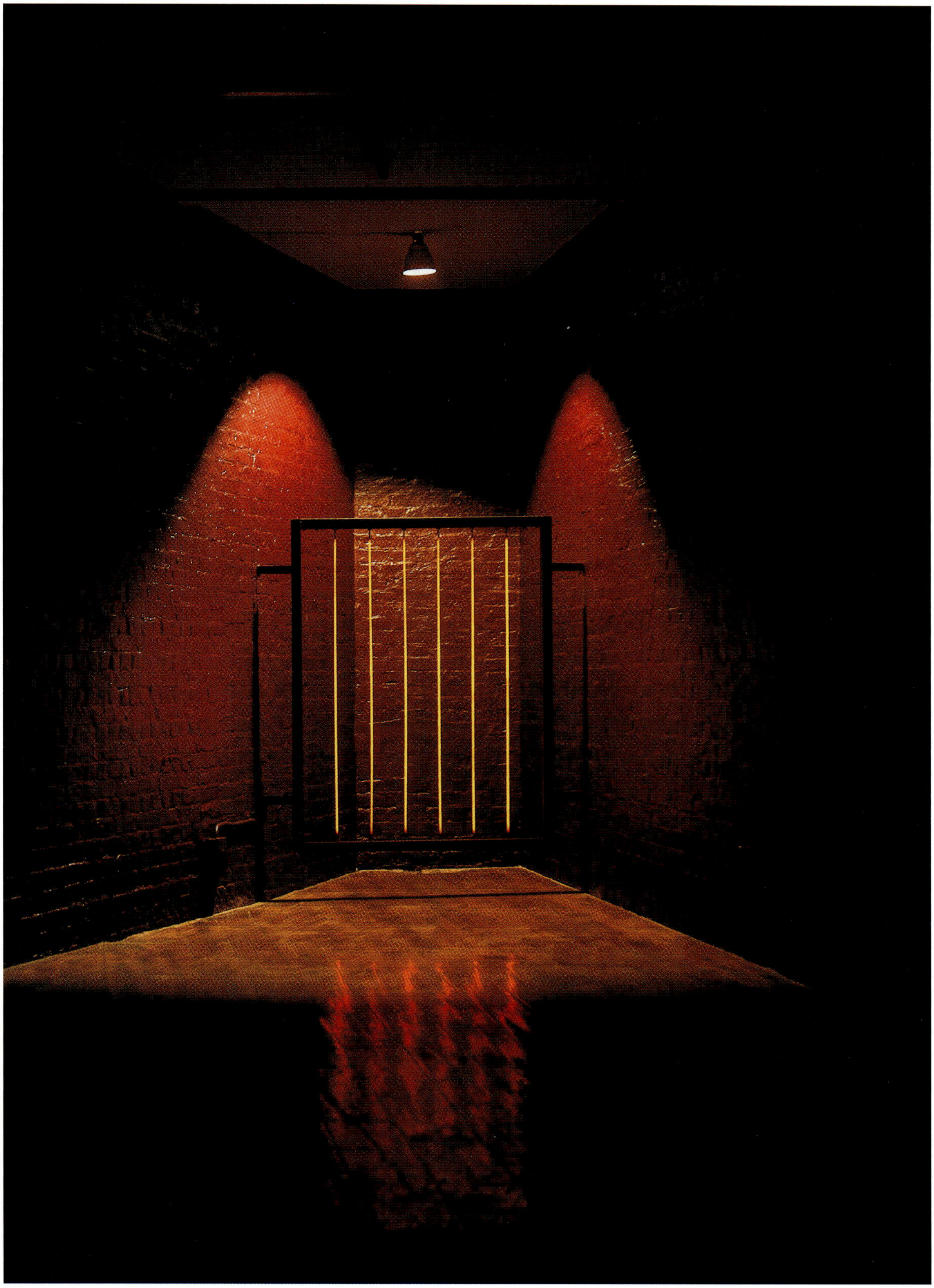

The Light at the End · 1989

Light Sentence · 1992 ▶

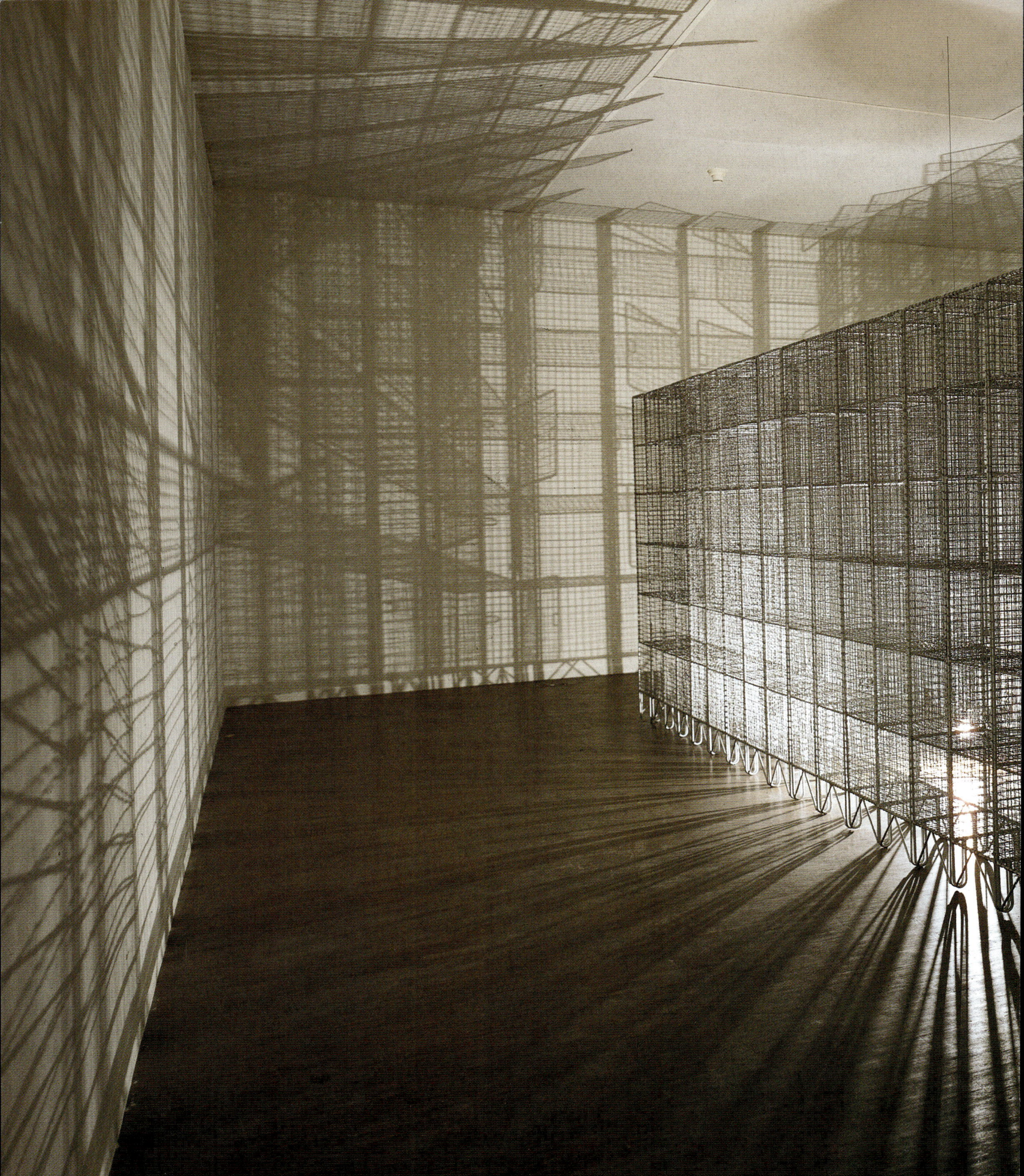

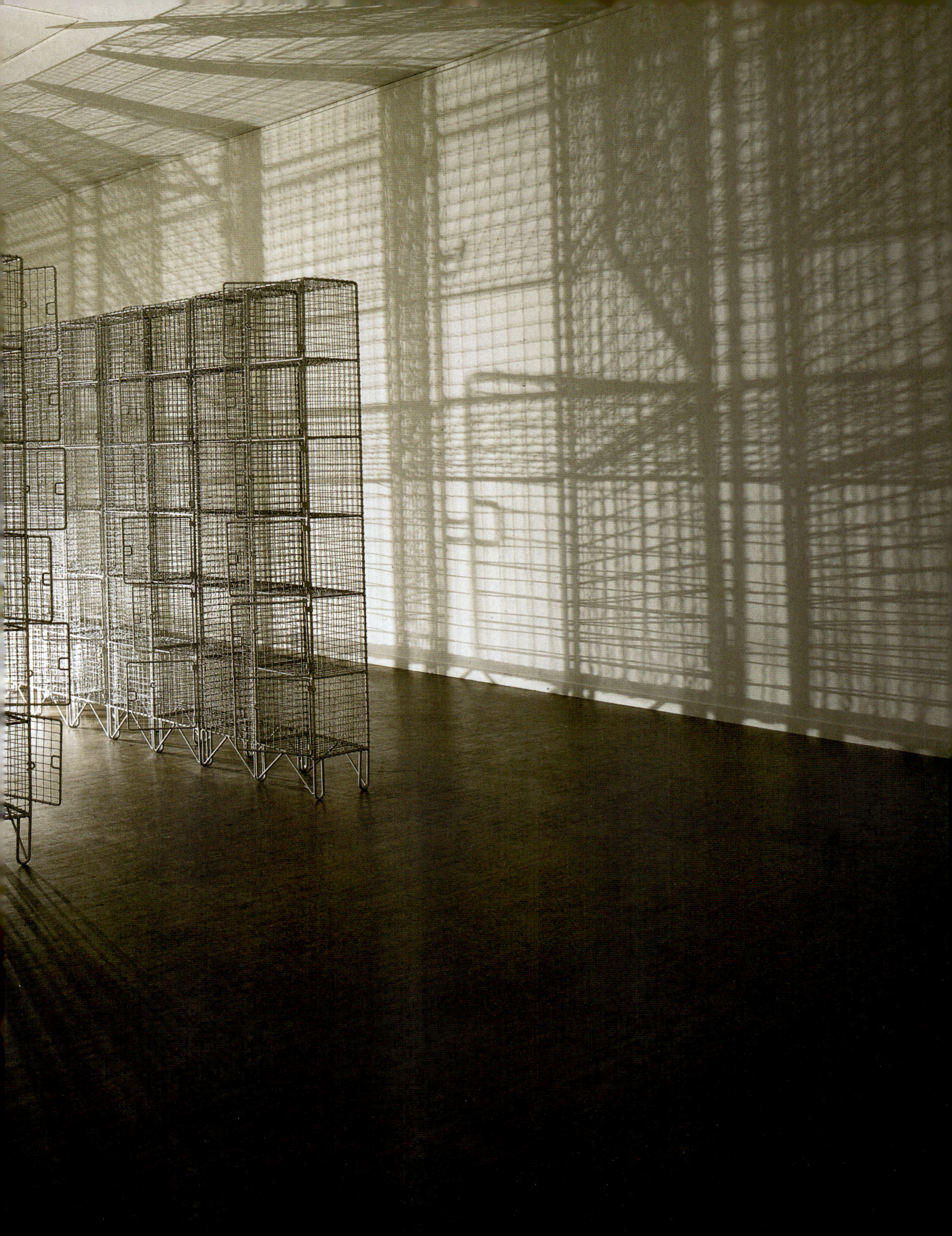

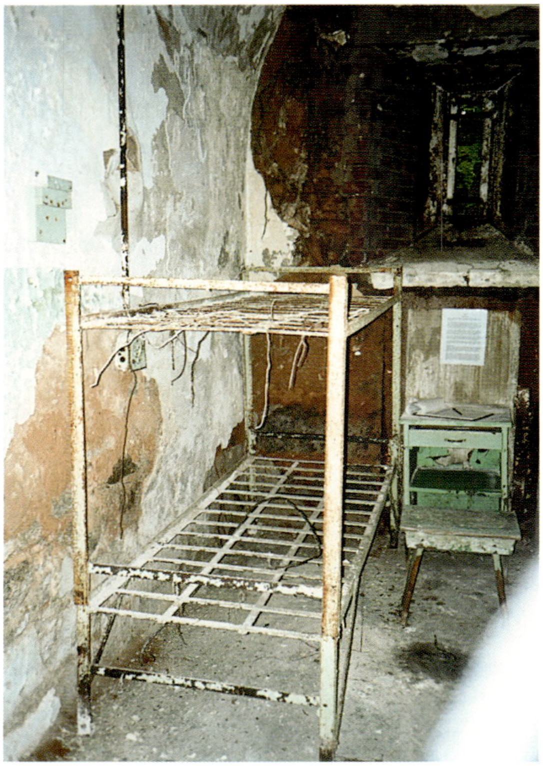

Eastern State Penitentiary · 1995
(artist's snapshot)

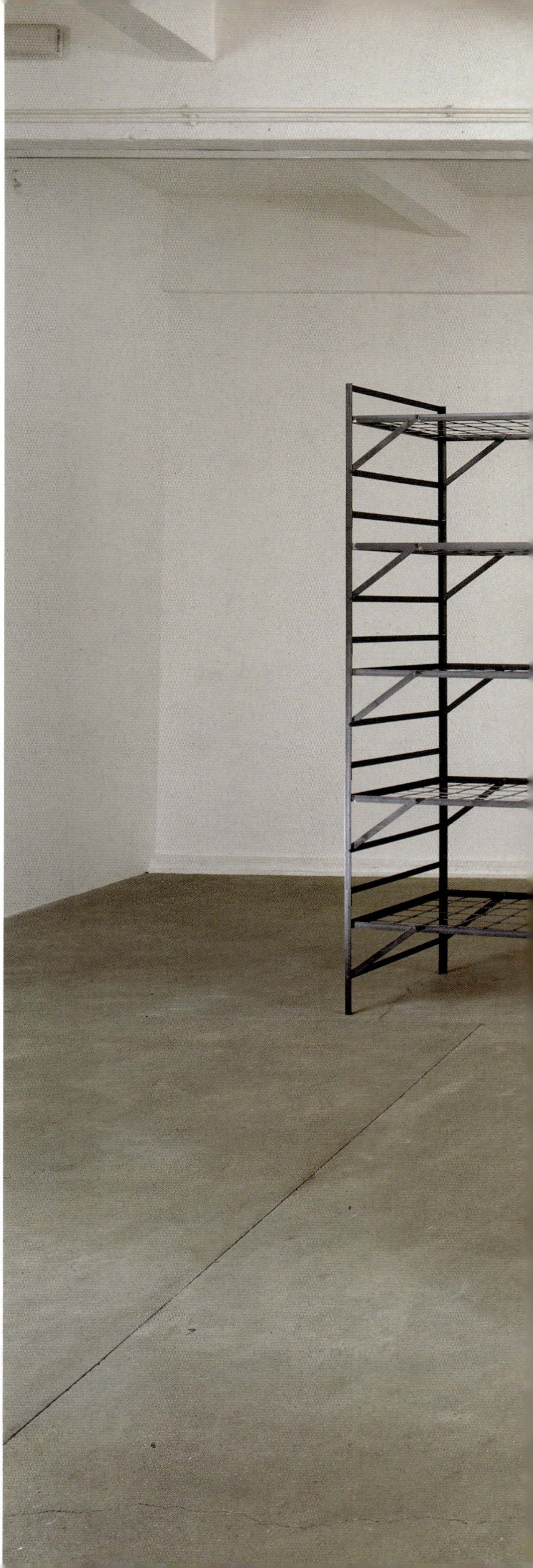

Quarters · 1996

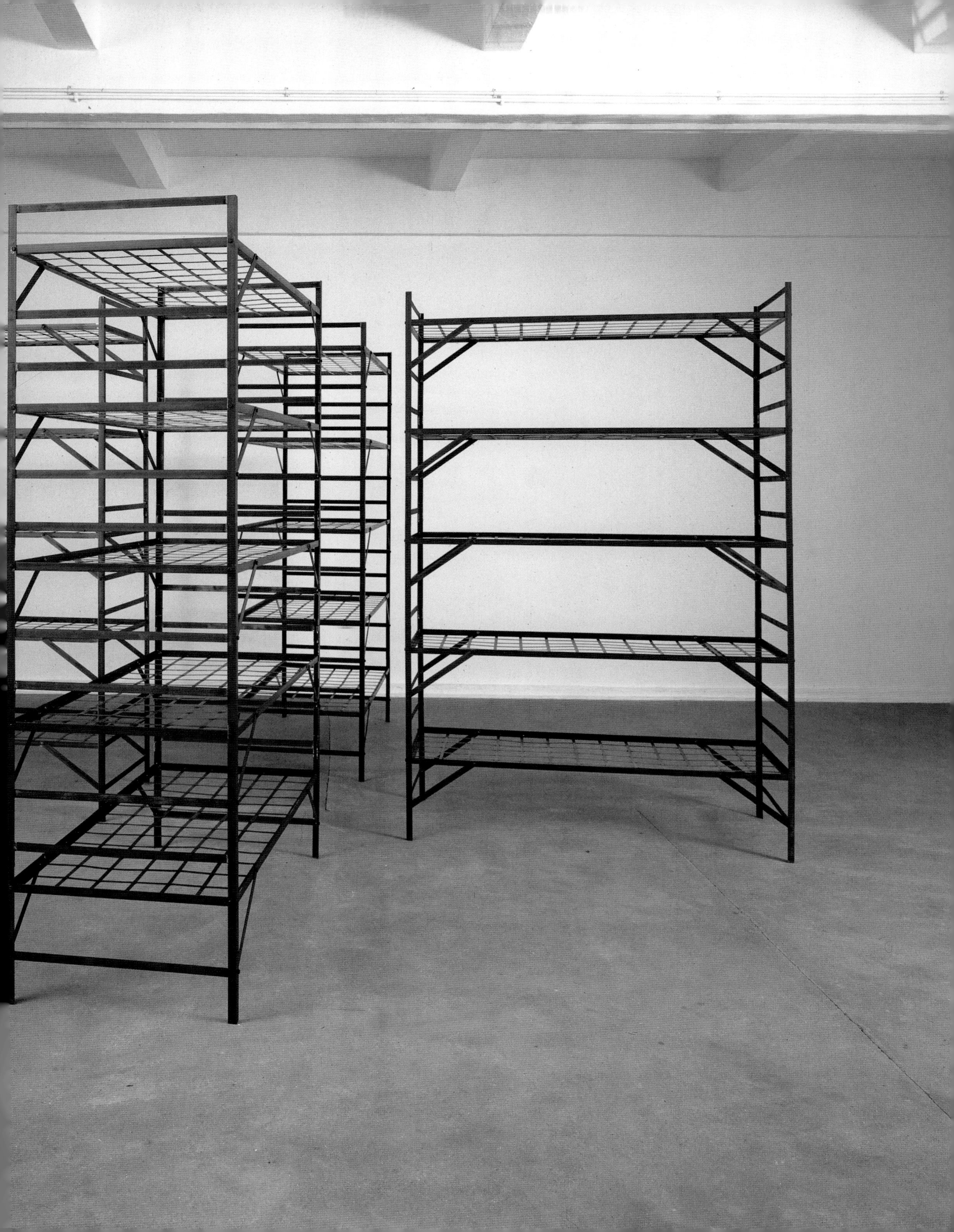

levels, becomes a Gulliveresque giant, a telescoping Alice: off with its head, body parts cropped by the moving light. The installation becomes a grotesque shadow play, echoing the abyss of modern mass housing. Hatoum has woven a grim sense of humour into the very fabric of this installation.

fig. pp. 18–19 The sombre 1996 installation *Quarters* is even more hard-hitting. Its component parts fig. p. 18 are made to scale, based on a photograph taken by the artist of a dilapidated cell in a Philadelphia prison. At first, the spectator can feel relatively detached, moving either physically or visually through the elegant geometry of the bed frames. However, as soon as one enters the axis of symmetrically aligned structures, there is an uncanny change of subject, as though the implacable gaze of another had gained the upper hand over one's own – there is a moment of *nunc stans*, of simultaneous attraction and repulsion, generated by the suddenly frozen spatial order that makes viewers stop in their tracks, only to pursue them further as soon as they leave the axis and the spell it casts. It is a kinetic work that has a shocking impact on our perception, generated in part by the viewer's own casual meandering and abrupt halt. In spite of the recognisable prison beds and the structural references to Minimalism, the uncanny gaze of surveillance is neither illustrated nor is it projected onto Minimalism, whose serial structures did not have this problem. Intuitively discovered in the act of creating the space as a petrified relationship, it is merely a question of how the roles should be allocated or swapped. But let us be under no illusion: a necessary passage, it becomes problematic only when frozen. The

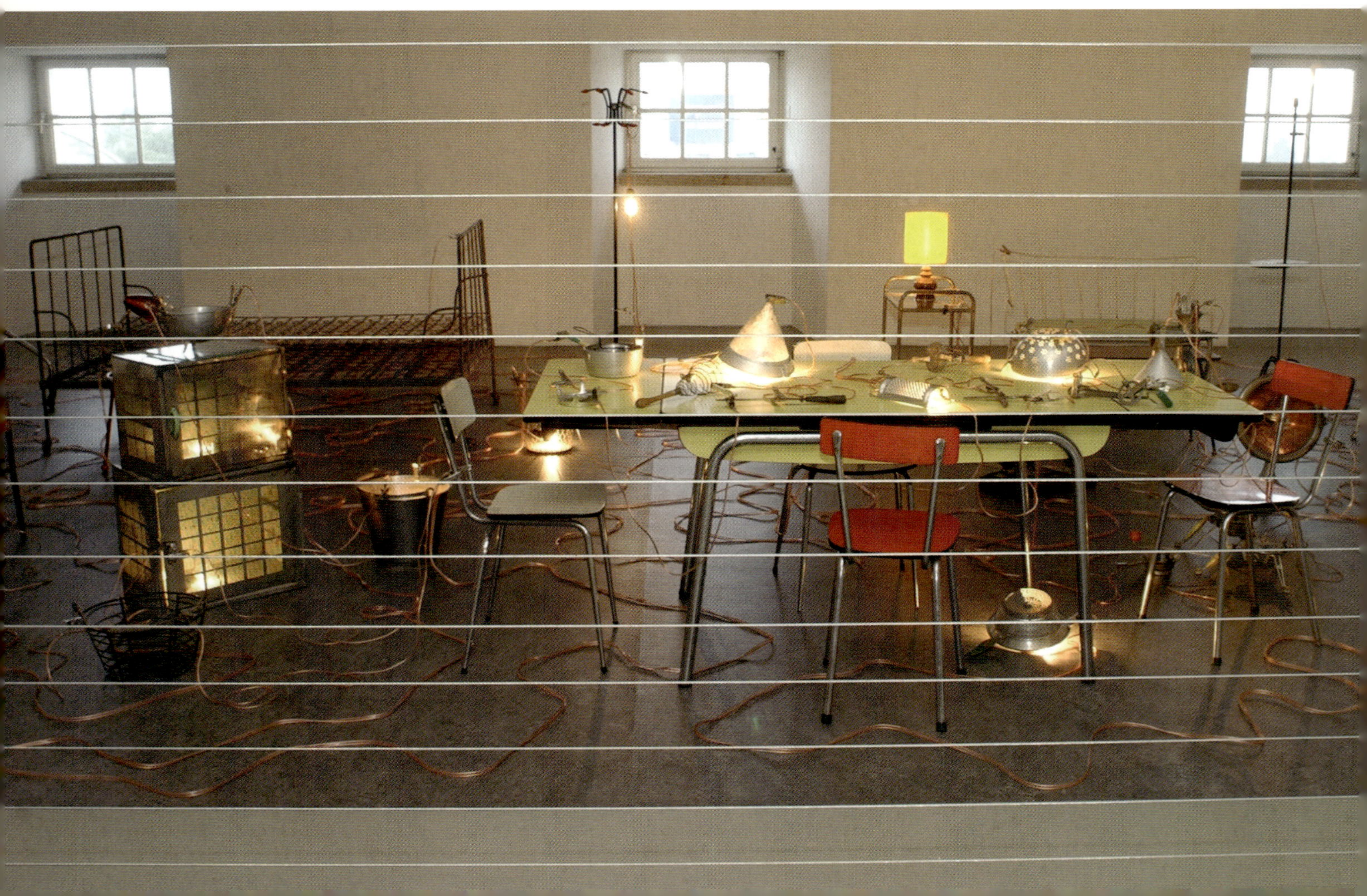

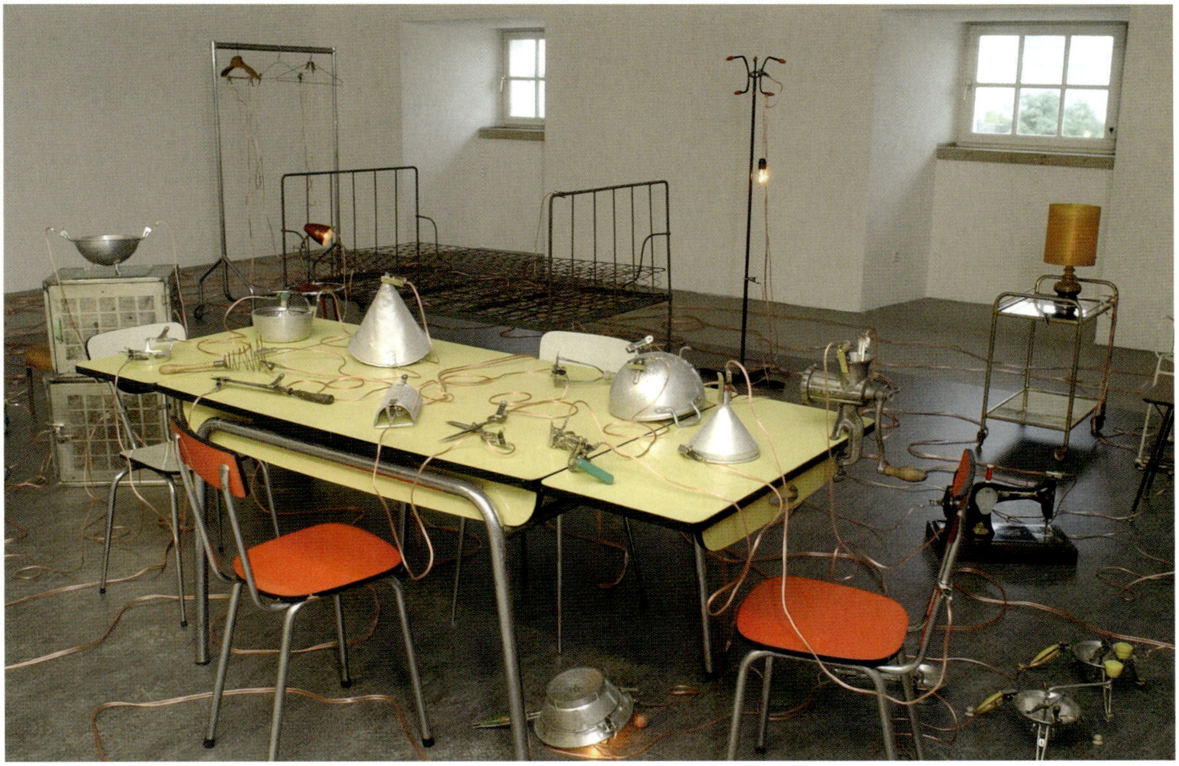

installation, however, with regard to the spectator, includes both: the active and the passive.

A skeleton is invariably associated with flesh, either directly or metaphorically. For the moment, let us consider the skeletal process in the sense of a paring-down. Hatoum has addressed and electrified the kitchen situation in three different variations: in 1999 with *Home* and with *Sous tension*, then in 2000 with *Homebound* (a larger version with some added furniture), which was installed at Tate Britain in the Duveen Galleries and also shown at 'Documenta 11' in Kassel, Germany. At the centre is a formica kitchen table with folding leaves and chrome kitchen chairs, while at the side there are an elegant armchair, a bench, two children's chairs, a clothes stand, a trolley, a standard lamp without a shade – all postwar furnishings from an era when elegance, functionality and stackability were in demand. There is also a metal bed, a metal cot, two small metal boxes with mesh apertures and a birdcage. There is not one single cushion or mattress, nothing soft – just the bare bones. This is less surprising in the case of the kitchen utensils: funnels, sieves, several Moulis-Julienne (French kitchen devices for slicing or shredding vegetables), cheese graters, tea strainers, a mincer, a working table lamp with a shade, and finally – looking somewhat forlorn amongst all this – the locomotive from a child's train set. The tableau is electrified by beautiful copper cables that weave their way across the furniture and floor and are kept carefully out of reach of the visitors by taut metal wires. Earthed as they are,

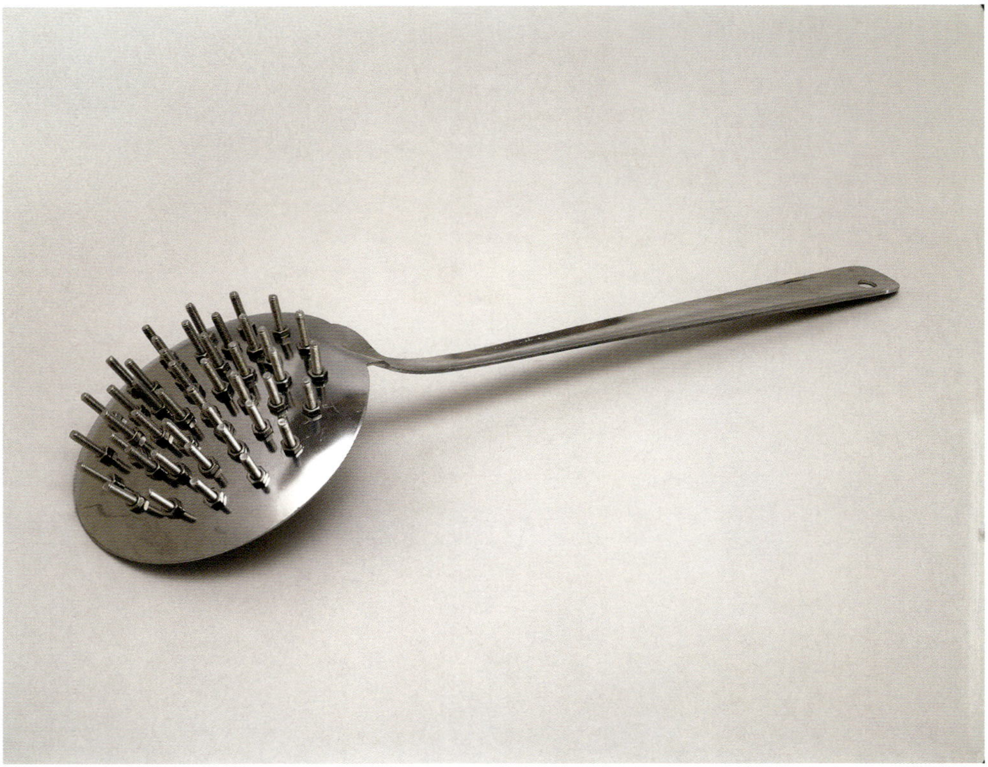

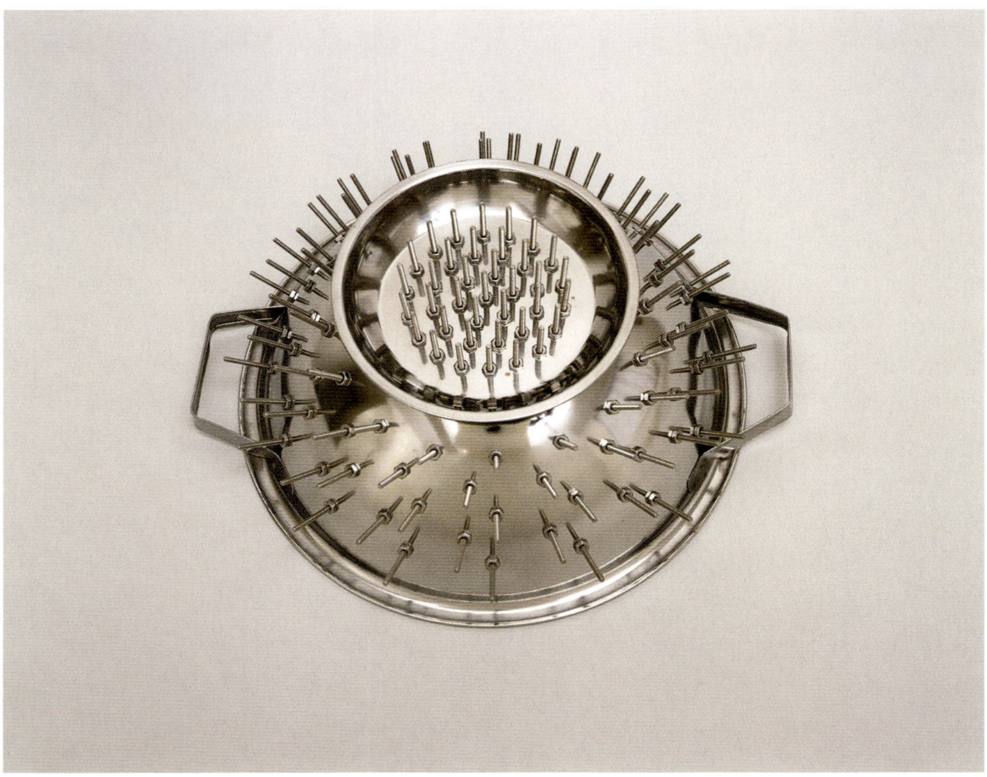

No Way · 1996

No Way III · 1996

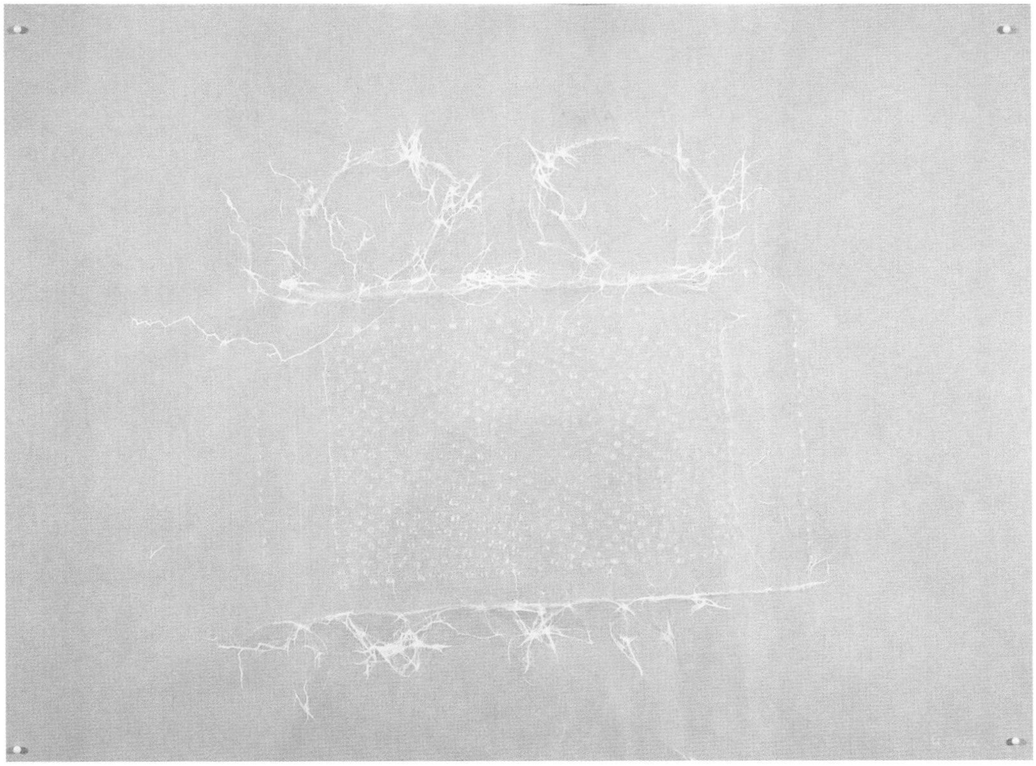

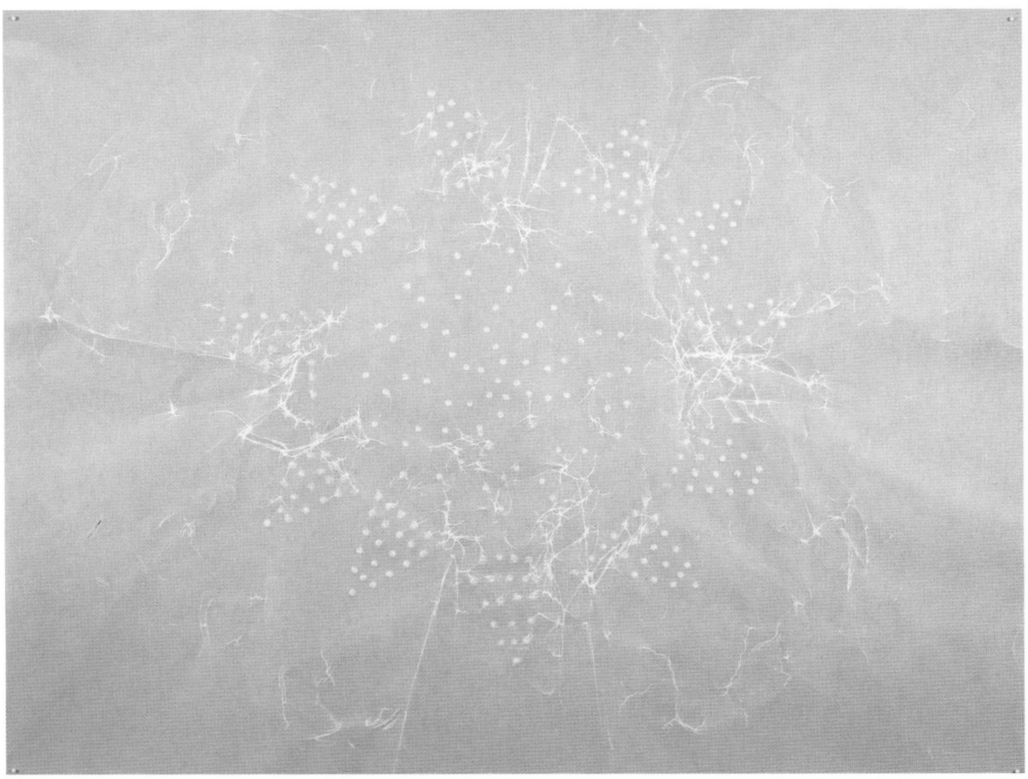

Untitled (grater) · 1996

Untitled (large Shaker colander) · 1996

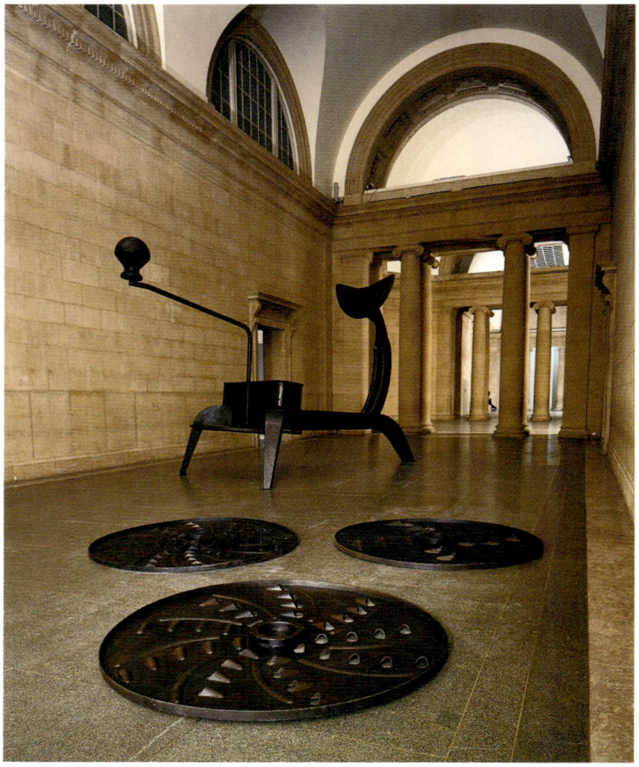

they could accidentally become conductors of energy. The computer-driven aleatory charges of energy are linked to loudspeakers, turning the whole installation into a *son-et-lumière* spectacle that crackles, hums and splutters in waves of sound that is menacingly pitched and raw. The title *Homebound* is sarcastically tongue-in-cheek, for this is anything but idyllic domesticity.

Kitchen devices are traditionally long-lasting. It was not until the late fifties that they, like shavers and dusters, became electric appliances with their working parts concealed in a casing. Before that, housewives had generally been deeply conservative – as was their cooking. The introduction of most of the kitchen devices featured in *Homebound* came during the great industrial age of the nineteenth century, when the all-purpose kitchen knife, the mortar and pestle, and the simple pot that was drained by tilting were ousted by a plethora of individually functional labour-saving items created in factories. Only the Mouli-Julienne appears to be an innovation of the fifties in France. Tinged with a nostalgic beauty today, all these things are the low-tech counterparts to more heavily high-tech industrial products that have made the commodified housewife into the 'low' derivative of the 'high' world of publicly respected business and representation. The installation of *Homebound* in the Neoclassical elegance of the Duveen Galleries provided a witty take on this situation, visually and acoustically underlined by an evident sense of danger.

The nineteenth century not only introduced new forms of control over the bodies of things, but at the same time brought with it a cleaving of the flesh from the bones. The skeletons of modern architecture were painstakingly clad in the classical garb of anthropomorphic stone facades intended to reflect human proportions. Only in civil engineering structures was it permissible for the bare bones of iron structures to show. One exception to this rule was the glass house, where the 'flesh' was on the inside; palm trees and other exotic plants from southern climes veiling the naked structure like fig leaves.

Consider a device that also emerged from the sidelines of industrial mass production and whose origins can be traced back to this period: the bottle rack. A pure skeleton-frame structure, sheer nerve paths of energy, it was destined to become the enigmatic icon of an era, thanks to Duchamp's readymade, with the status of a *cargo* that defied any signifier.

Hatoum uses the 'assisted readymade' in the sense that she minimally alters everyday objects or reproduces them in unlikely materi-

La grande broyeuse (Mouli Julienne x 21) · 2000

Divan Bed · 1996

als or, in the case of a readymade enlargement, creates a shift of function or addressee. However, this does not apply to *Homebound* – an object installation in which the very austerity of the objects puts paid to any sense of cosiness. The bottle rack can help us here if we grant it some recognisable form as a simple bottle rack rather than as a readymade: it resembles the corset of a graceful lady, albeit with treacherous thorns, like a sombre signifier of nineteenth century literature's notorious tendency to despise and fear the feminine. In *Homebound*, Hatoum not only touches upon a biographical resistance to the traditional female role, but also addresses the unresolved power struggle between the private and the public, and, with that, the gender issue that is the other side of the same coin. It is the same 'current' that breaks through one way or another, electrically or emotionally. There is more than just a touch of dark humour here, depending on whether one actually feels threatened or enjoys the frisson of danger.

. pp. 20–21

Against the towering Neoclassical columns, pilasters and vaulting of the Duveen Galleries, *Homebound* seemed positively Lilliputian. The electric and acoustic confrontation between *Homebound* and the surrounding space had its counterpoint in *La grande broyeuse* shown at the same venue. This sculpture, more than four metres high, whose title is a reference to Duchamp's *Broyeuse de Chocolat*, is a ready-made enlarged: a *Mouli-Julienne* scaled up to twenty-one times its original size and proportional to the accompanying heavy-duty. Malevolently destructive, it is capable of 'shredding' anyone who might stray too close. Looking up at *La grande broyeuse*, the Duveen

fig. p. 24

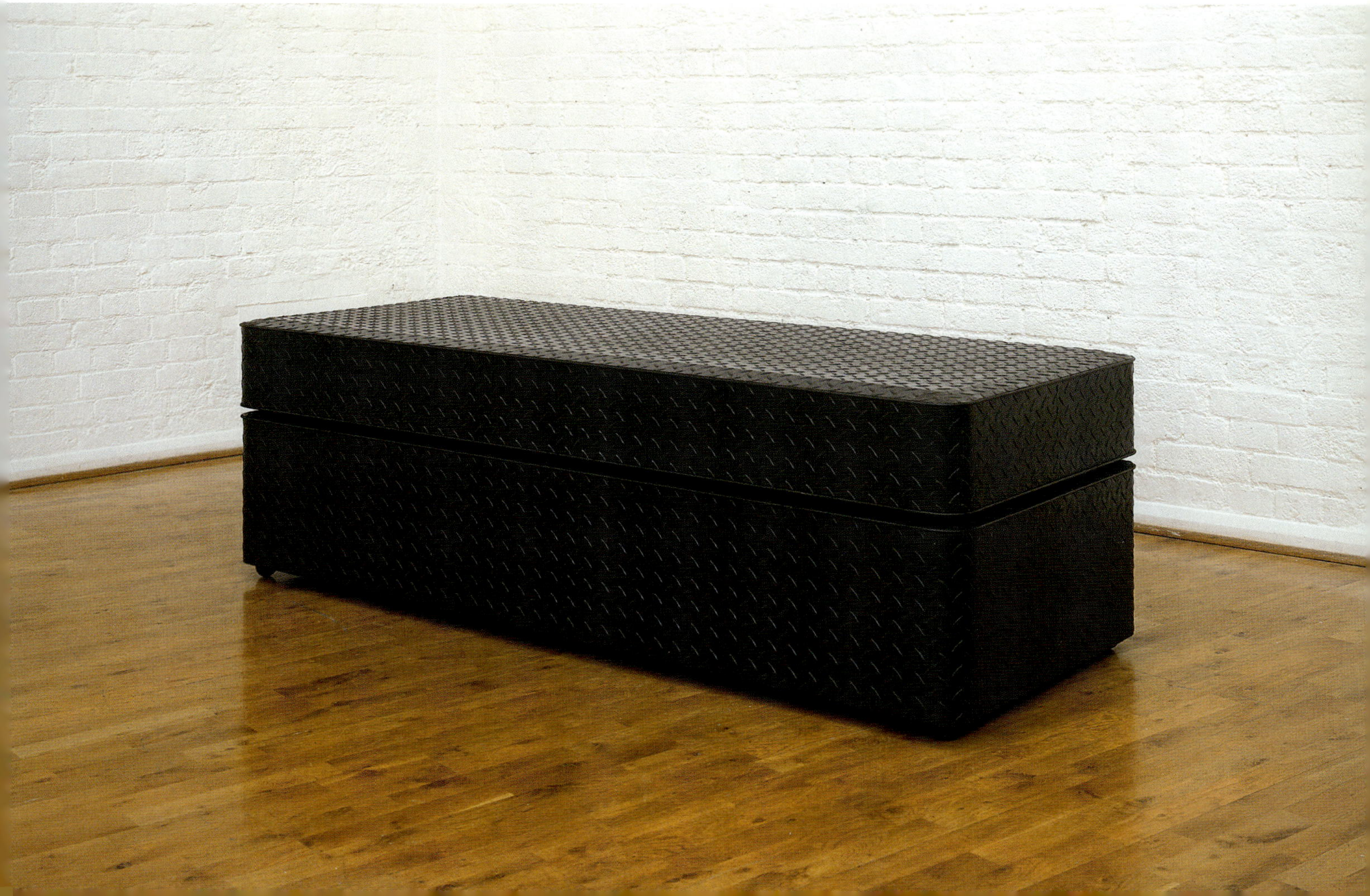

Galleries were drawn into our gaze as well, and their ostentation seemed further heightened still, especially in the view through the columned portals. *La grande broyeuse*, by contrast, seemed comparatively small, but the spatial tension kept the architecture at bay, preventing us not only from identifying too closely with the sublimity of the space, but also from indulging in any other sense of awe. Thus, the spectator was caught between two fronts in a productive way. Intuitively, in both installations, the space became a crucial aspect of the constructed situation, and so, paradoxically, became 'involved' in the conflict.

fig. pp. 54–55

Now to some assisted readymades in the form of objects with added flaws. *Balançoires en fer* (1999) turns a swing into a dangerous duet as soon as we notice the sharply honed edges on the inside. *Divan Bed* (1996) replaces the soft upholstery with implacably hard steel plates. Anyone aware of Magritte's paraphrasing of David or Manet, in which he replaces the female figure with a coffin, is likely to want to lift the lid of this sarcophagus. *Incommunicado* (1993), a tubular steel hospital cot, promises anything but tender loving care: instead of slats or springs, there are sharp, thin metal wires spanned across the base, suggesting that any baby placed there might be sliced mercilessly into pieces like a hard-boiled egg. This gloomy 'hard' version has a counterpart in the fragile glass, ethereality and baselessness of *Silence* (1994), and then there is *Marrow* (1996), a 'soft' version of flesh-coloured latex that chills you to the bone: instead of a child, it is the cot that sinks whimpering to the ground. A 'soft' object for adults,

fig. p. 25

fig. p. 6

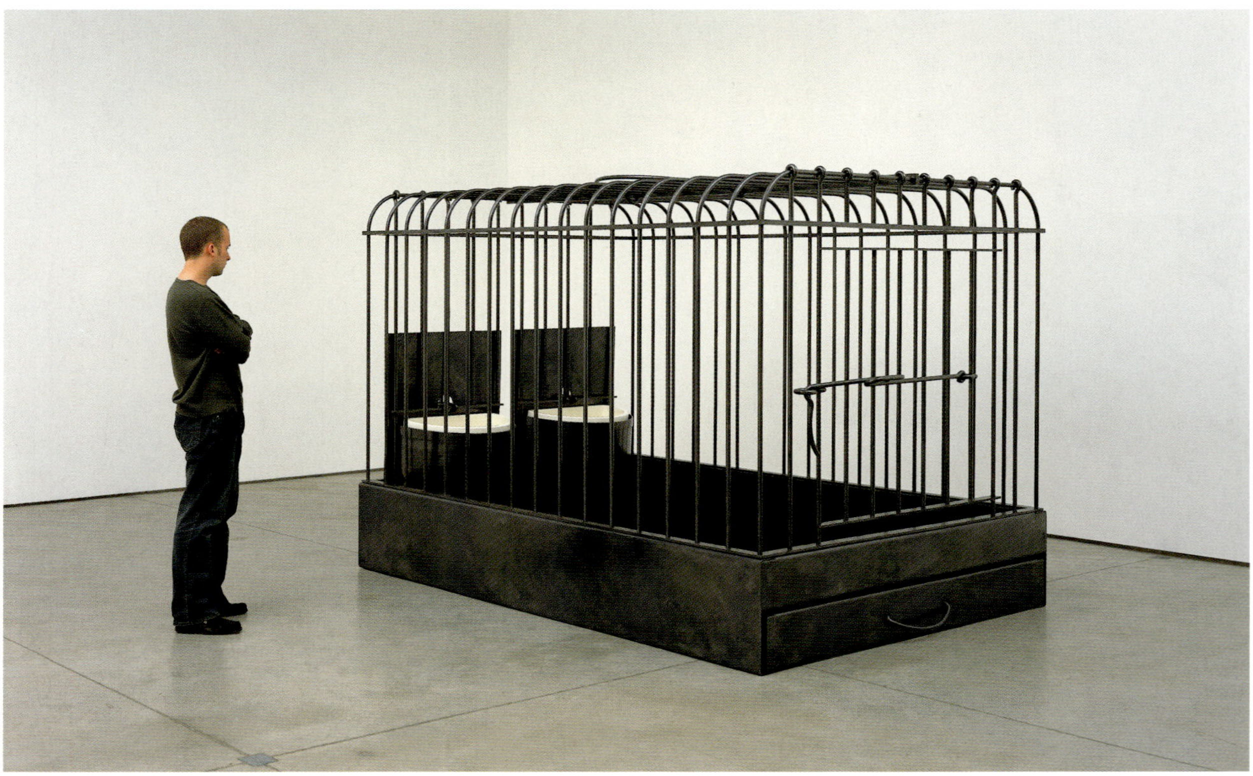

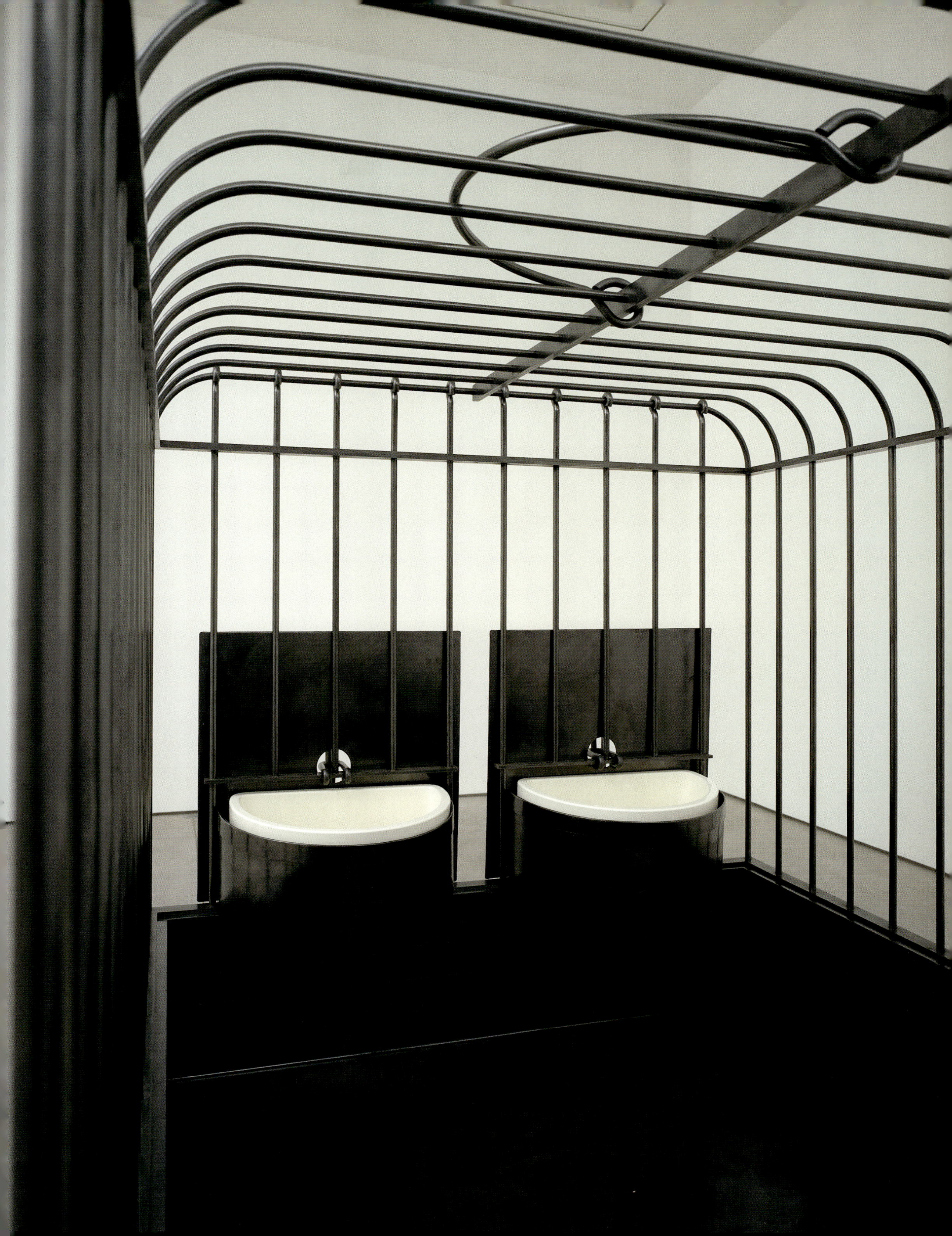

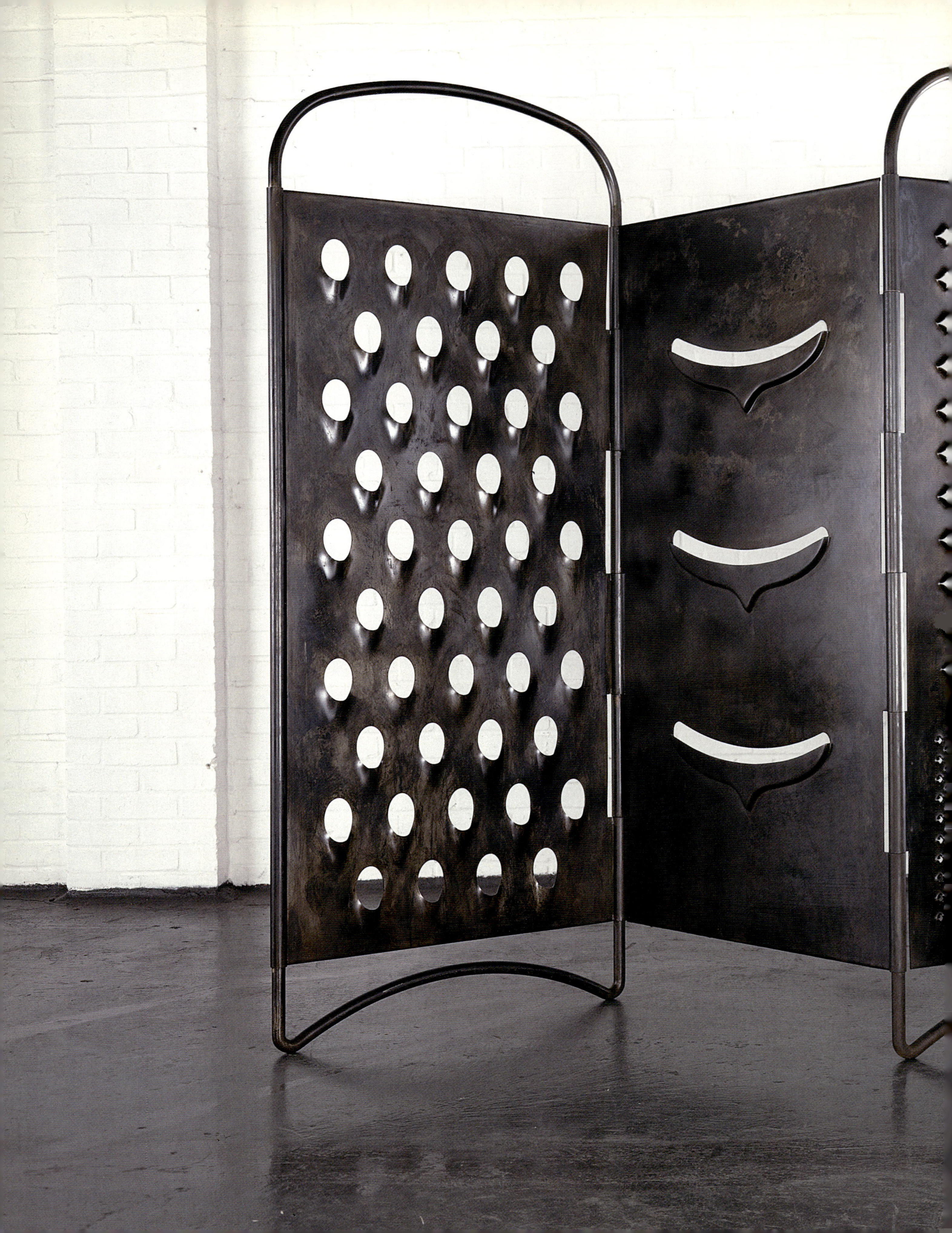

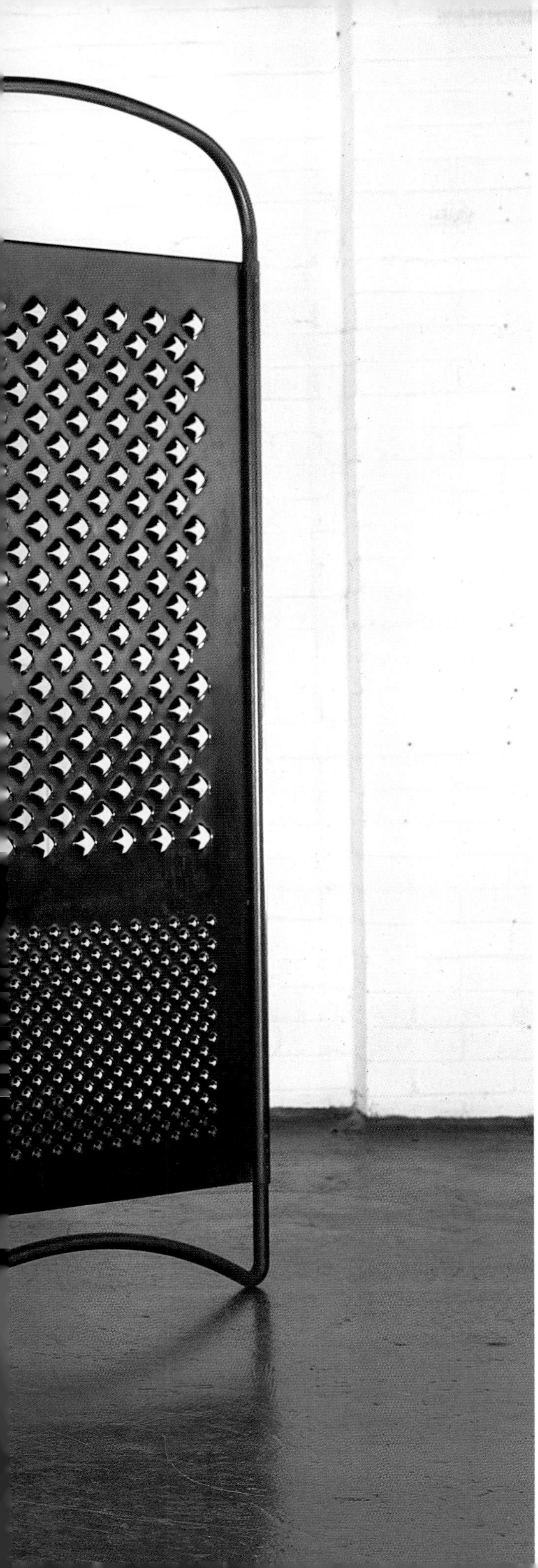

Untitled (crutches) (1991–2001) leaves us with a rather comical feeling. The crutches imitate the gait or movement of a cripple leaning against a wall and slipping to the ground, and at the same time suggest a perplexing lack of support. More perplexing still is *Untitled (wheelchair)* (1998) in which a wheelchair is fitted with sharp steel knife blades instead of rubber grips. Whether it is the wheelchair user or their companion who is threatened by these remains a moot point. The objects bear witness to an atavistic terror that turns from catatonic rigidity to instability, from hard to soft. Whether it is about ourselves or others, about perpetrators or victims, or about both, and whether one is merely the flipside of the other, remains unclear. The answer is left to our own emotionally charged projections.

fig. p. 33

fig. p. 31

But beyond primordial reactions, between menacing rigidity and formless acquiescence, be it voluntary or forced, there seems to be no third way – the consequence of a tense relationship between reason and emotion, body and mind, and perhaps even between the western world and the unfortunate rest, when there is no longer any alternative to these extreme reactions. The industrial readymades, with their material and details altered, set a disquieting and ironic counterpoint to their formal perfection.

Two examples of the conflict between mind and passion are worth noting here. In *Sweet Temptations*, a play by Jan Fabre (1991), two identical naked men are seated in wheelchairs. One of them says hesitantly that he has recently read a scientific study claiming that owls are not birds – a claim that deals a shocking blow to our notion of reason embodied by the flight of the Owl of Minerva. Rebecca Horn's film *Buster's Bedroom* (1991) is set in the soporific tedium of a strange rest home by the name of Nirvana House. One of the patients sits permanently in a wheelchair, dressed in red – the colour of passion – concentrating her energies on training her immobility, and fuelled by a tumbler of whisky affixed to the wheelchair. The wheelchair itself becomes her downfall when, in pursuit of her rival, lashing out hysterically with a whip, she rises from the chair only to be knocked down by it as it rolls away and sent tumbling into the swimming pool, breaking her spine and drowning ignominiously.

With 'enlarged readymade' objects, viewers are offered a further physical dimension for their projections. fig. pp. 26–27 In *Cage-à-deux* (2002) there is room for two to lie down and rest, with water basins as pillows for their grim nightmares – a strange bed indeed, apparently abandoned by the birds who have flown the cage through the large spaces between the bars. In *Grater Divide* (2002), a grater scaled-up to the size of a paravent, there is nothing to temper the sense of tension before or behind the folding screen. fig. pp. 28–2 Moreover, it contains another aspect that was also present in *Quarters* (1996). fig. pp. 18–1 The holes of the grater are eyes whose malevolent gaze meets the gaze of the spectator in a domestic variation of the publicly invasive and surreptitiously controlling gaze. Here, as in *Homebound*, there is no distinction between the public and the private; instead, the question is raised as to the extent to which they collaborate. It is a question also asked in *Doormat II* (2000–01) which beckons with the word 'welcome' only to reveal its hard metal pins.

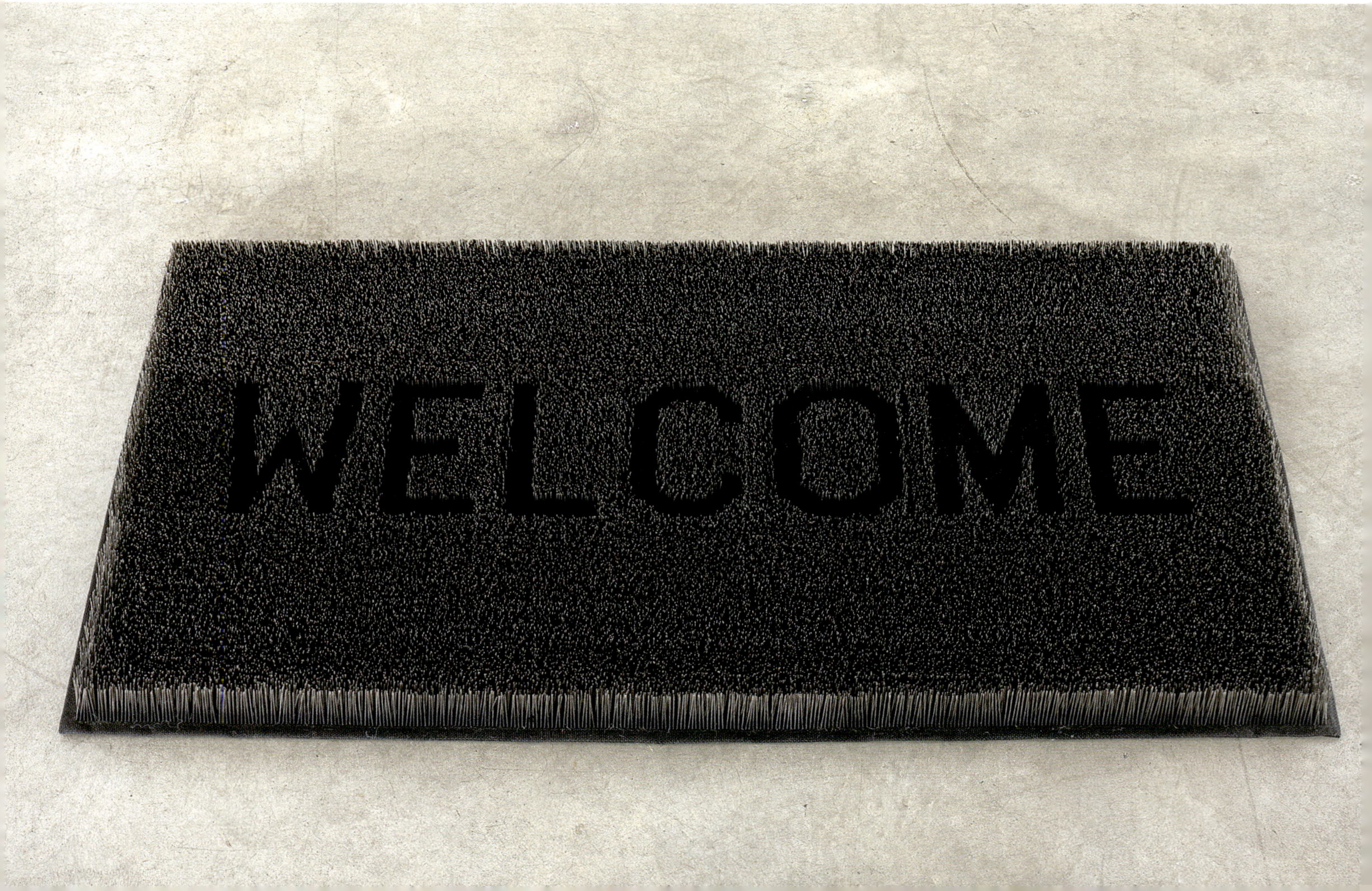

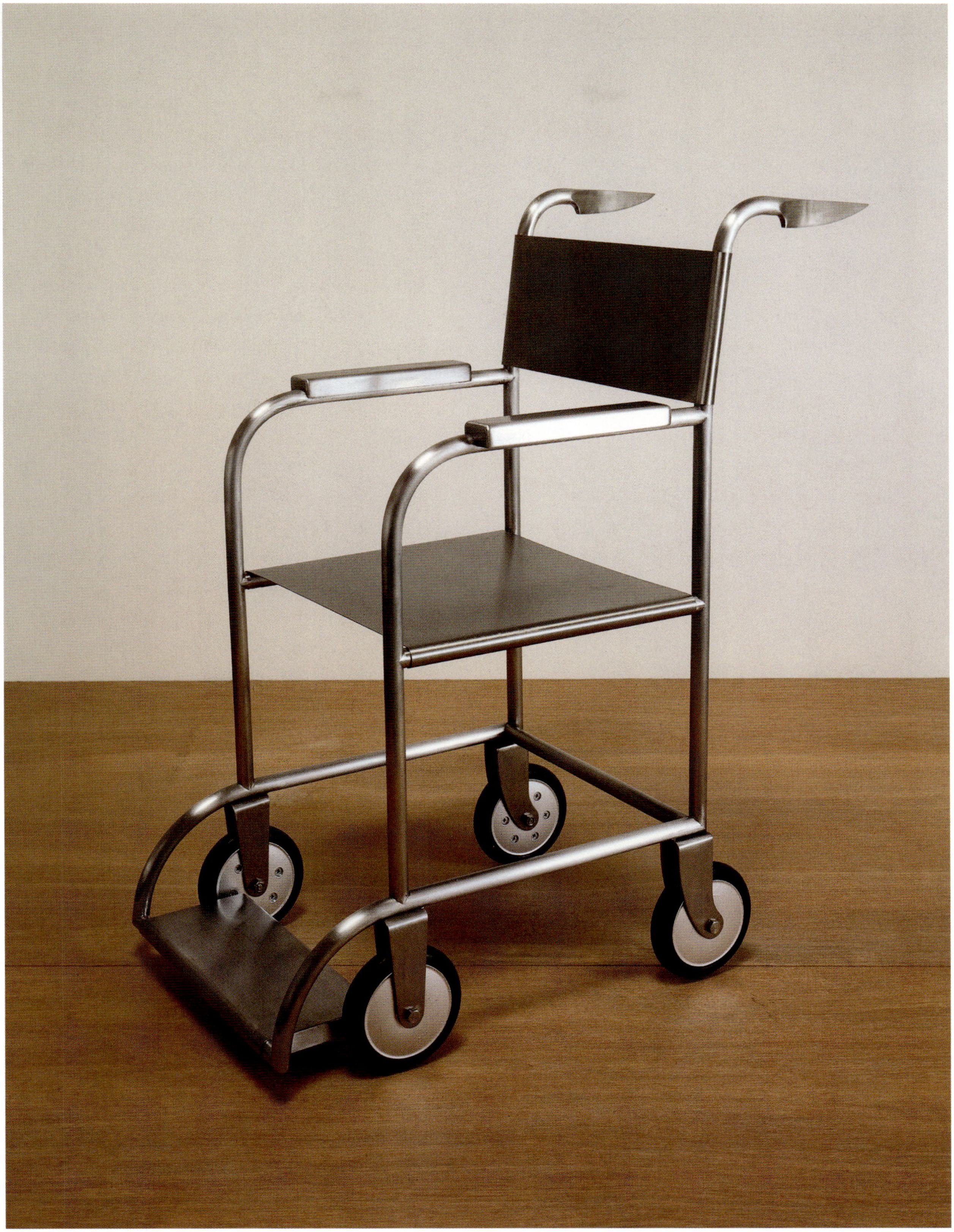

Doormat II · 2000–01

Untitled (wheelchair) · 1998

Penetrating one's own body with diagnostic instruments is a risky borderline experience. Meret Oppenheim and later Isa Genzken had their skulls X-rayed in profile. Pipilotti Rist has had the inside of her body filmed endoscopically, though, as I see it, protected by the irony of the camera image. Hatoum's installation *Corps étranger* (1994) – a longstanding wish eventually realised at the Centre Pompidou – combines close-ups of the body's surface with intrusions into every orifice. It is in every respect a visceral journey: an excursion into the morphological unknown of the interior, complemented by sound recordings, an audiovisual journal of an inner beyond in which all symbolic detachment meets its limits.

fig. pp. 46–47

Here, I would just like to touch on the issue of the spectator's involvement. Once the camera eye – itself a *corps étranger* – has entered the body – another *corps étranger* – the spectator becomes an uneasy witness, caught on the narrow rim of a deepening crevice as though the floor itself had been shifted to the upper edge, and drawn into the circular projection of images of a body that, even as a *corps étranger*, is a physically tangible reflection of our own lives. This subject shift leaves us with the disturbing feeling that our own bodies are not unaffected by what is happening in the body of another. We are surrounded by quadrophonic speakers that make it difficult for us, standing there as we are with our own bodies in the midst of it all, to associate the sounds with the images, and each spectator experiences it differently, depending on whether this view into the body of the opposite sex – again, a *corps étranger* – or indeed into the body of another of the same sex is perceived as fascinating or repulsive, and also on whether anyone else – any other *corps étranger* – is present as a witness in the room. The feelings this triggers defy description. They are ineffable. Our sense of shock at discovering something beyond a symbolic order cannot be expressed or shared in words. The possibility of experiencing it without words and sharing it physically is provided by the carefully considered form of the installation, which is entered through two narrow apertures, axially aligned.

Hatoum has taken a similarly stringent approach of remarkable subtlety in a piece which forms the male counterpart to *Corps étranger*. In *Testimony* (1995-2002) there is no penetration. Instead, the view is from the outside and instead of looking down we look ahead. In a darkened room, a video projector on a socle casts a moving image on the wall at short distance. It is a circular detail of a scrotum, its skin reacting to minimal changes in temperature, set in shadow like stars seen

fig. p. 42

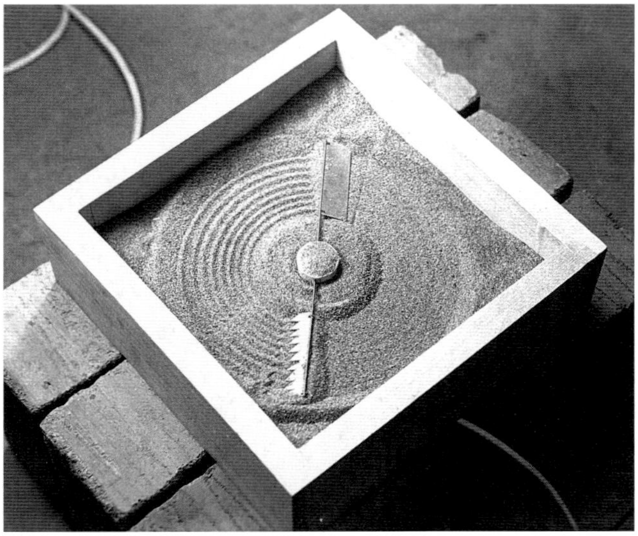

Self-erasing drawing · 1979

in a gloomy night sky, with a simultaneity of proximity and distance that bears no relation whatsoever to a pornographic close-up. In Ancient Rome, men appearing in court would place a hand on one testicle when taking an oath. Hence the title *Testimony*, which subtly shifts this memory, to which we are witnesses.

. pp. 48–49 *Deep Throat* (1996) without emphasising gender, blends humour with uneasiness: on a table set for one, the plate is used to serve up not food, but images from an endoscopic video of the digestive tract.

Hatoum's incredibly tender, ephemerally fleeting yet meditative objects do not stand in contradiction to the dangerous territory trodden by her risky, provocatively shocking and menacing works. On the contrary, I find them mutually enhancing as opposite sides of an alert and courageous mind.

On a small weaving loom similar to one the artist herself used as a child, she has woven pieces barely the size of a palm using human hair, sometimes her own: *Untitled (hair grid with knots)* (2001) and *Untitled (grey hair grid with knots)* (2001). fig. p. 34 fig. p. 35 The ephemeral grid of hair, hardly a material easily woven, has been painstakingly fixed before being removed from the supporting frame of the loom, at which point its tautness relaxes slightly. The warp and weft of this unusual yarn can be followed with the eye, starting at the top right and ending at the lower left with a rolled-up or wavy hair that hangs down as though the fabric were a temporary interruption of a freefall through the endless void, as though this fragile something were borne along by nothingness. In an extremely calm and meditative installation at the Beguinage St. Elisabeth in Kortrijk, fig. p. 73 little balls of the artist's own hair, which she had collected over the years and shaped with great tenderness into tiny spheres, were loosely scattered on the floor like stellar constellations. They are shaped with such infinite care as though a mysterious breath of gentle wind had wrapped them like an ethereal shell around an empty core. In the sublimity of their transience and fragility, they bear an affinity with the woven hair. One year later, in *Why not squeeze*, Hatoum placed two of these almost weightless balls of hair in a birdcage. The title and the work itself are a reference to Duchamp's birdcage *Why not sneeze, Rrose Sélavy*, whereby the pun is more than just a witty play on words. Things so fragile tend to trigger destructive urges; it is the art of remembrance and the task of civilisation to resist these urges. To keep something of oneself in this way combines the

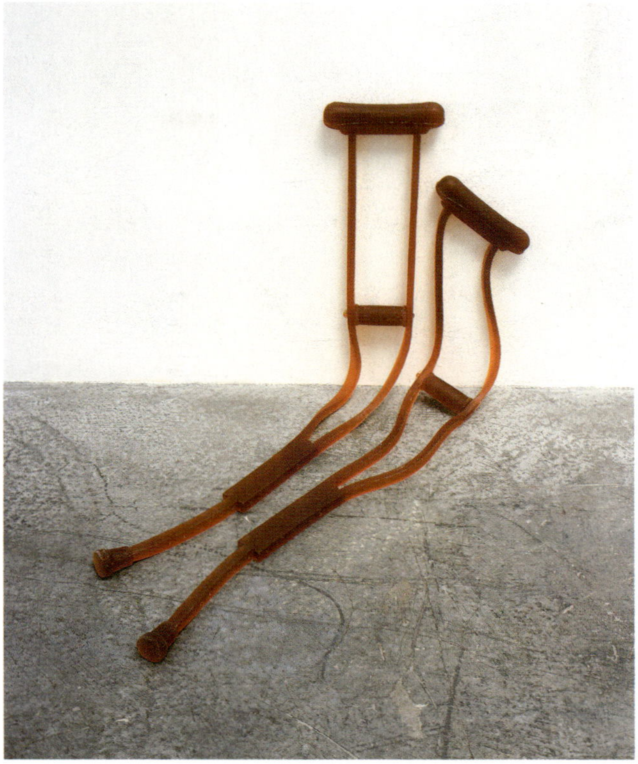

Untitled (crutches) · 1991–2001

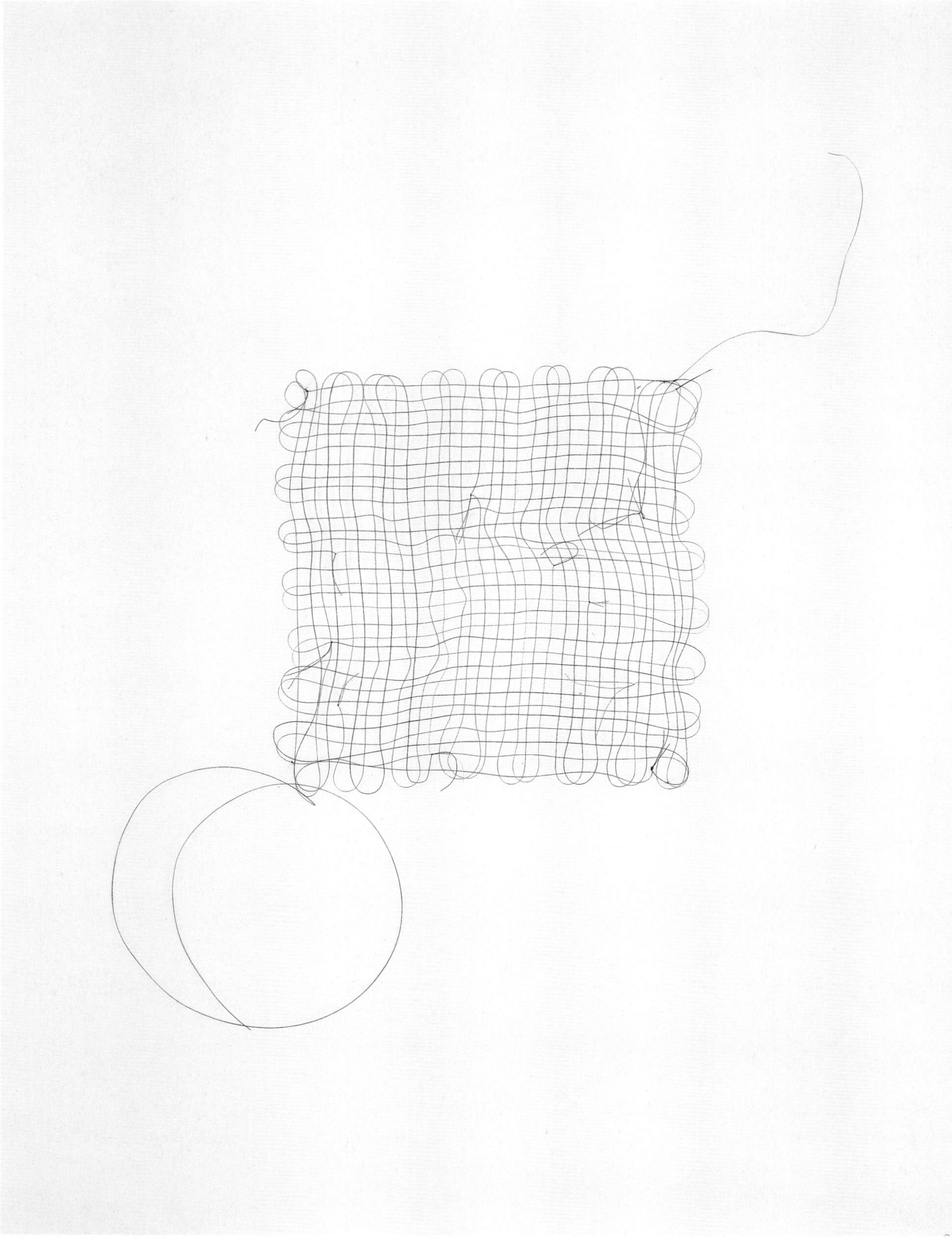

Untitled (hair grid with knots) · 2001

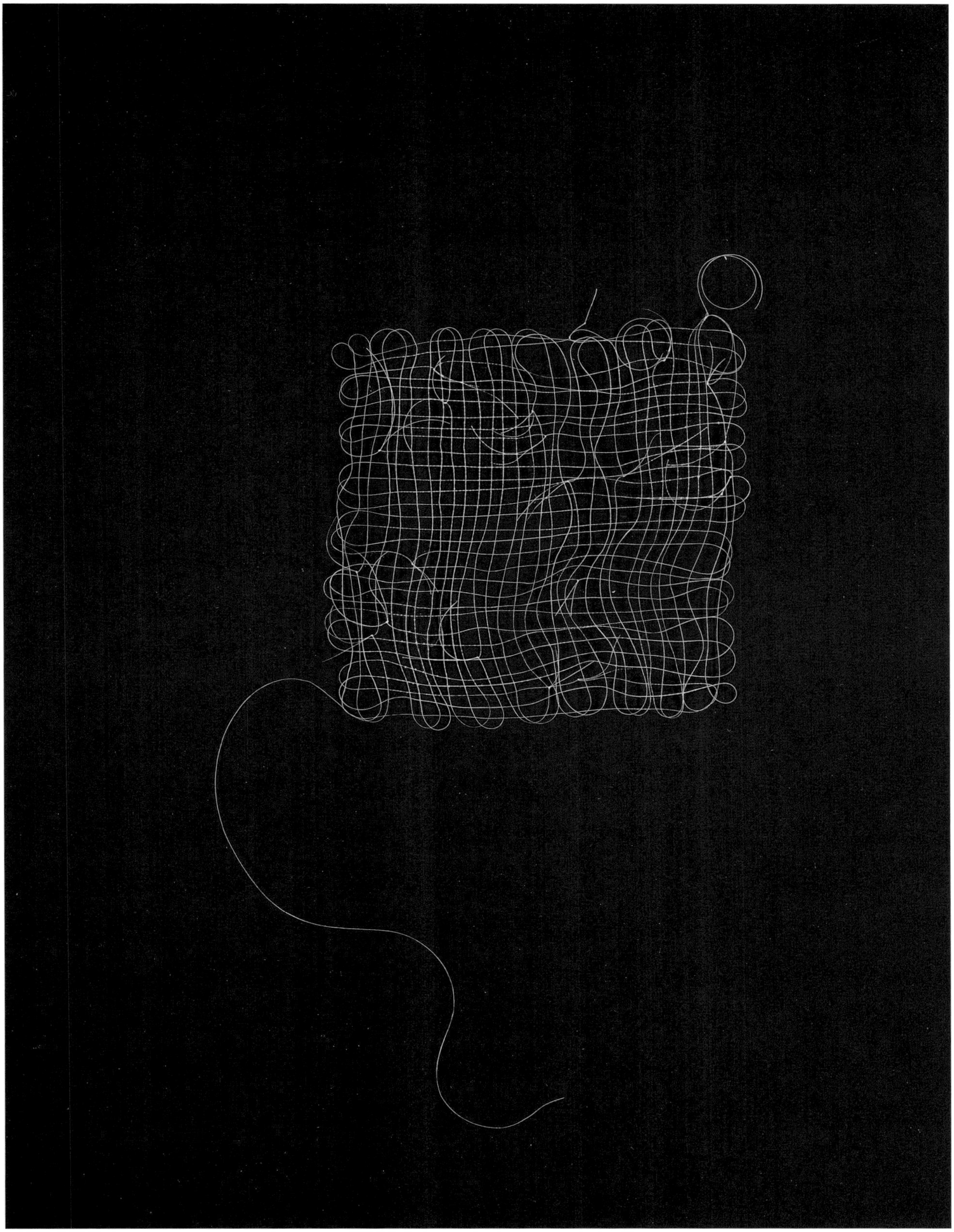

Untitled (grey hair grid with knots) · 2001

intimate with the public, the fragility of self with the fragility of culture.

This intimate and meditative act of keeping something that has been removed from one's own body, and giving it a new form at a certain remove of time, harbours a chance: in the balls of hair and woven hair, a loss is transformed into the material moment of a symbolic presence. *Self-erasing drawing* (1979) with a rake revolving slowly on a circular field of sand can also be regarded in terms of this meditative remove. In 1994, Hatoum created a large public version of this work entitled + *and* – (shown in Japan and later destroyed). The current exhibition presents a reconstruction of + *and* – (1994–2004). It is installed in the atrium of the Galerie der Gegenwart, where visitors to the exhibition can look down on it from several floors up, but may also approach it directly. The slowness of the circular movement through the sand, slower still towards the outer edge, does not resolve the paradox of + *and* –, but expands it in time.

fig. p. 32

fig. pp. 4–5

The same meditation on the transience or endangerment of form is found in Hatoum's recent drawings, created in 2003 for her exhibition in Oaxaca, Mexico: *Hair Drawing*, *Skin, nail and hair*, *Blood Drawing*, and *Untitled (brain)* as well as *Hand Made Paper*. The first of these have hair, others have a shred of skin, a single fingernail and dried blood on little strips of paper mixed directly into the paper pulp. For the last two, Mona Hatoum developed a new technique of embroidering the screen. The drawing appears as a subtle relief, ephemeral as a watermark – albeit created by an inverse technique – on the

fig. pp. 52–5

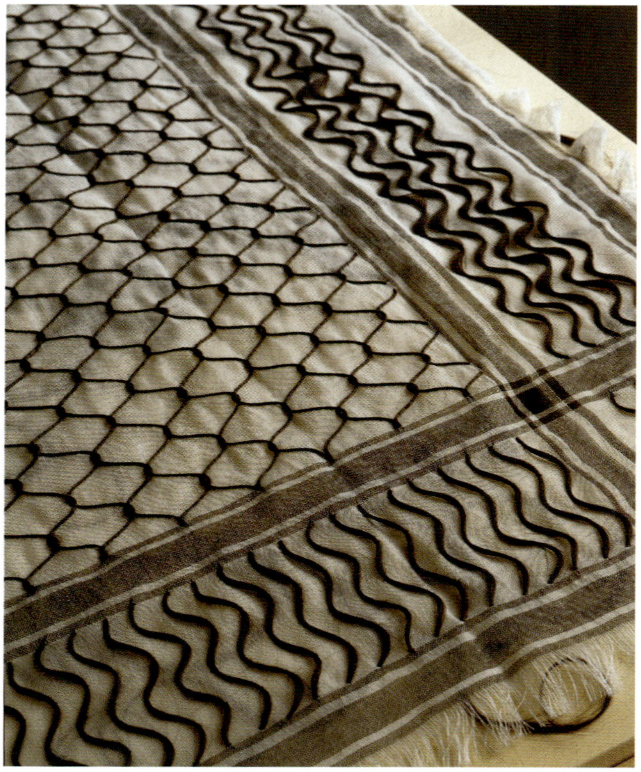

Keffieh · 1993–99

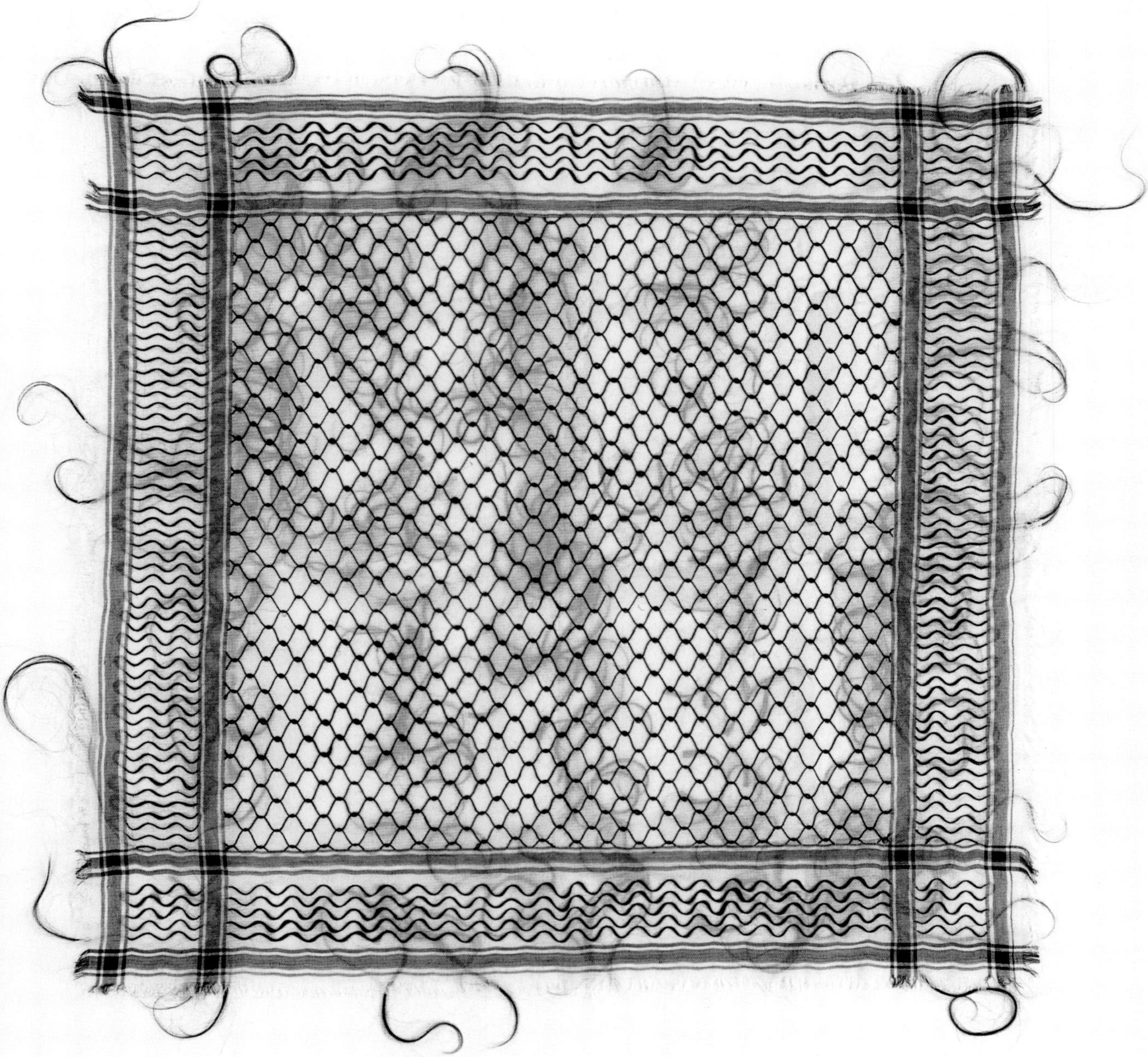

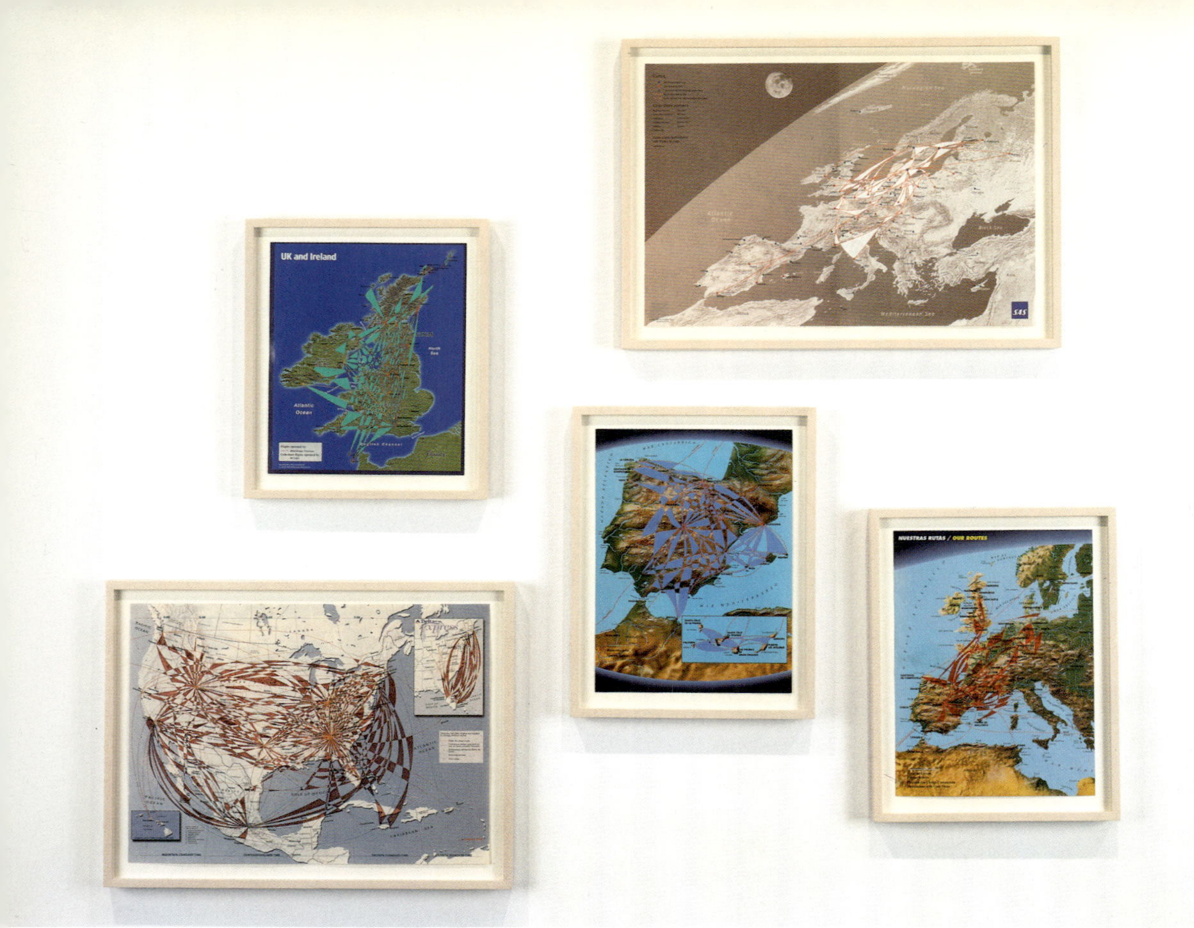

paper that she has carefully peeled from the screen once it dried.

Many of Hatoum's works self-evidently address the dramatic situation of the Other with great care and keen observation. One work that fig. pp. 68–69 springs to mind in this respect is *Present Tense* (1996), a field of soap bars, of the kind still made today from pure olive oil by Palestinian artisans in Nablus. The scattering of disconnected territories into which Palestinians were pushed by the Oslo Agreement is mapped out on the soap in tiny red beads. As we try to follow these dotted boundary lines like so many droplets, we lose track of them, and move along the fringes of islands as though on paths that carry the here and now along with them instead of cutting through it. In *Routes II* (2002) rounded segments have been shaded in between the curved lines of the flight routes abstractly spanned across countries and continents, bringing the airspace to life as though it were filled with gently billowing sails.

In *Traffic* (2002) we are horrified to discover two bunches of women's hair spilling onto the floor out of the two shabby suitcases that are standing close together. Shocked at seeing this hair 'in the wrong place', we are left wondering where these suitcases might be taken by customs officers, just what kind of traffic is involved here, and how the cases and hair came to be divided or duplicated in the first place. Another work that addresses the theme of the Other is *Drowning Sorrows* fig. p. 57 (2001) with its tenderly empathetic, clownishly tottering array of sliced-off tequila carteritas or flasks of the kind that some poor devils in Latin America still carry around in their

Routes II · 2002

hip pockets, albeit uncut and half full. So too does *Every Door a Wall* (2003), in which a fine voile curtain is printed with a newspaper report showing the X-ray scan of illegal immigrants smuggled inside a truck. Hung in a corridor, where the work and the information it contains can be easily 'pushed aside' by the visitor, it illustrates the extinction of these figures, captured by an eyeless, technically invasive gaze and reduced to schematic negatives, before they are forcibly deported to their mandatory homeland.

Mona Hatoum: The Entire World as a Foreign Land – the title of the exhibition at Tate Britain refers to a remark by Edward Said, with whom the artist discussed exile and home. According to Said, 'The exile knows that in a secular and contingent world, homes are always provisional. Borders and barriers, which enclose us within the safety of familiar territory, can also become prisons.'[1] I would like to take up this point in order to add a further angle to my theme of Being Involved. The Entire World as a Foreign Land: even 'home' is an exile, the first in which we are expelled from a mythical paradise that lives on in our collective or individual imagination. The second exile as a forced move to a foreign land opens up the wound of the first exile, but also provides a chance – admittedly an immensely difficult one – of confronting the issue, whereas the invisible wound of the suppressed first exile can have hauntingly unresolved and devastating consequences. The question here is how these exiles correlate in the depths of experience and whether they might even be linked to a third exile – the exile of gender or sexual iden-

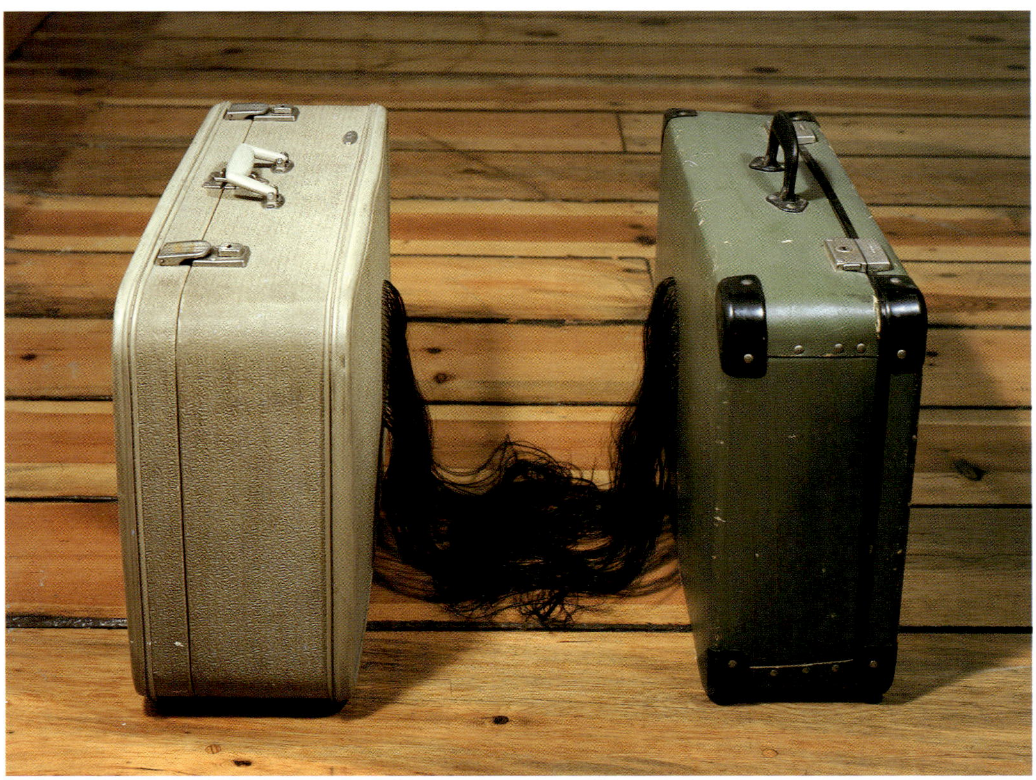

tity, which might lead out a myth-making lack of differentiation by way of struggles that are anything but harmless.

Translation from the German by Ishbel Flett

Note

1 Edward Said, 'Reflections on Exile', in *Granta* 13: After the Revolution, September 1984. Cited in exh. cat. *The Entire World as a Foreign Land,* London, 2000, p. 36.

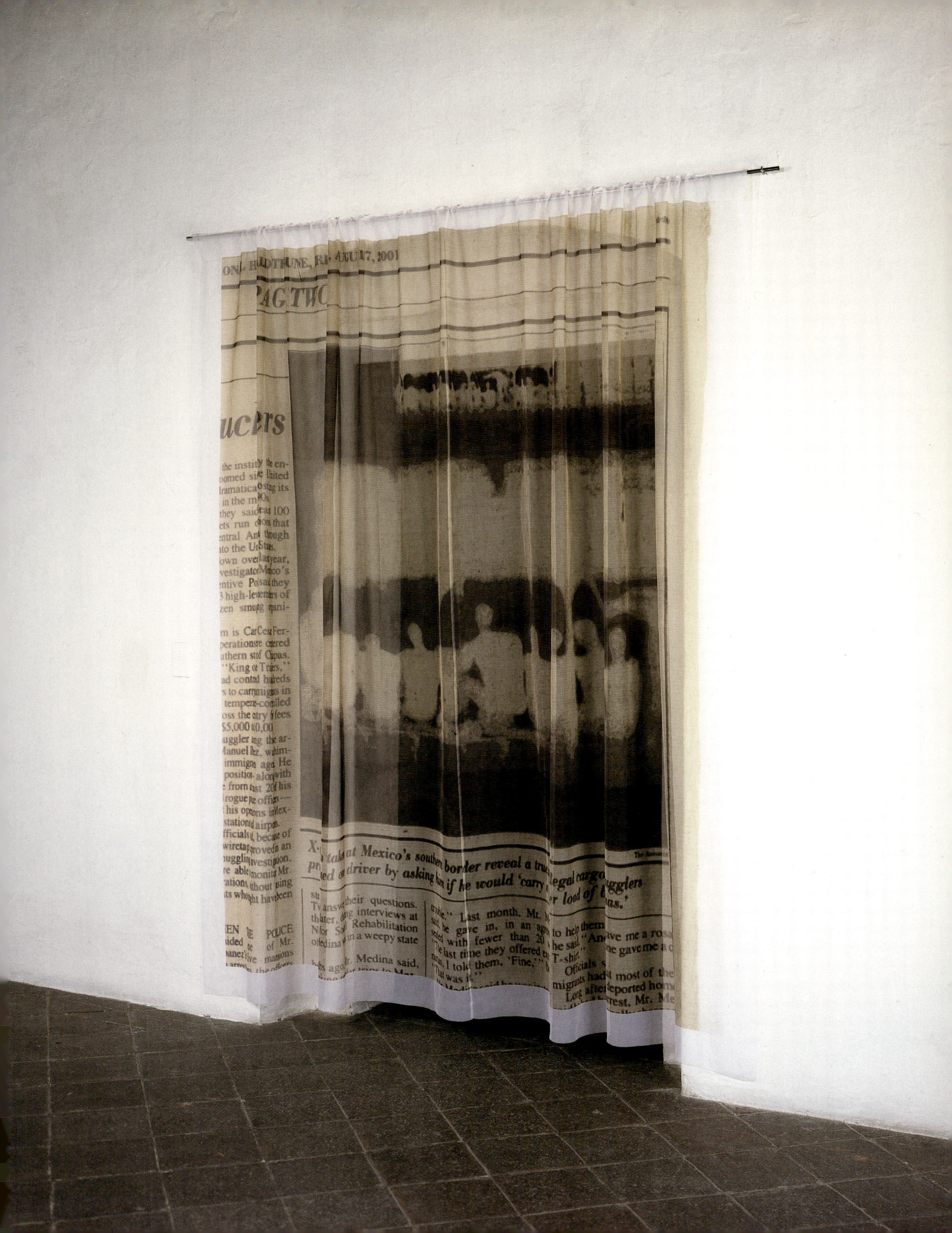

AUGUST 17, 2001
at Mexico's southern border reveal a tru
driver by asking him if he would 'carry
Last month, Mr. M

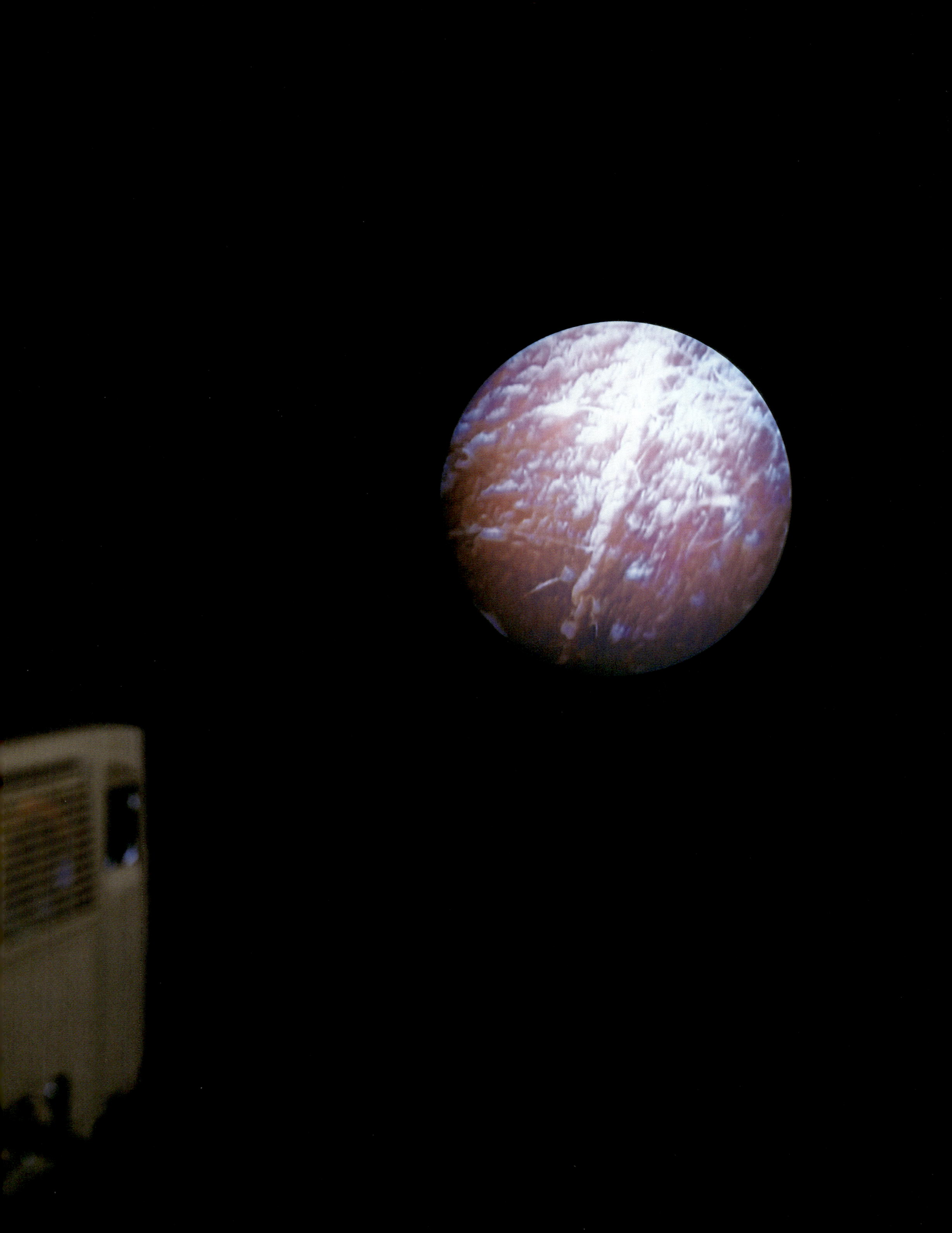

Volker Adolphs

The Body and the World

The body is of key importance in the oeuvre of Mona Hatoum. She has experimented with the body, using hair, nails and body fluids as source material in her works on paper right from the start of her artistic career in the late seventies. In the eighties she took the radical step of using her own body in performances. Then, towards the end of the eighties, she started creating installations in which the body appears only fragmentarily or is alluded to by objects it uses. These works, in particular, trigger an intense response in the spectator.

Hatoum has given a number of explanations for her interest in the body as a crucial coordinate of art. As she remarked in a 1996 interview, 'I come from a culture where there isn't that tremendous split between body and mind. When I first went to England it became immediately apparent to me that people were quite divorced from their bodies and very caught up in their heads, like disembodied intellects.'[1] For Hatoum, however, the integrity of the human being is inextricably linked with the unity of body and mind. It is for this reason that she has always emphasised the physical aspect of her art – not just by addressing the physical senses in her work, but also by developing the artwork as an event or as a body in physical space. 'I did not want my work to be one-dimensional in the sense that it just appeals to the intellect. I wanted it to be a complete experience that involves your body, your mind, your emotions, everything.'[2] On the basis of this significance of the body, the artist, especially in her early works, has used the body as a metaphor for social struggle and for the inhumane violence to which people are subjected; later, with the awareness of the threat of AIDS, imbuing her works with a palpable sense of our vulnerability and mortality.[3]

If a work of art is to be more than merely self-referential, relating instead to our experience of the world and of life itself, it has to be based on the body. Hatoum has described the body as a 'starting point' and as the 'axis of our perceptions'. 'We relate to the world through our senses ... Meanings, connotations and associations come after the initial physical experience.'[4] In her approach to the body, Hatoum poses the fundamental question of the role played by the body in terms of how it constitutes the seemingly ever less tangible self confused by the complexity of an increasingly globalised, networked, virtual world and disoriented by computer-simulated spaces and visual worlds. Perhaps the body, as the last authentic locus of the subject, is able to retain the integrity and identity of the self and self-awareness because it constitutes the specific, the immediate and the tangible that define the boundary between the self and the world as the Other. In spite of the significance that the body possesses in terms of the individual as entity, Hatoum does not perceive the body as a protected and inviolable whole. She shows the body threatened by manipulation and injury, as an object of surveillance, as foreign matter. Yet even though – and perhaps precisely because – the body appears to be endangered, vulnerable and reduced to fragmentary forms, Hatoum renders it visible as something concrete and factual. It is no fiction, but a reality, inextricably linked with our existence in the world.

It was while she was a student at the Slade School of Art from 1979 to 1981, in particular, that Hatoum developed a keen political awareness of the power of bureaucratic institutions, feminist and racial issues, cultural alienation and the relationship between the western world and the so-called third world. In her performances, she used the body as a vehicle for the investigation and representation of social violence.[5] While these early works, in spite of their explicit reaction to political reality, already strive towards a broadly general concept of the structures of order and power with which the individual has to contend, her objects and installations from the late eighties onwards are stripped even further of any specific narrative references. The theme of aggression, threat and control is ever present, but it is formulated now with more subtle and even intense and contradictory feelings of attraction and repulsion.[6] The artist no longer appears in person in the work, but involves details or fragments of her own body in lieu of every other body, or uses objects that stand for it. This detachment from the self as performer provokes and activates the spectator's sense of physical self-awareness all the more. Hatoum describes this as a shift 'from a situation of representation to a desire to create an actual and real situation that the audience could experience directly for themselves. I wanted to explore the phenomenology of the space and materials to create a direct physical interaction.'[7] This goes as far as confronting the individual with his or her self in the mirror inscribed with the words:
fig. p. 12 *You are still here.*

One of Hatoum's most important works on the significance of the body is the 1994 video installation *Corps étranger.* Even in her video fig. pp. 46–4
and performance works of the early eighties, she had already experimented with the theme of observation and surveillance, with other works such as *Deep Throat* developing from fig. pp. 48–4
it. An endoscopic camera explores the surface of the artist's body and suddenly enters through various orifices to explore the inner labyrinth of the body. The alien eye presents seductively beautiful yet horrifying landscapes, cavities and tunnels of shimmering tissue and blood-red flesh. Seen up close, each detail is distorted and magnified into a monstrosity. If the body is the scale, it is destroyed here by the simultaneity of macrocosm and microcosm, distance and proximity, exterior and interior, attraction and repulsion. The body, surveyed with seeming objectivity and thoroughness, never appears as an entity in itself, but dissolves into the component parts of individual images. Although all the parts of the body are shown with the utmost clarity, the body as whole cannot be seen. Carried along by the movement of the camera, our eye finds no point of orientation, our seeing comes to no conclusion.

The gaze is never neutral and innocent. Even the seemingly impartial, scientific eye of the camera, detached from the human body, reveals itself as the gaze of constant surveillance, as an invasion. It is the *Corps étranger,* the foreign body within our own body. The eye of the camera penetrates the body at its most vulnerable points, where it interacts with the world, occupying and violating its identity. Hatoum's body, presented as object, is turned inside out and made public; it is no longer the guarantor of a subjective experience of self, no longer part of the entity of

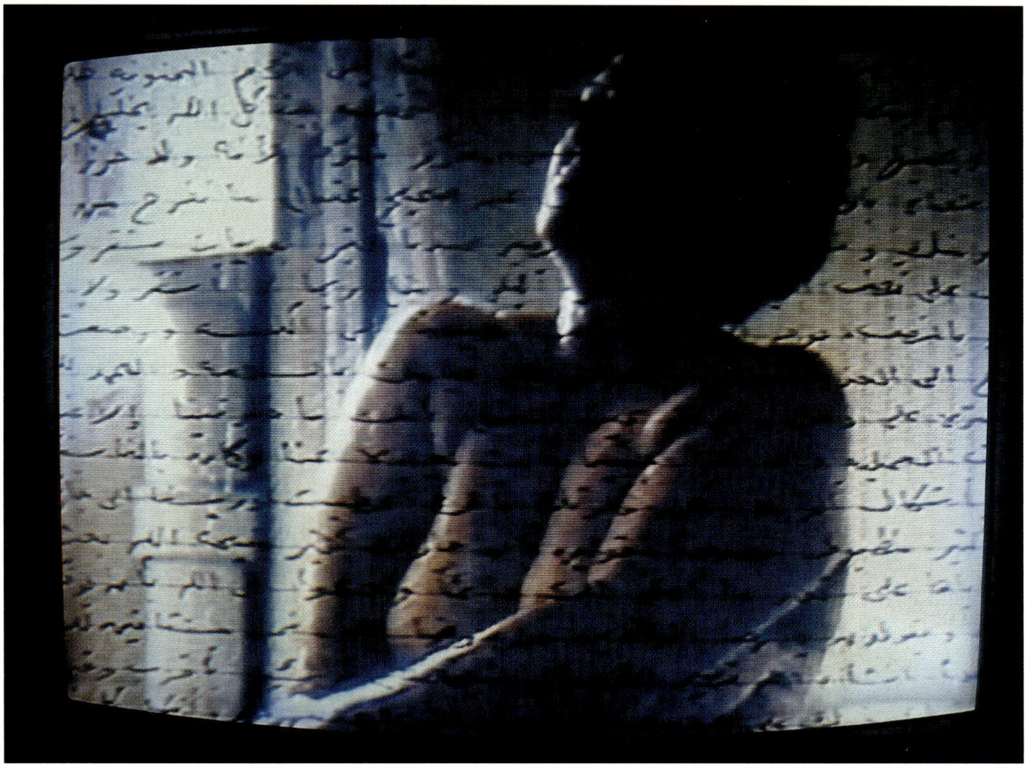

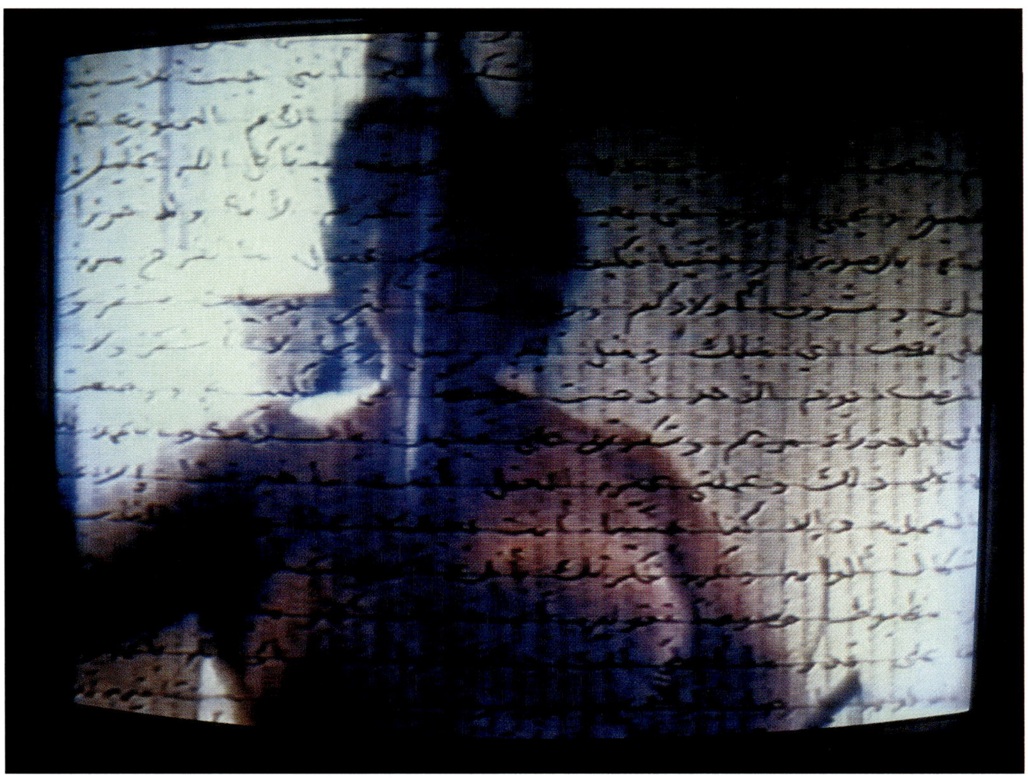

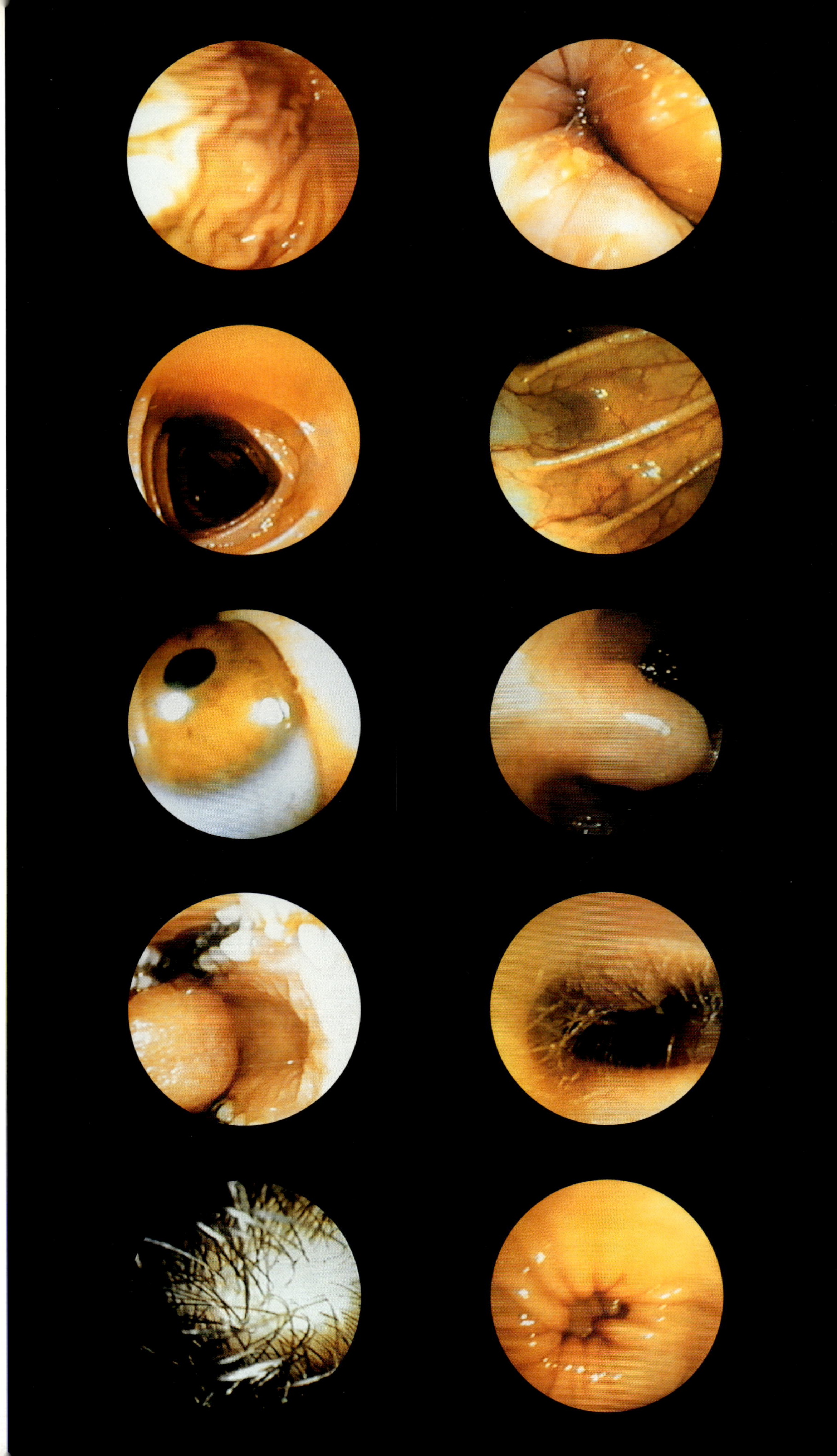

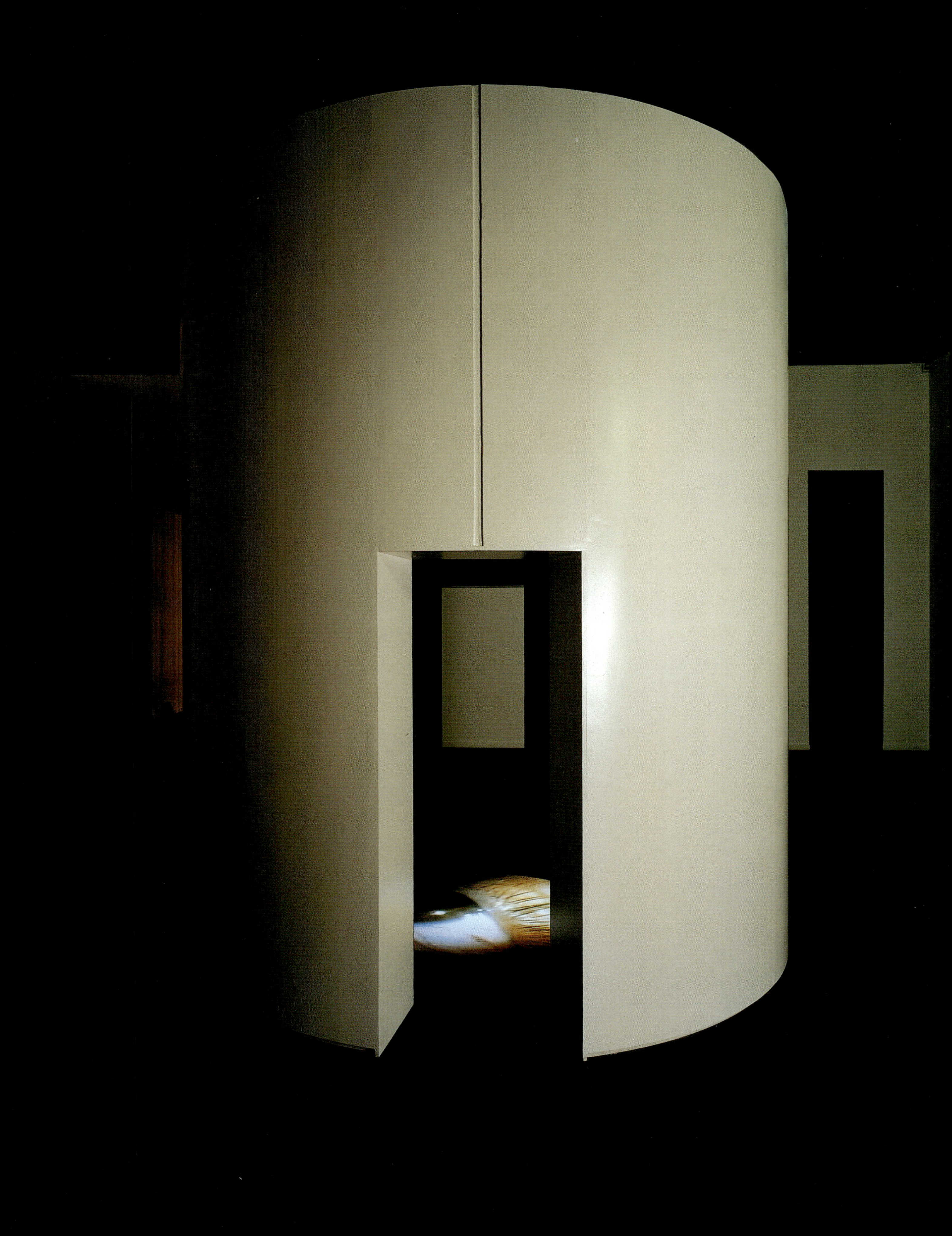

body and mind, but – even for the artist herself –an unfamiliar and soulless territory. 'I wanted the work to be about the body probed, invaded, violated, deconstructed by the scientific eye.'[8] *Corps étranger* is not intended as a self-portrait of the artist. The images projected could belong to any human body. Even the gender of the body is of secondary importance, although the images trigger an awareness of sexuality, of entering the womb, of a nakedness that goes under the skin and no longer corresponds to any ideal of beauty. Hatoum uses her own body to show it and perceive it as the Other. She becomes a spectator, experiencing the otherness of her own body just like any spectator does, as a *Corps étranger* in every sense.

Hatoum makes the situation more daunting for the spectator by enclosing the installation so that the viewer is surrounded by walls that leave only a small area to stand on. The spectator thus becomes a prisoner of the body viewed inside; a prisoner of his or her own gaze. Watching the changing images on the floor, gazing into an abyss that threatens to swallow you up, the pleasure of looking and of visually recognising things becomes an unbearably angst-ridden magnet. The spectator is confronted not only with a visual experience, but also with an acoustic one. Overwhelmed by the alien and familiar sounds of the body, the beating of the heart, the murmur of internal organs, we sense that this journey into the depths of another body is destabilising the very ground beneath our own feet. In paradoxical simultaneity, we identify on the one hand with the artificial eye of the camera that has taken control of the body, while on the other hand losing all control as we tumble into that body.

When Hatoum uses fragile traces of her body, stripped of all individuality, such as her

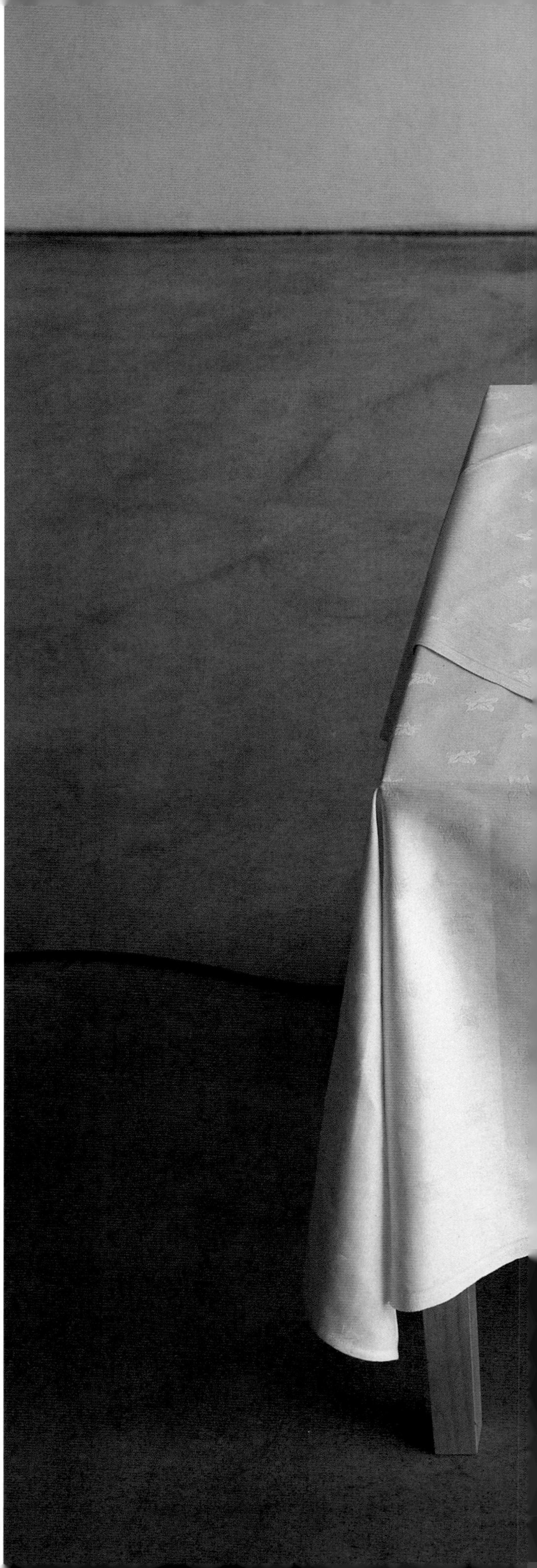

 ◀ Corps étranger · 1994   Deep Throat · 1996

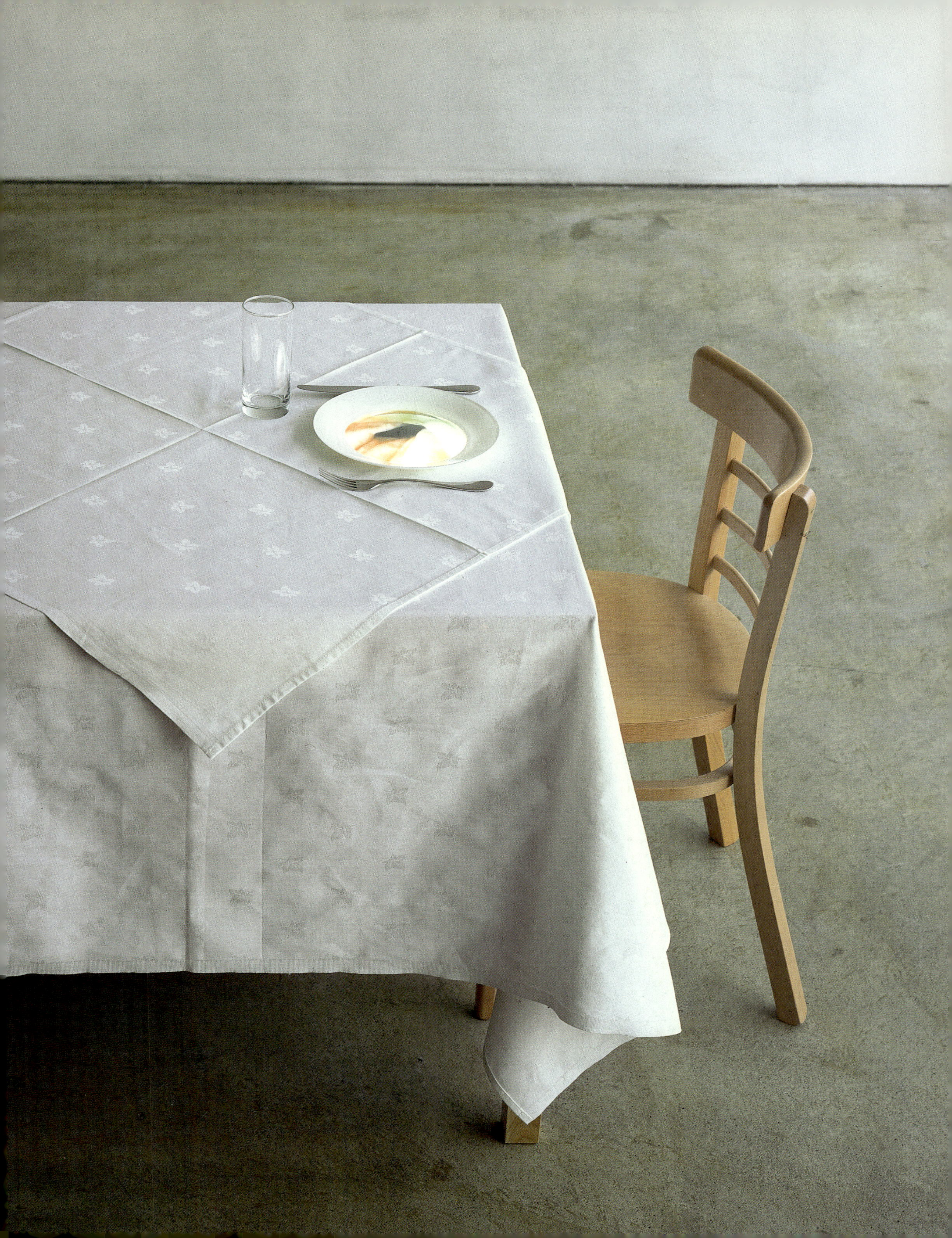

fig. p. 74 pubic hair in *Jardin Public*, or her blood and skin in works on paper, she is also focusing on the bodies of others, albeit in a different way. fig. p. 45 In *Measures of Distance* she shows the naked body of her mother, ample yet vulnerable, in which her mother is actually recognisable as a fig. p. 42 specific individual. In *Testimony*, by contrast, only the rosy skin of an anonymous scrotum can be seen, while some photographs taken in Jerusalem show the carcasses and entrails of dead animals. The corporeal appears associatively when the eye perceives a chain of colourful buttons as an umbilical cord *(Umbilicus)*.

However, the body can be both present and at the same time absent simply by dint of the presence of the objects that normally surround it. Beds and wheelchairs of steel, crutches of rubber, or oversized household utensils all point to the body's everyday activities, and underline its neediness and limitations. It is only on second glance that the objects freighted with our collective memories reveal their latent violence. Nothing is as it seems. The child's cot becomes a prison and fig. p. 6 an instrument of torture when the mattress is replaced by razor sharp wire. The friendly *Welcome* on a doormat is transformed into a fig. p. 30 threat by pointed metal pins. Two swings in complex interaction are capable of cutting the potential users' legs, while the handles of a wheelchair are knife-blades that might injure fig. p. 31 the potential helper. Household utensils are fig. pp. 20– electrified, enlarged beyond the scale of the human body, made unusable, mutated into weapons. Everyday things that normally serve our well-being, and which we usually associate with homeliness and protection, suddenly

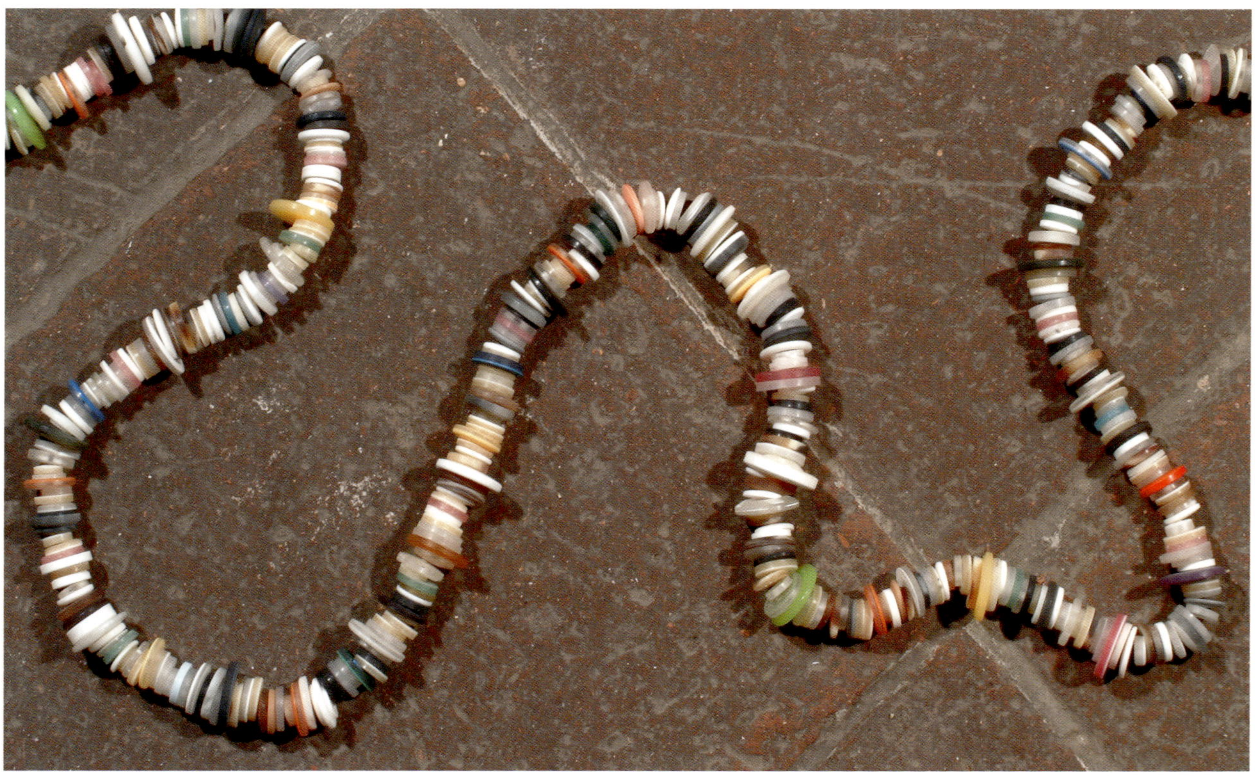

 Umbilicus · 2003

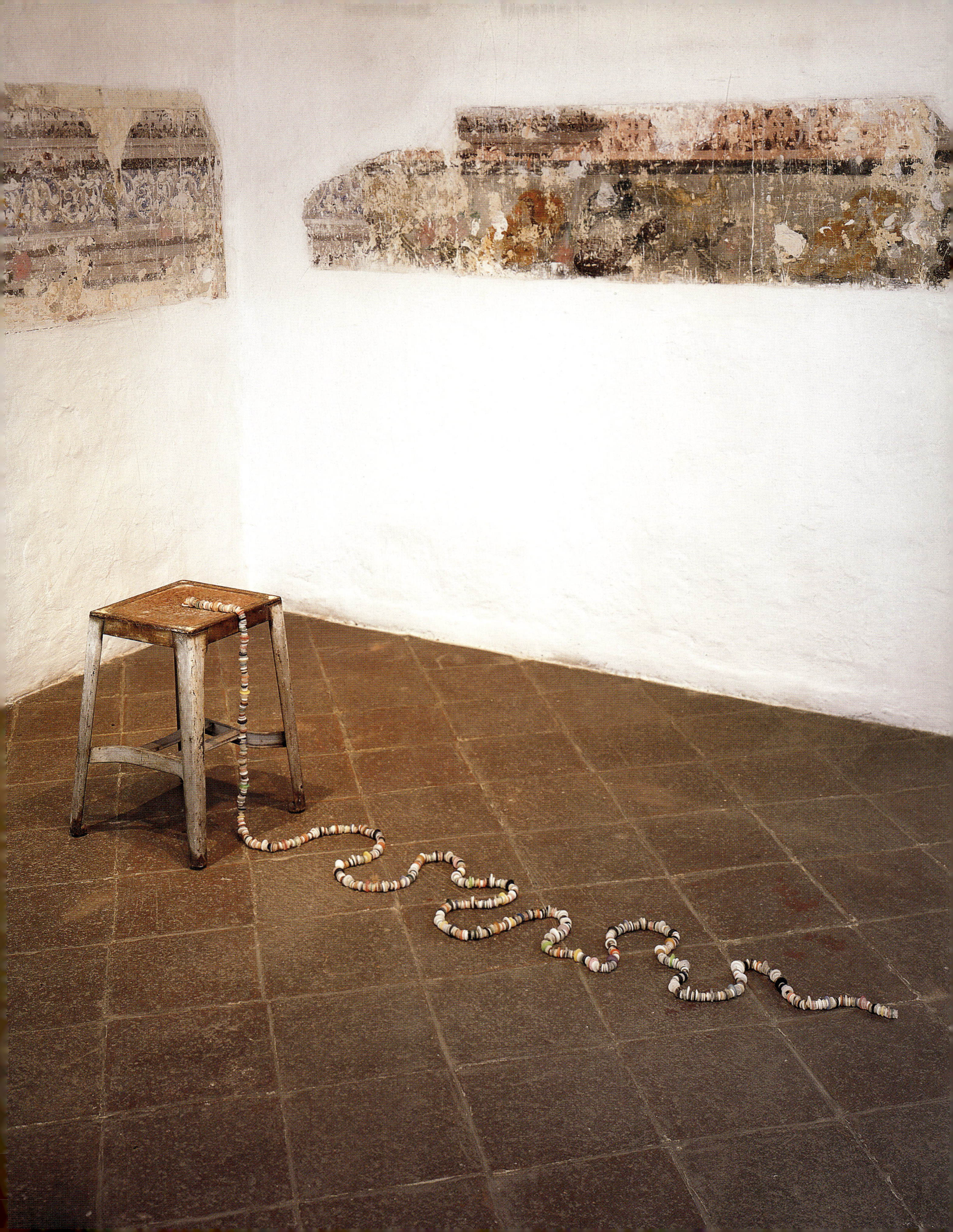

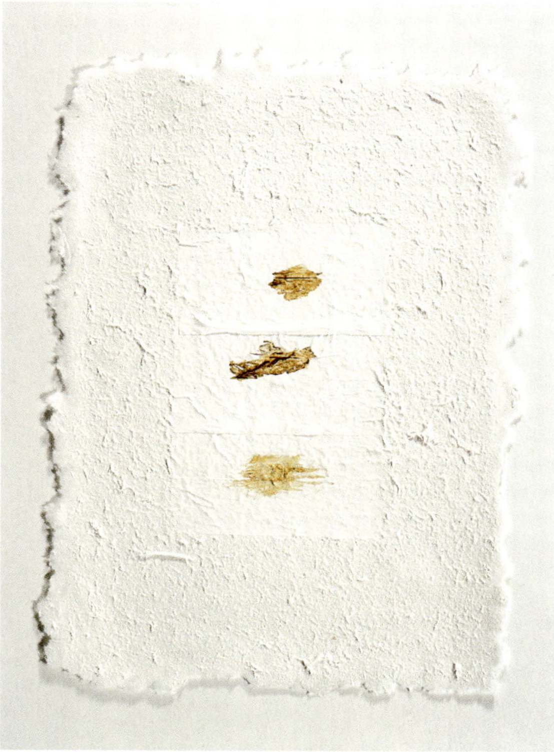

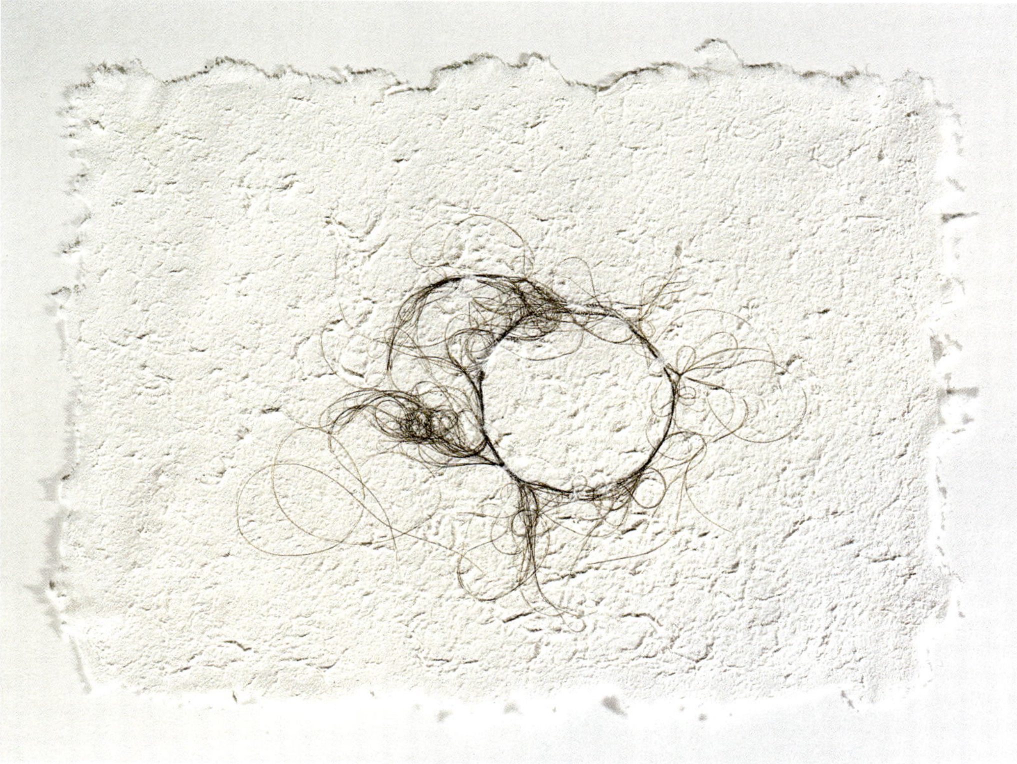

Skin, nail and hair · 2003

Hand Made Paper · 2003

Blood Drawing · 2003

Hair Drawing · 2003

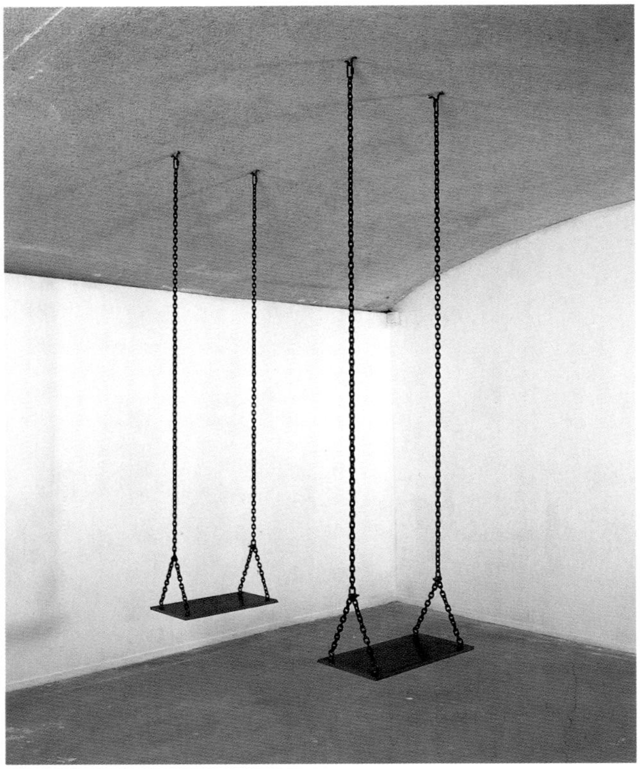

appear as menacing. Even the large-scale in-
fig. pp. 16–19 stallations such as *Light Sentence, Quarters,*
fig. pp. 26–27 *Cage-à-deux* express the horrors of a life lived in uniformity, under external surveillance and organisation, pressed into standard units. While the notion of cells and emergency accommodation readily springs to mind, these works are also based on real experiences: Light Sentence, for instance, is based on the artist's observation of low-income housing on the outskirts of major European cities.[9]

Hatoum does not present the threatening aspect of these works with pathos and admonition, but at times with a sense of humorous detachment. Rather than portraying her own feelings, she seeks to trigger existential feelings in the spectator. When we look at her work, we are struck by its formal clarity and almost cool precision. Yet instead of perceiving this clarity and coolness as an isolating aspect that distances us from the work, we find it becomes a vehicle by which the physical and psychological effect of the work is heightened. By taking an approach that is both emotional and detached, Hatoum succeeds in portraying the terrible as beautiful and the beautiful as terrible, arousing expectations and disappointing them at the same time. Hard and rigid materials are juxtaposed with ones that are soft and fluid; the timeless perfection of objects, seemingly untouched by life, bearing a certain affinity to Minimal Art's approach to form and material, and the intimacy and vulnerability of the body exposed to the effects of time and decay, become mutually and causally interrelated. While Hatoum's works may sensitise our perceptions, they do not aim to shock or injure, but appeal instead

Balançoires en fer · 1999

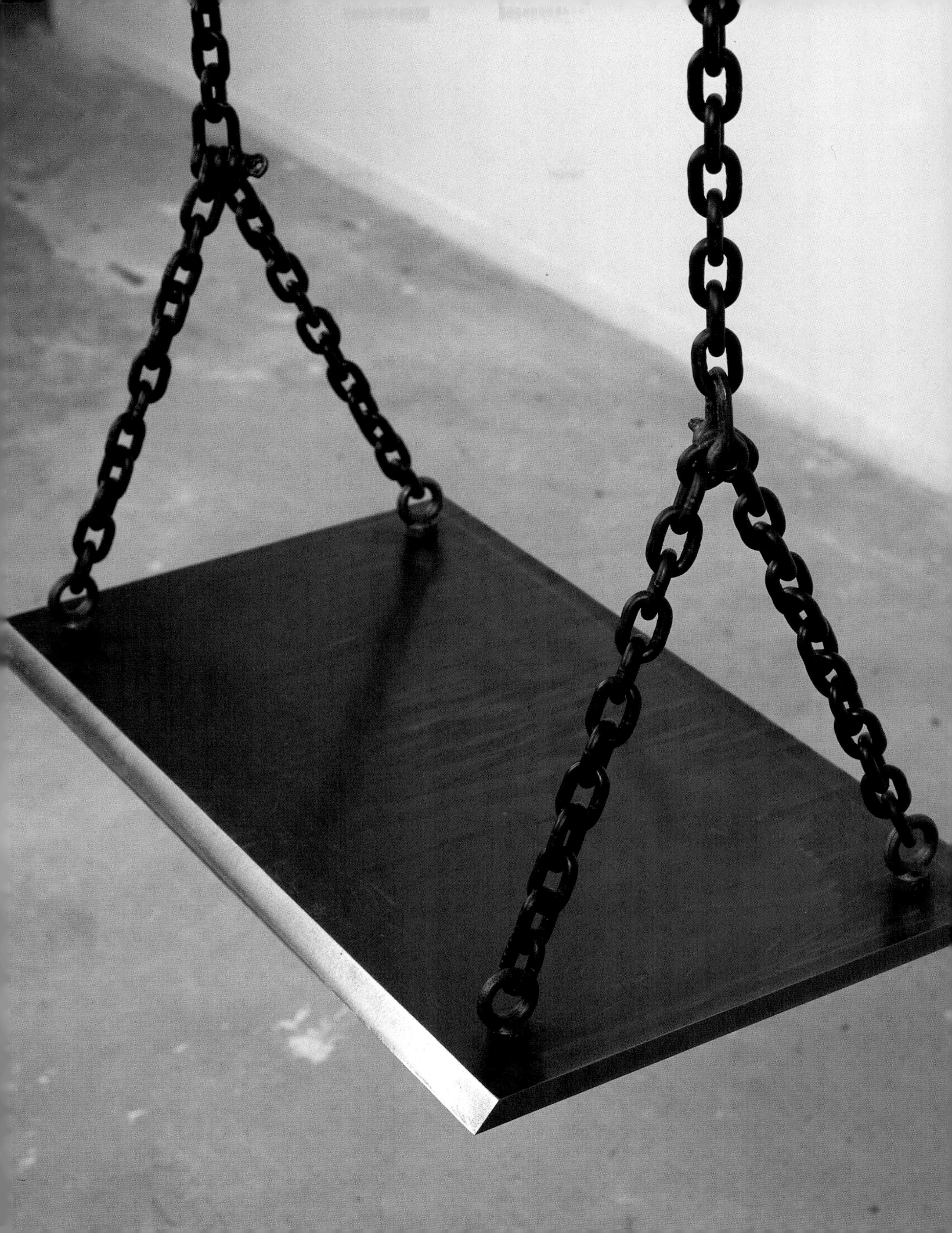

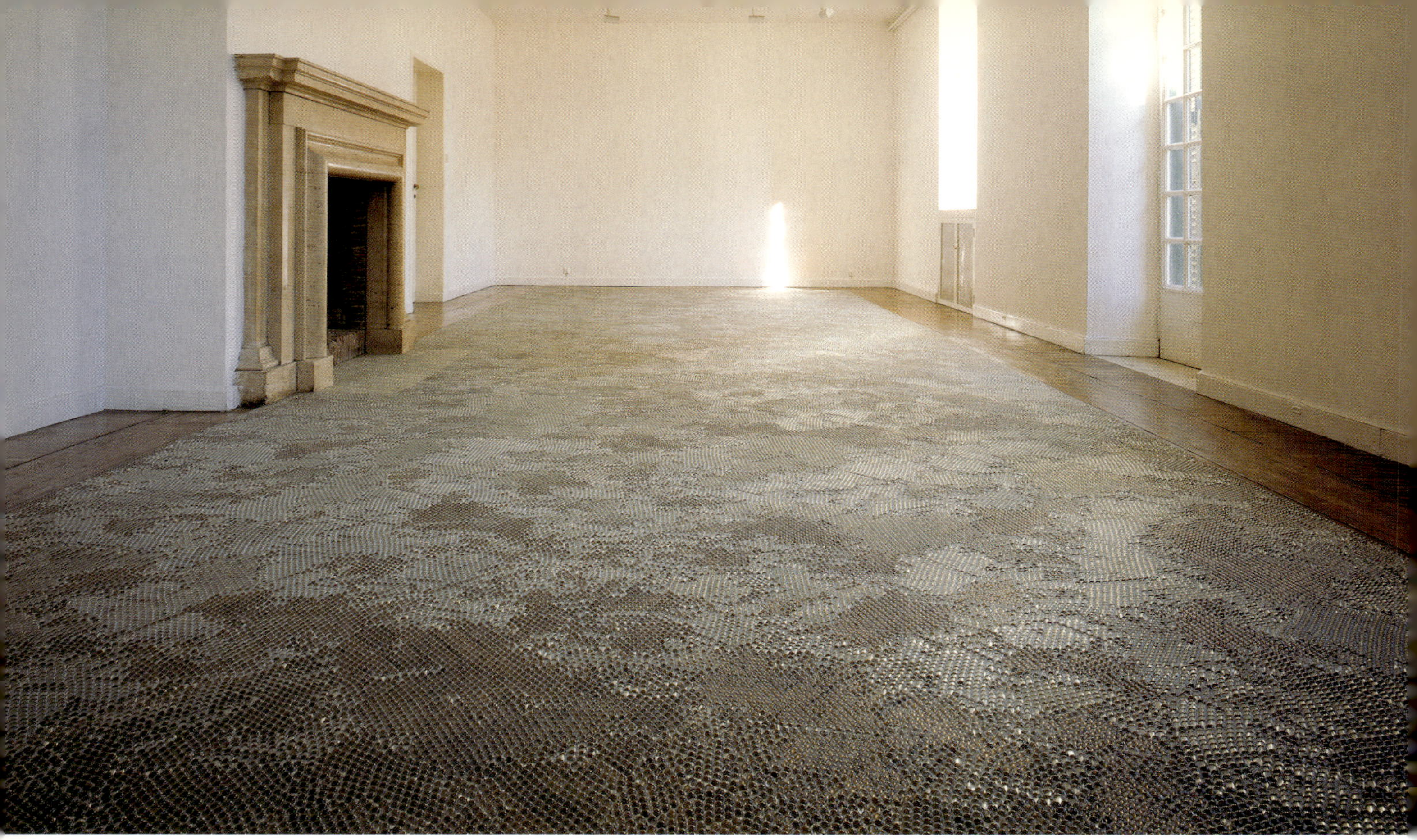

to our powers of imagination. The experience of being both perpetrator and victim, a feeling of aggression and pain, leaves a lasting impression in the mind of the spectator.

The self exists only in terms of its relation to, and separateness from, the surrounding world. While the body, through the senses, defines the receptiveness of the self to the world, absorbing and exuding energy, it also defines the insurmountable boundary between the self and the world that is crucial to a sense of identity and self-awareness. It is this boundary that makes it possible for a dynamic relationship to occur between self and world in the first place, thereby enabling an awareness of identity. Our reciprocal relationship with the world and our separateness from it show that the world as the Other is also a constant and crucial aspect of our identity. Hatoum works in this highly charged area between the body and the world. Most importantly, she has analysed the problematic and violent side of this relationship. The world restricts the body's potential for movement or penetrates it. As individuals, we stand on unsteady ground *(Marbles Carpet)*, never certain of our place, and are constantly on the move *(Traffic)*. Living far from her homeland, Hatoum addresses in her works her own experience of exile and rootlessness, the feeling of being 'out of place'[10], albeit without ever seeking to illustrate her personal fate in these intense images of alienation and loss.

fig. p. 39

Time and again Hatoum has addressed the issue of boundaries, always with the existence of cultural, ethnic, sexual, economic, physical and psychological limits in mind, and probably also with a certain fear that breaking down

Marbles Carpet · 1995

the boundary is more likely to result in the destruction of the other than to create greater unity. She questions the drawing of boundaries g. pp. 68–69 in specific situations, as in *Present Tense*, and puts it into context in its inevitable relation to boundlessness, for one cannot exist without the other. The finite-infinite form of the circle contains within it the simultaneity of the limited and the limitless. Gloves sewn together grasp endlessly and aimlessly at one another g. pp. 58–59 in *Chain*, and bottles of wine become a *Vi-* fig. p. 61 *cious Circle*, their corporeality emphasised, when the necks of the bottles are pushed into the deep dimple in the base of the next bottle.

Even the horizon is a boundary that divides the world. Hatoum has created one of g. pp. 62–63 toy soldiers in *Horizon:* the figures blend in the distance into a line, and the eye perceives them individually only at close quarters. Apart from the narrative significance of this endless martial chain of mutual threat, the work also addresses the confusion of seeing and of a shifting zone in which our perception alters from one view to another and one thing becomes another. In this way, Hatoum provokes the movement of seeing and, with that, the movement of the spectator in the space. The ambivalence and shifting of our perception is also addressed by Hatoum in other ways. The horizon provides a point of orientation for our perception and is indeed the very basis on which the body takes its conscious place in the world. And although, or perhaps because, Hatoum materialises the horizon with her toy soldiers, she makes us realise that the horizon is immaterial – it is a construct of the mind that makes space tangible in terms of up/down, here/there, renders it visible and allows us to

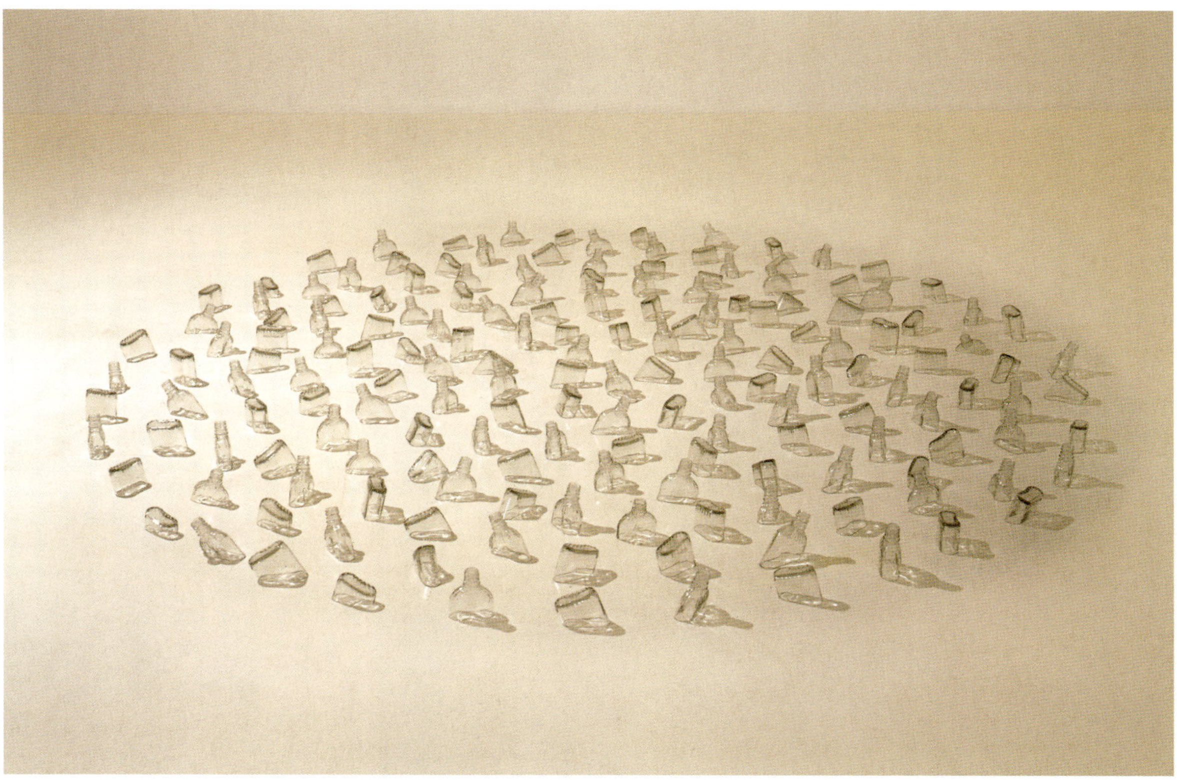

Drowning Sorrows · 2001

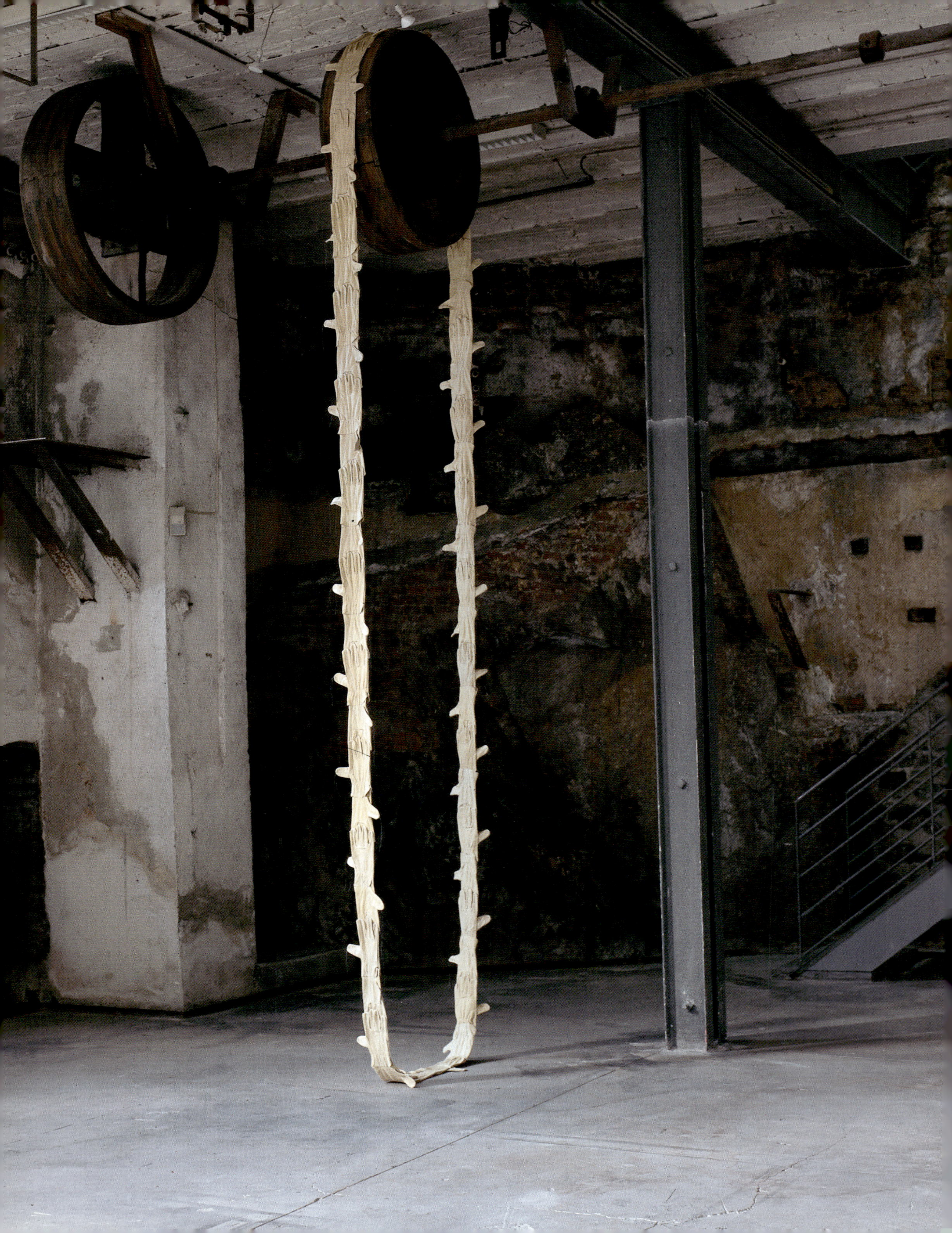

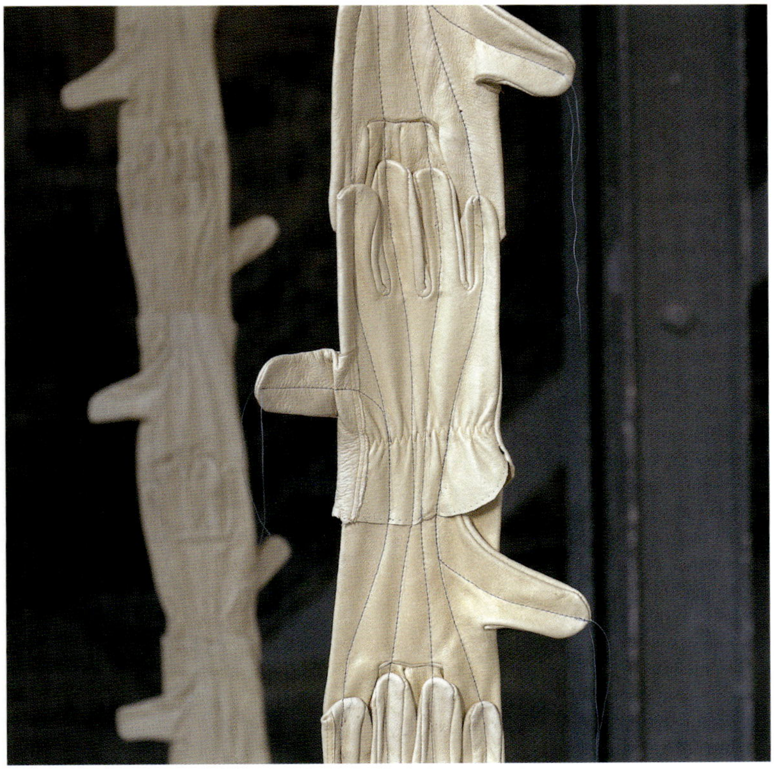

see ourselves in relation to it, but at the same time denies us proximity, keeping us at a distance as it runs into infinity.

Although the body and the world are, by necessity, fundamentally different, they are perceived in the works of Hatoum as one and the same. One's own body is no less alien, unstable and insecure than the world itself; an unexplored landscape, a bounded space that is both protective shell and inescapable prison, a boundless expanse that is both liberating and frightening. The journey through the body becomes as much of an odyssey as any journey through the world. In her works, Hatoum has found exemplary ways of imaging the complex experience of the body in the world on which the self depends, and of showing how we are bound to the body, not only in and with the world, but also against the world, and how we are bound to its abilities, its failings, its mortality – it is through the body that we are here, and with the body that we pass away.

Translated from the German by Ishbel Flett

Chain · 1999

Notes

1 Mona Hatoum in a 1996 interview with Claudia Spinelli, in Michael Archer, Guy Brett and Catherine de Zegher, *Mona Hatoum,* London 1997, pp. 134-141, (this quote p. 141).

2 Ibid., p. 141.

3 See the artist's statements in the interview with Claudia Spinelli, p. 140, and in her interview with Michael Archer, in Archer, Brett and de Zegher 1997 (see note 1), pp. 8-30 (this quote p. 8).

4 Mona Hatoum, interview with Michael Archer, ibid., p. 8.

5 On the performances, see the essay by Christoph Heinrich in this publication, pp. 82-129.

6 Mona Hatoum has repeatedly stressed this simultaneity of attraction and repulsion, seduction and resistance (see also the interview with Janine Antoni, first published in *Bomb* magazine, no. 63, spring 1998, later in Mona Hatoum, exh. cat. Centro de Arte de Salamanca 2002, pp. 117-131; this quote p. 130).

7 Mona Hatoum in the interview with Claudia Spinelli (see note 1), p. 134.

8 Mona Hatoum in the interview with Janine Antoni (see note 6), p. 128.

9 Mona Hatoum in conversation with Doris von Drathen, in *Künstler: Kritisches Lexikon der Gegenwartskunst,* issue 51/18, Munich 2000, p. 14.

10 Mona Hatoum in the interview with Michael Archer (see note 3), p. 9.

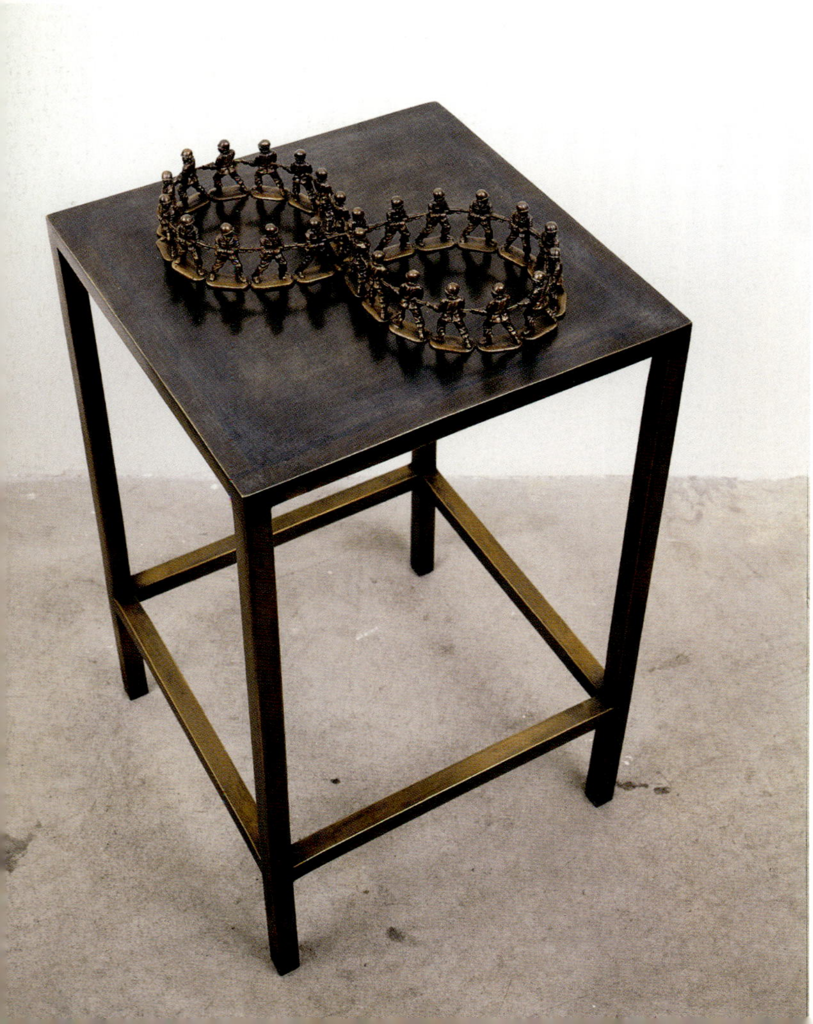

∞ (Infinity) · 1991–2001

Vicious Circle · 1999

Horizon · 1998 ▶

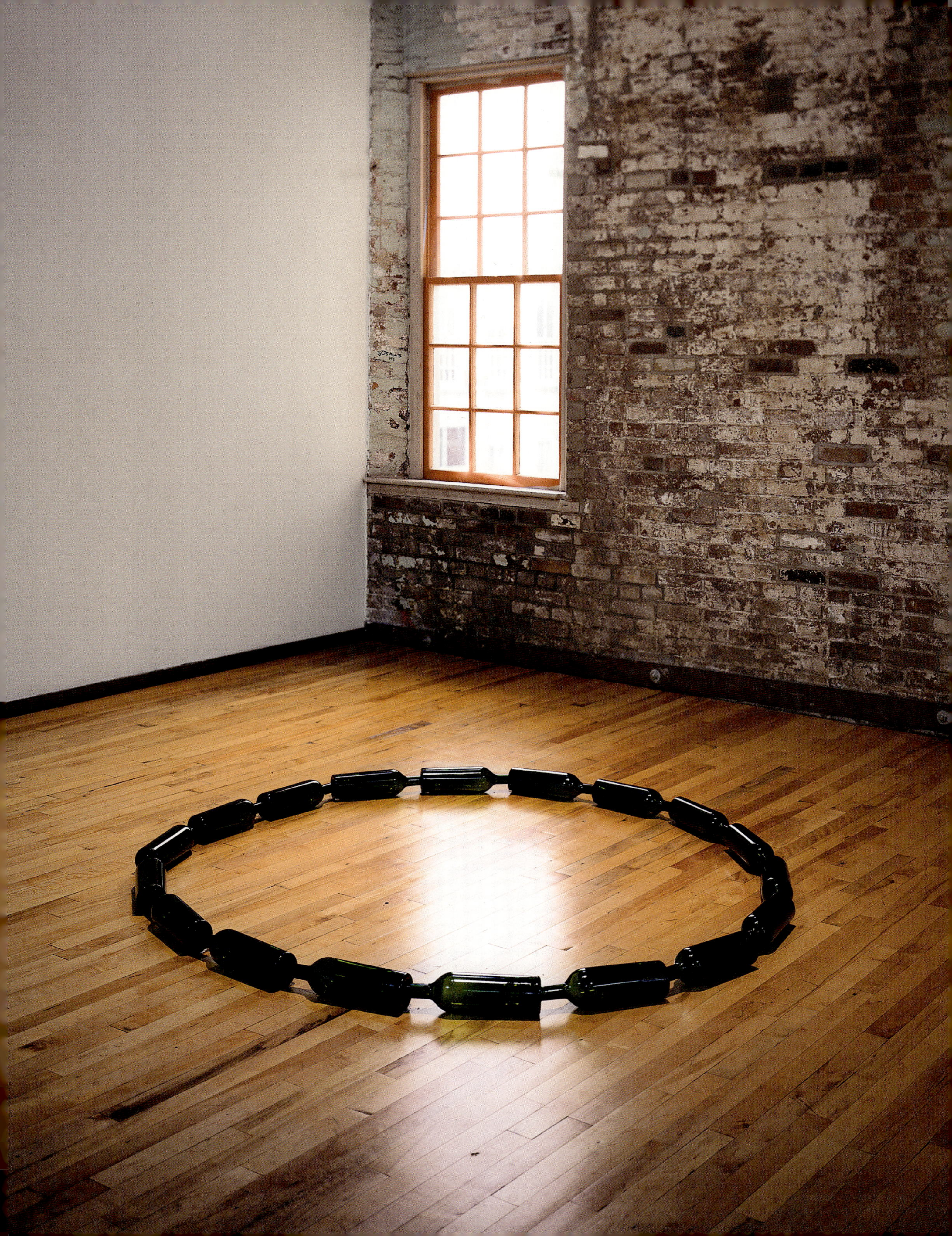

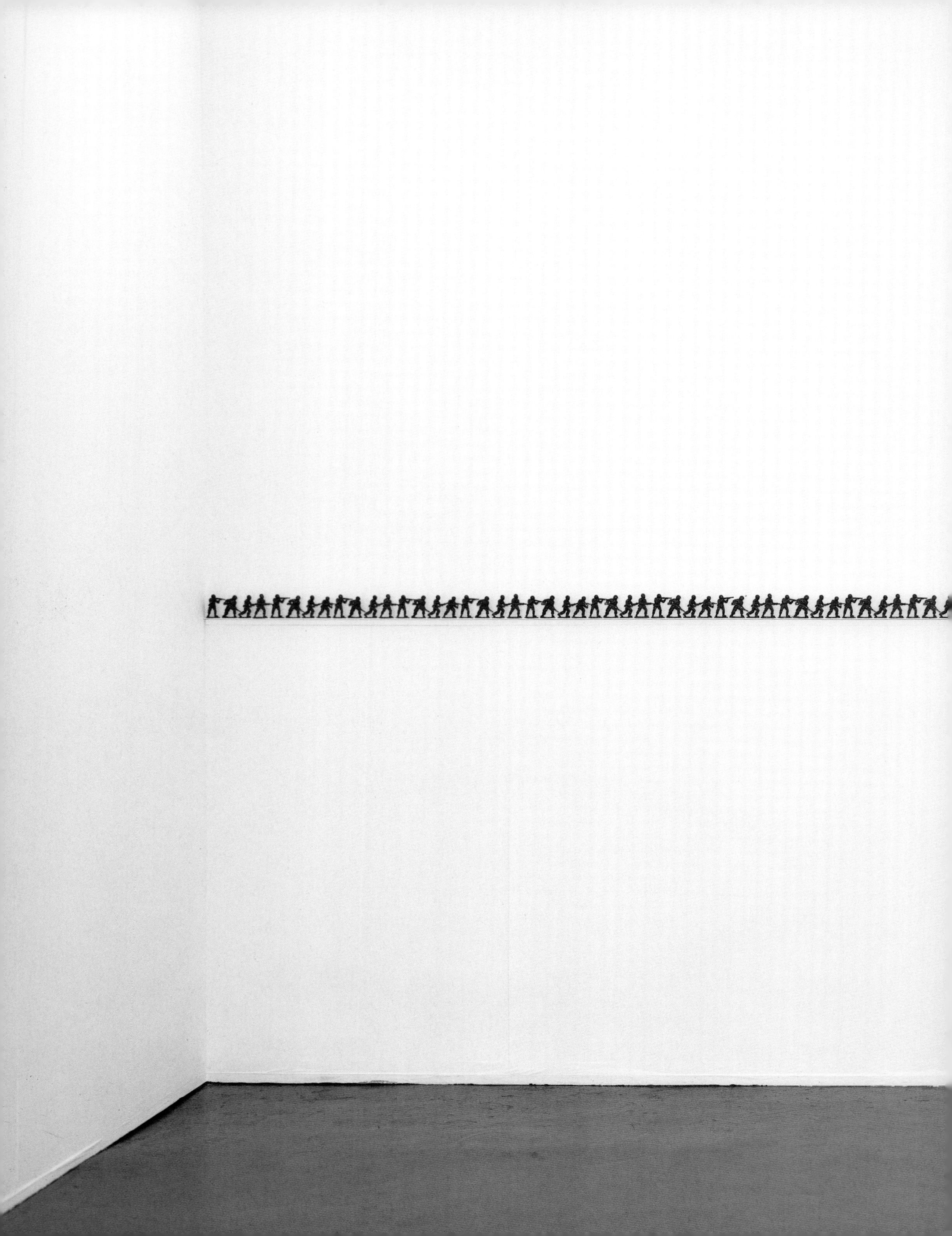

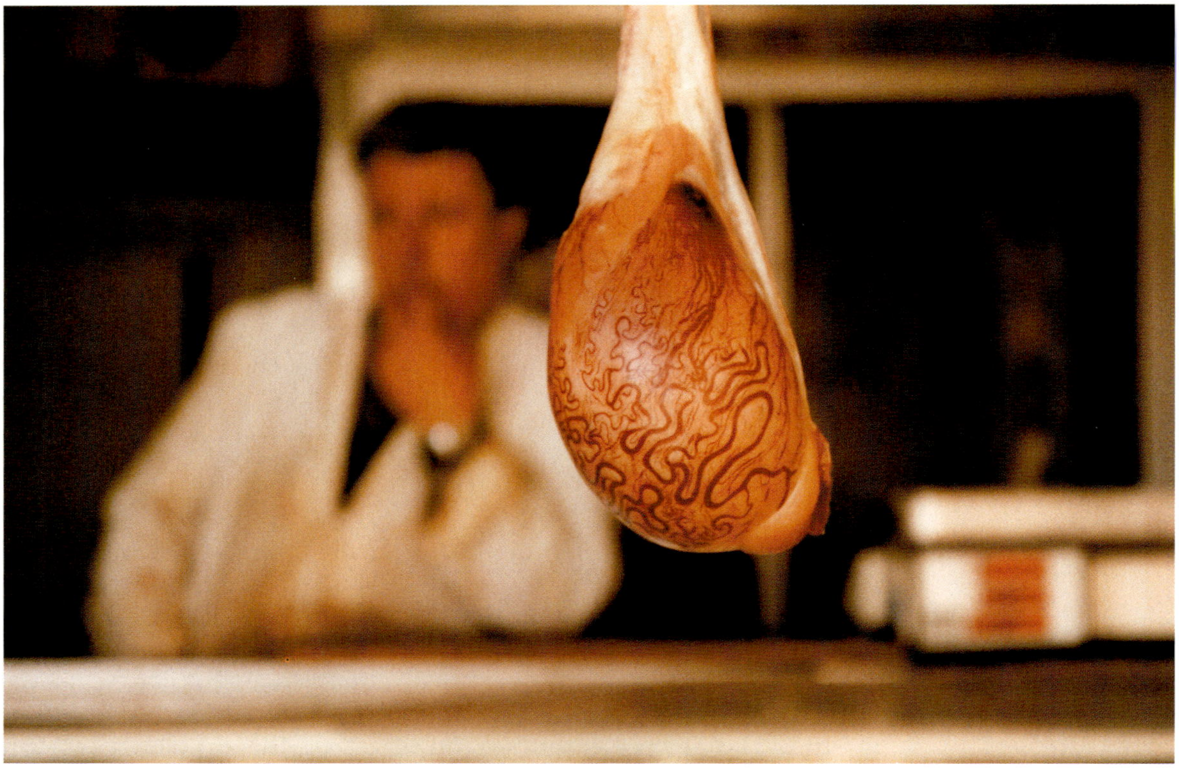

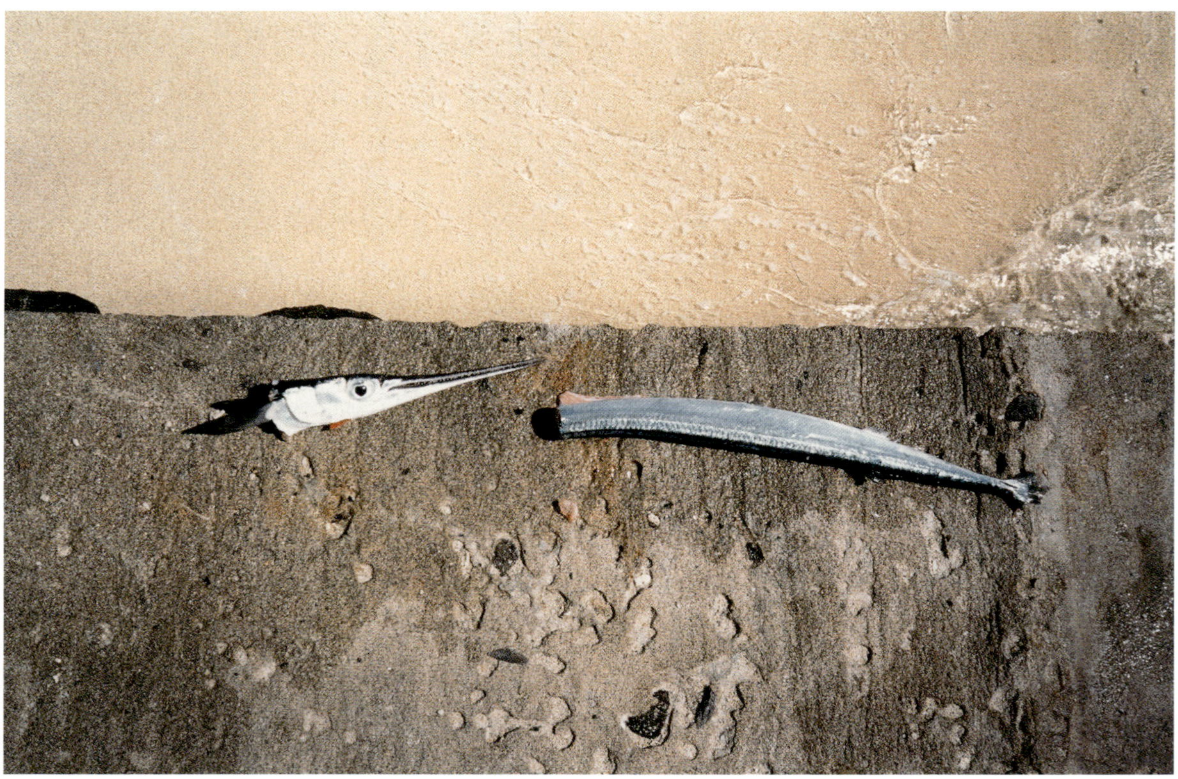

Baid Ghanam (sheep's testicle) · 1996

Garfish (Bequia) · 1996

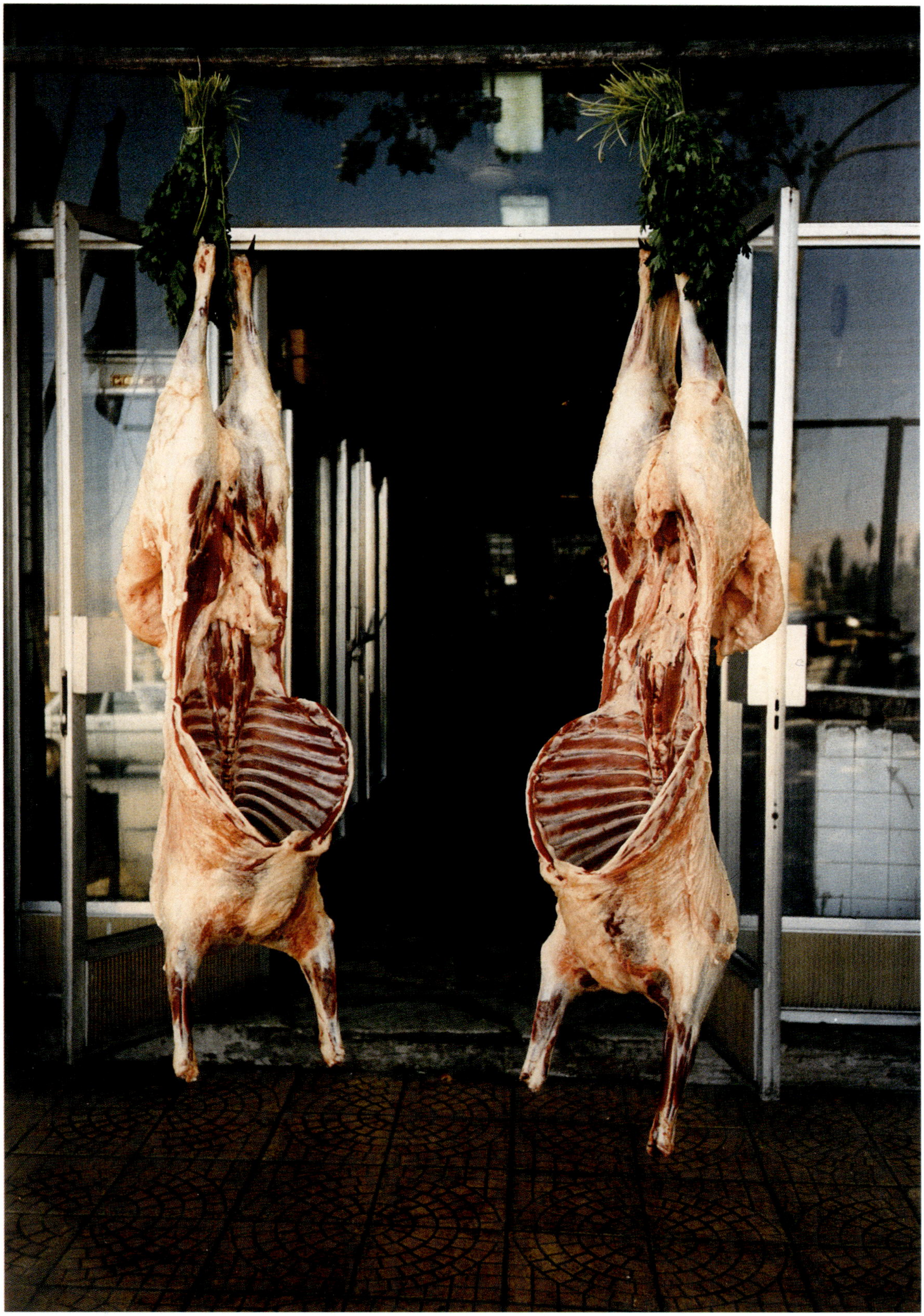

Carcasses (Baalbeck) · 1998

Nina Zimmer

Epiphanies of the Everyday Materiality and Meaning in Mona Hatoum's Work

'I find that my greatest difficulty and the really most painful and difficult part of my work is draining and ridding my mind of that burden of meanings which I've absorbed through the culture,' said Carl Andre in an interview in 1970.[1] He thus gave expression to a tendency that was characterised by its reduction of artistic means to simple geometric forms, which were often used in series and made of simple industrial materials. This reduction went hand in hand with the utopian concept of an art that was totally self-referential, and thus broke with the centuries-old art history principle of making meaningful statements. In the artistic system of Minimal Art, achieving meaninglessness was the objective, cultural neutrality, the nirvana.

Mona Hatoum belongs to a generation of artists who, through a discourse with this artistic position of the sixties, have not only taken their own standpoint on it, but also strictly differentiated themselves from it. Whereas the point of departure in a number of her works is a formally-reduced aesthetic marked by geometry and serialism, her main focus returns again to the production of meaning. She thus reverses minimalist principles and arrives at new possibilities of expression through her specific handling of materials.

The Light at the End was created by Hatoum as a site-specific installation for the Showroom Gallery in London in 1989. An iron frame subdivided by six equally spaced electric heating rods stands before an acutely angled corner of a room. The rods are powered, and electric energy is converted into heat and light. The impression made by the regularly positioned, yellowish-orange glowing rods – reminiscent of serial arrangements – suddenly changes the moment the viewer comes closer to the work and feels the heat from the rods on his or her skin. Through its physical presence, the grid of rods, which hitherto functioned as a vertical structure, unavoidably acquires certain associations with pain and torture. Thereupon, one reads it in physical terms and estimates, for example, that one's head would fit exactly between the rods, and that a person could squeeze into the space between the work and the floor – with unpredictable results. Consequently, the system of *The Light at the End* thus undergoes a reinterpretation, becoming a concrete, tangible image of physical danger. The fascinating thing about this work is the way the different layers of meaning are actually triggered by different senses: whereas initially the viewer may visually associate the work with Minimalist neon sculptures, at the level of the skin's sensitivity to different temperatures, a completely different, emotional and physical response is evoked. fig. p. 15

Hatoum has made repeated reference to the Minimal Art of the seventies: 'I had a long relationship with Minimalism at the time before starting to make work that was more conceptual.'[2] Apart from a few exceptions, this connection has not found expression in texts on her work.[3]

Hatoum's oeuvre to date can be divided into her early work, especially characterised by performances, and a phase after 1989, initiated by *The Light at the End*, where she worked predominantly with installations.

g. pp. 16–17

Light Sentence, a 1992 installation is structurally similar to *The Light at the End*. It consists of wire mesh lockers placed in the shape of a U. The material is of industrial origin, a circumstance Mona Hatoum – like many Minimalists – discloses.[4] Instead of using material that refers to its own specific qualities, she chooses objects that were made for a specific purpose – products – whose everyday context she includes in her work.

The mesh is based on a square pattern, and the basic locker element is cuboid. The geometric perfection of the ensemble is only disturbed by open doors and their locking mechanism. From the ceiling hangs a naked, moving light bulb that slowly descends, touches the floor, and topples over slightly, before slowly rising up again with a gently swinging movement. The light from the bulb casts a dense network of shadows through the wire mesh of the lockers onto the surrounding walls. Because the source of light is moving, these shadows are constantly changing. What at first seems restricted and reduced – an installation composed of cuboid modules – is transformed into a dramatic scenario. The emptiness of the lockers is countered by an abundance of superimposed shadows on the walls, bundles of lines fan out only to recede again, to correspond with the movement of the bulb. The beauty of this shadow play, however, is overlaid by other associations: the descent and ascent of the naked bulb has something unrelenting about it; lockers are normally havens of the private in institutional contexts like the military, or prisons. These lockers are made of wire mesh so that their potentially dangerous contents can be kept under permanent surveillance. In this installation, the ray of light from the bulb, which penetrates everything like a searchlight, represents the authoritarian gaze.

The impression this work makes is not produced by the qualities of the material used. Instead, the work thrives on the many and varied images and associations which these materials have in the everyday lives of the viewers and which they bring to the work. Hatoum was thus able to greatly extend the range of materials she could avail herself of for her art. Moreover, with this method she is able to use materials that have traditionally male connotations, for example steel, as well as materials traditionally associated with women like hair, soap or glass beads. She thus playfully disregards the aesthetic of Minimalism, whose materials very deliberately expressed power and masculinity.[5]

The way the image of this installation is given concrete content remains, to a certain degree, open. Mona Hatoum: 'A work of art has two aspects: the natural, physical aspect, which I think of as the conscious aspect that the artist can manipulate and shape; and then there is the very complex cultural and unconscious aspect of the artwork. This is rich and full of meanings and associations, and it is as impossible to explain fully or comprehend as an individual or the social subconscious. Years after making this work, I still discover interesting associations, sometimes pointed out to me by viewers.'[6] In another interview she explains the work in a more political way as an indictment of torture and oppression, but rejects a too strongly directed interpretation: 'The political issues are quite important but I do not like to deal with them in a didactic way.'[7]

To a certain extent, Hatoum steers the reception of her works through the titles she

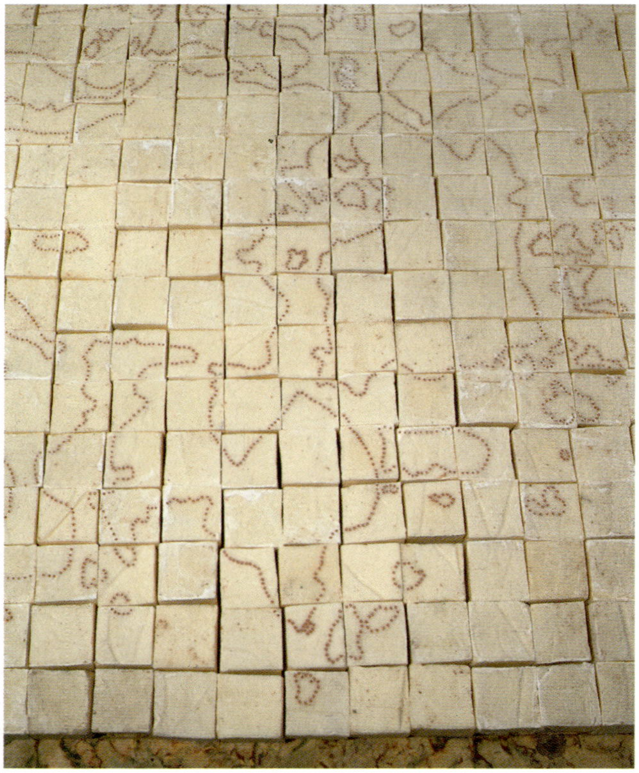

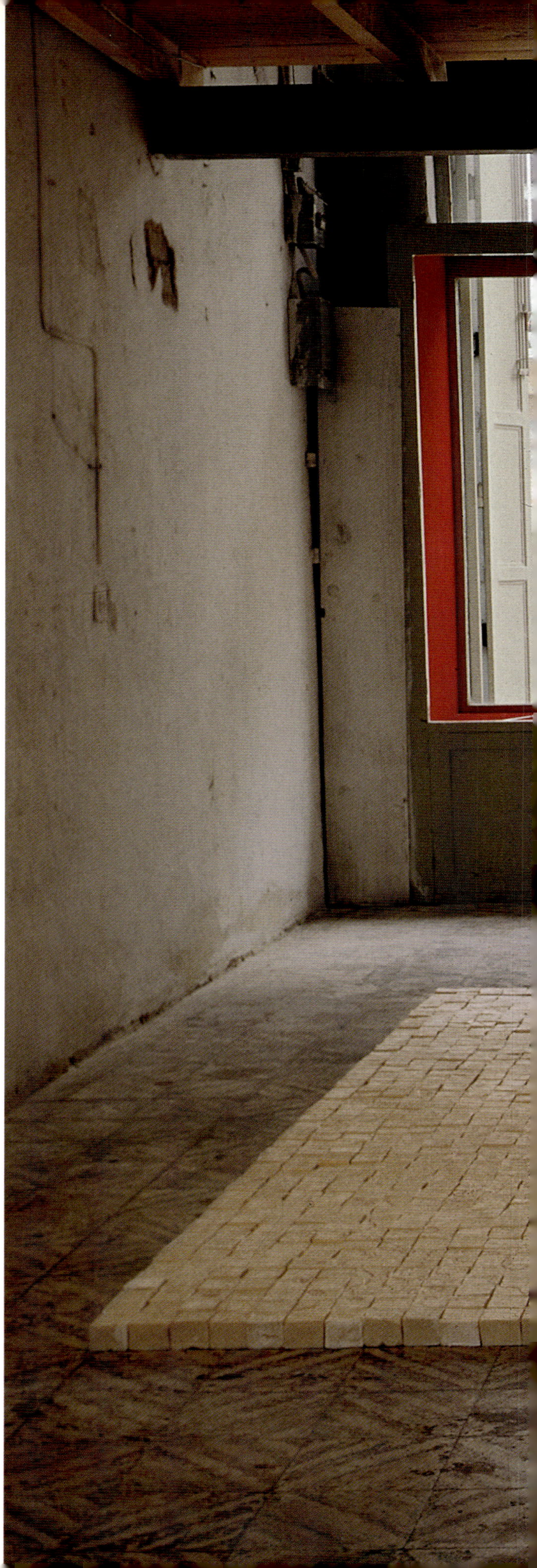

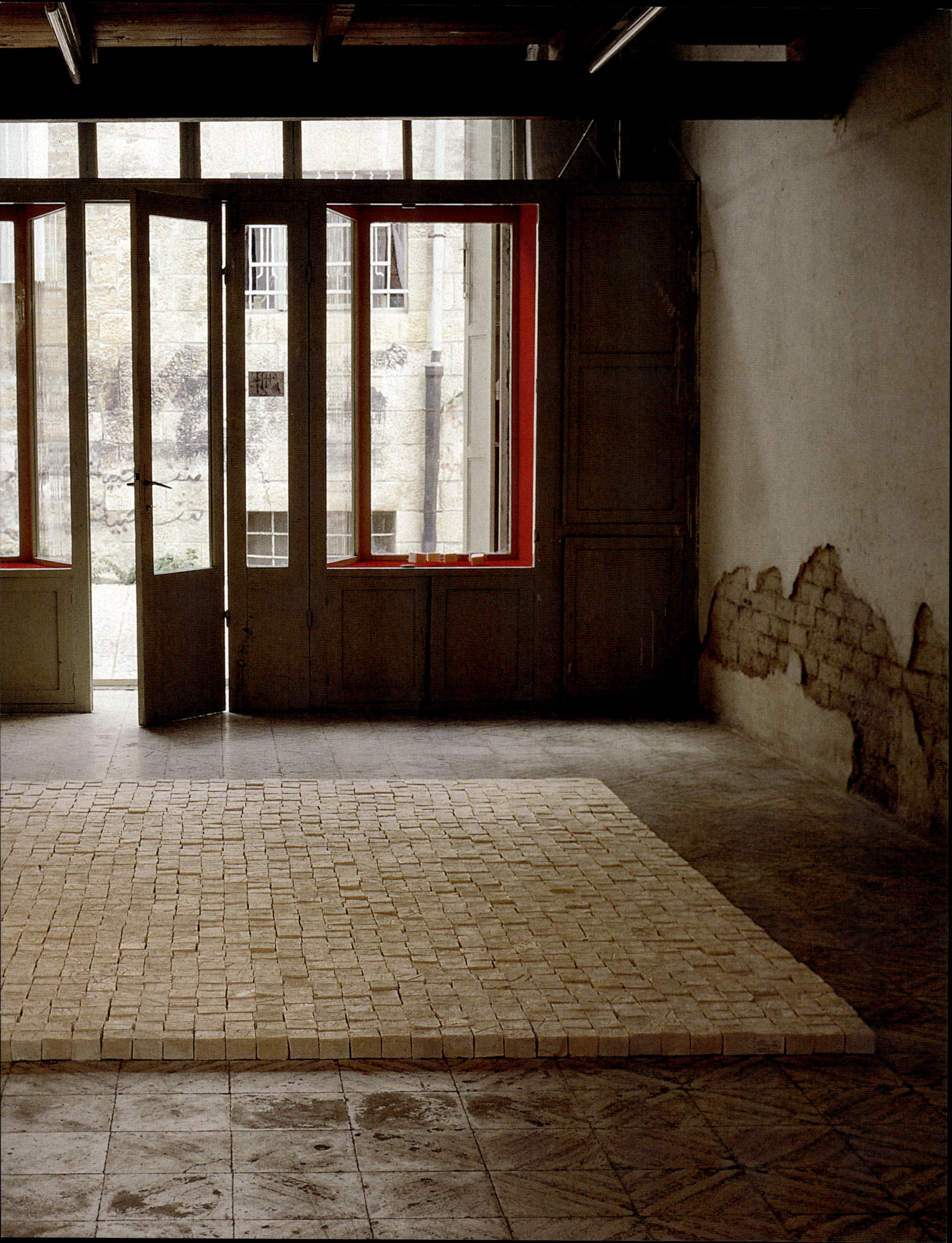

chooses. These are often complicated plays on words pre-supposing a familiarity with the English, sometimes also the French[8] and Spanish languages and their etymologies.[9] The title *Light Sentence*, for example, may function as follows: 'light' can mean both the opposite of heavy and also the opposite of dark, so that here the word conjures up both a 'light punishment' and a 'punishment by light', associated with forms of torture using light; the expression 'life sentence' also resonates in this title. *The Light at the End* plays with the phrase 'the light at the end of the tunnel', a promise of hope, which is thwarted by the dangerous light from the glowing hot rods.

The artist thus linguistically reconstructs her artistic approach in the installations: she puts forward a certain familiar linguistic image (or an easily read artistic form). At another level the experiences of the viewer are added, resulting in the first impression being edged out and the need to construe a completely new reading. James Joyce described this moment, for literature, as an 'epiphany'[10], a sudden shift of meaning or an endowment of meaning through a visual manifestation. Originally derived from the appearance of God in Catholicism, Joyce profaned the term, using it to designate a moment of insight that endows meaning. This moment of recognition, when one meaning changes into another, is possible several times in Hatoum's works. The process takes place as the viewer engages with the work, yet it is not automatic. Instead, it always remains dependent on the viewing subject's knowledge of the world[11] and life-world[12] experiences.

The intersubjective treasure trove of experience with which Hatoum works is, at least in part, culturally encoded. In exhibitions in which the artist has been successfully participating for years in Europe, North America, the Middle East, Japan and Latin America, the viewers from the different countries and cultures bring ever-new experiences with them to the artworks.

Present Tense, a work Hatoum created and exhibited in Jerusalem in 1996, is also based on a modular structure using block elements. The formally minimalist arrangement becomes charged with meaning through the choice of material: the artist uses blocks of Nablus soap, a traditionally Palestinian product made of potash and olive oil. Mona Hatoum arranged the blocks of soap in a square on the floor. She cut notches into the surface into which she then pressed little red beads. These dots made up lines that, from above, can be read as the outlines of a map. It is the map of the Palestinian state as envisaged by the Oslo Agreement of 1993. The outlines show the disjointedness of this potential state, which looks more like an archipelago than a territorial state. Just how sensitive the topic of drawing maps is in this conflict can be seen from comparative studies of Palestinian and Israeli school textbooks carried out by independent institutions, which analyse the respective maps used as to their ideological thrust.[13] fig. pp. 68–6

The map agreed upon in Oslo was largely unknown to the Western public. Yet the map problem had an impact even on Germany, where a discussion emerged on the outline maps of the Middle East used in television news bulletins. The conflict arose through their graphic simplification, the reproach being that this falsified matters upfront, as it suggested a continuous, autonomous, Palestinian region, which did not exist in that form.

Given that the title of Mona Hatoum's work, *Present Tense*, unites contradictory aspects, it is capable of aptly characterising the relationships between the two parties. Not only does it play on the grammatical term 'present tense' for the present, it also points to the prevailing 'tense' situation. Furthermore, there are the associations with 'present' which means both to give a gift and to present arms.

As the examples so far have illustrated, a formal point of departure for a number of Mona Hatoum's works is her links with Minimalism.[14] By means of reduced forms, regularity, and the repetition of modular structures, she presents the viewer with a level of reception which at first is neutral in meaning, only to arrive at the actual significance of the work on another level of understanding, a level complemented by evocative elements like the title and the choice of a material whose everyday context provides a wealth of allusions.

With this approach, the work of art is no longer graspable in all its depth and richness at first glance, being one of the criteria for an aesthetics of autonomy as demanded by Modernist Art criticism. In the installation, the viewer is exposed instead to a situation which is created by the artwork, which he or she completes, bringing his or her own very personal experiences and interpretations. This mutual process can be understood as the production of meaning, but also as the subversion of meaning.[15] It is because Hatoum includes us as viewers into the production of meaning in this way that her works are capable of affecting us so directly.

Hatoum reverses Minimalist aesthetics and the 'burden of meanings', which Carl Andre thought he had shaken off once and for all, returns: and her works reverberate with political, psychological, feminist, social or cultural meanings that alternate or complement one another.

Translated from the German by Pauline Cumbers

Notes

1 Interview with Phyllis Tuchman, *Artforum,* vol. VIII, no. 10 (June 1970), pp. 55–61, p. 59.
2 Interview with Michael Archer, in Michael Archer, Guy Brett and Catherine de Zegher, *Mona Hatoum,* London 1997, p. 10.
3 One chapter of Judith Marth's dissertation deals with this issue (Judith Marth,*Von der Performance zur Installation am Beispiel Mona Hatoums,* dissertation, Hamburg 2003, typescript, pp. 107–117; at this point I would like to thank the author for placing her as yet unpublished work at my disposal), as does the essay by Lynn Zelevansky in the exh. cat., *Sense and Sensibility: Women Artists and Minimalism in the Nineties,* Museum of Modern Art, New York 1994. In her essay, Zelevansky designates Minimal Art as the art movement that influenced the second half of the twentieth century as decisively as Cubism the first half. This analogy clearly illustrates Zelevansky's claim that Minimal Art had an epoch-making theoretical and formal influence on the art of the nineties.
4 Brett in Archer, Brett and de Zegher 1997 (see note 2), p. 68.
5 See Anna C. Chave, 'Minimalism und the Rhetoric of Power', *Arts Magazin* 64, no. 5 (January 1990), pp. 44–63.
6 Interview with Michael Archer in Archer, Brett and de Zegher 1997 (see note 2), p. 25
7 Interview with Claudia Spinelli in *Kunst-Bulletin* (September 1996), p. 17, reprinted in Archer, Brett and de Zegher 1997 (see note 2), pp. 134 f.
8 For example, *Vidéau,* which plays with the French word 'eau' for water and 'video'. See also the meaning of the title *Testimony,* as discussed on p. 33.
9 In the case of the title *Jardin Public* Mona Hatoum was interested in the etymological link between 'public' and 'pubic'. Interview with Michael Archer, in Archer, Brett and de Zegher 1997 (see note 2), p. 25.
10 Cf. Maurice Beja, *Epiphany and the Modern Novel,* London, 1971, p. 72: 'The word of course refers to the manifestation of Christ on the 12th day, January 6th, the Feast of the Epiphany. ... Joyce did not know Greek, but he may have known the original meaning of [Greek epiphany]: a manifestation, striking appearance, esp. an appearance of a divinity, according to the OED, which also relates to the verb to manifest. In English, the word has for the most part kept its theological context, although the OED does cite figurative adaptations of it. The attempt to determine sources for it other than the ecclesiastical one for Joyce's application of it have proved unconvincing.'
11 Semiotics, hermeneutics and psychology emphasise that understanding works, signs and text requires activating a 'knowledge of the world'. A particular feature of this expression is the inclusion of a pre-scientific and pre-predicative understanding of the world and of the self, and a knowledge of action that embraces not only practices and capacities but knowledge about forms of actions, situations, cultures, cultural differences and the behaviour appropriate to these. Cf. Günter Abel: *Sprache, Zeichen, Interpretation,* Frankfurt am Main 1999.
12 The term life-world goes back to Edmund Husserl.

Husserl characterises the life-world as the 'style of the experience world as a way of being', as the 'world of sensibility', the place of subjective-relative experiences, which appear as self-evident. Cf. Edmund Husserl: 'Phänomenologie der Lebenswelt', in *Ausgewählte Texte II,* ed. by Klaus Held. Stuttgart 1986, pp. 55–79.

13 Center for Monitoring the Impact of Peace (CIMP), *Jews, Israel and Peace in the Palestinian Authority Textbooks and High School Examinations,* November 2001, and *Arabs, Palestinians, Islam and Peace in Israeli School Textbooks* and other studies published on the institute's homepage, see http://www.edume.org/reports. Also, Jonathan Kriener, 'Die palästinensischen Schulbücher und ihre Kritik durch CMIP', in *Palästina Journal* 47/48 Majallat Falastin (Zeitschrift der Deutsch-Palästinenischen Gesellschaft), December 2001, pp. 26–31, and in *Israel und Palästina* (Zeitschrift des Deutsch-Israelischen Arbeitskreises für Frieden im Nahen Osten), January 2002.

14 These could also include *Short Space,* 1992; *Untitled,* Mario Flecha Gallery, London, 1992; *Socle Du Monde,* 1992/93; *Quarters,* 1996; *Current Disturbance,* 1996; *Divan Bed,* 1996, and others.

15 Juliane Rebentisch, *Ästhetik der Installation,* Frankfurt am Main 2003, p. 59.

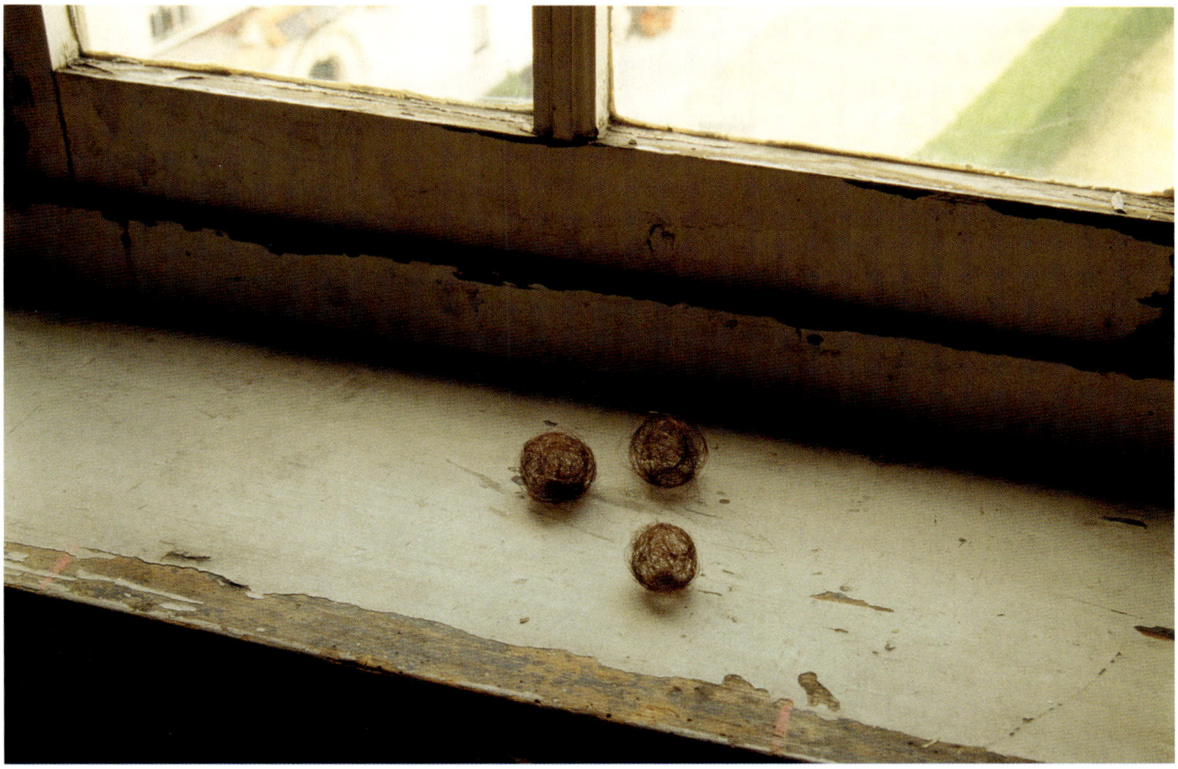

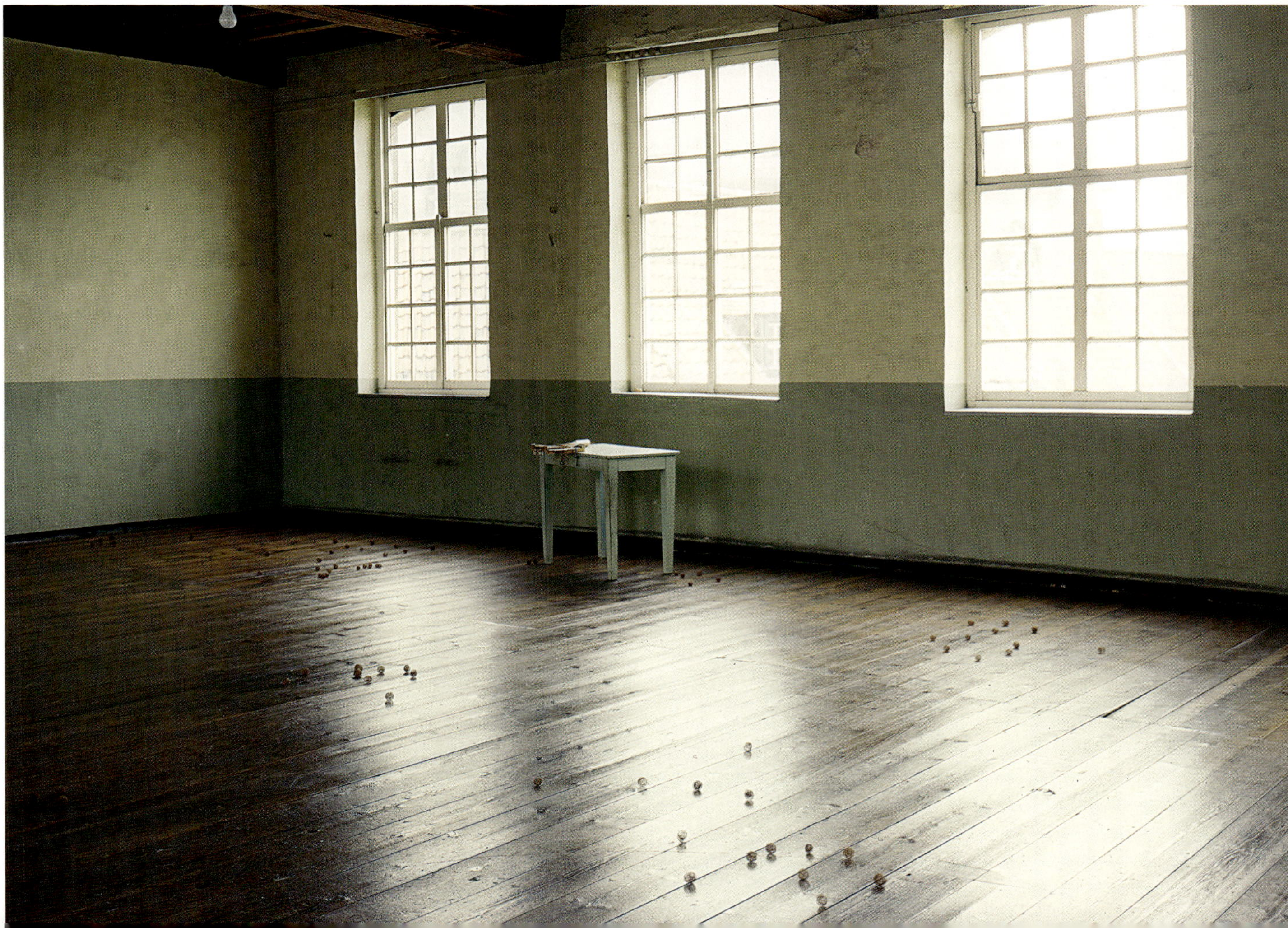

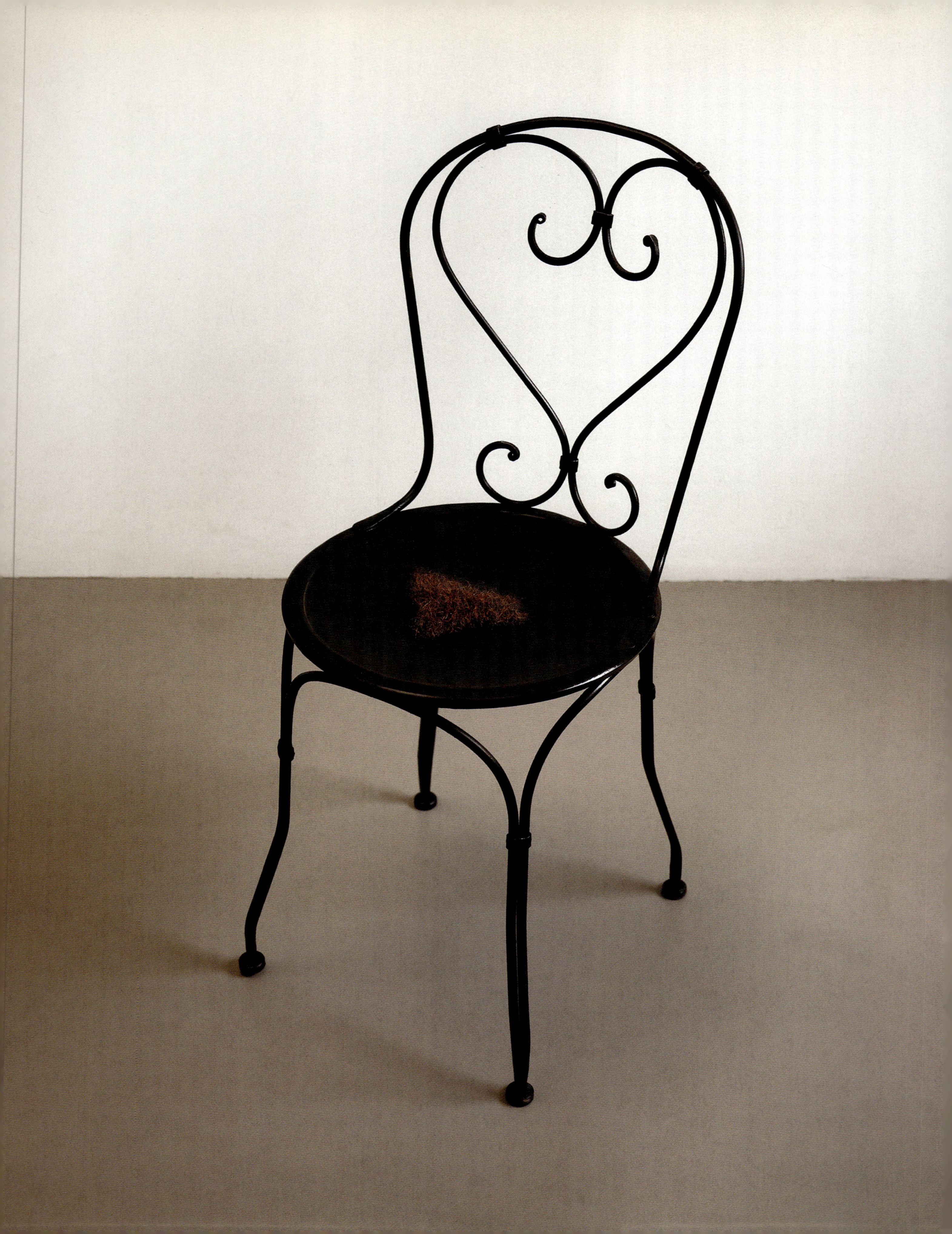

Richard Julin and Elisabeth Millqvist

Notes on Hair

The work of Mona Hatoum encourages an active engagement on the part of the viewer and invites a simultaneous and layered viewing experience: an intense physical reaction and, subsequently, an unravelling of possible meanings. What we are confronted with – the actual material that the work is made from – is often all too familiar having been selected from our everyday life. On second glance, however, abstract notions are evoked. The sensual is repulsive and physical presence is coupled with absence. Hatoum intelligently creates this ambiguity to move us in directions we haven't found ourselves in before.

Hair as material occurs in Hatoum's works from the late seventies to the present. Looking at the works that include hair as integral material we asked ourselves as viewers: what reactions are evoked by hair? We have chosen to concentrate on situations where we encounter hair in everyday life, rather than myths and other literary references. In the works where hair is a common denominator the content deals with a wide range of themes. Therefore we found it adequate to present reflections on hair as fragmented text notes, not as specific interpretations of works. Acknowledging that the same is valid for Hatoum's art as with complex systems – the whole is greater than the sum of its parts.

Hair plays a part in the creation of identity. It is the part of the human body that is easiest to change in our efforts to express our social affiliation. The role played by hair extends beyond the sensual and the aesthetic, it also serves as a guardian of social norms such as those pertaining to race and gender. The Western ideal is the dominant one. The first black millionairess in the US made her fortune with tongs that flatten out frizzy hair. Paradoxically, this invention was a development of the electrical technology used to curl the straight hair of Western women.[1] We shape our appearance in order to embody various ideals and to show who we want to be. In the video installation *Women Who Wear Wigs* (1999) by the artist Kutlug Ataman, four women are portrayed discussing when, where, why and how they wear wigs. One of the women is a terrorist and has to conceal her appearance, another is an orthodox Muslim student who is not allowed to wear the veil at school, one of them wears a wig so as to hide the fact that she has lost her hair following chemotherapy and one is a transsexual prostitute. They wear wigs as disguise, as a form of submission or because of illness.

There is a fine line between what is attractive about hair and what we find distasteful. The images we see of bodies in the mass media today are most frequently devoid of all body hair, apart from what is to be found on the head. The rules pertaining to hair are strict, we have to know where it is supposed to be and work to keep it under control. Plucked, cut, shaved, dyed, permed or straightened – hair has to be shaped. The views held by the

Jardin public · 1993

members of a Swedish school-class are presented in a doctoral thesis on the processes that create gender identification among teenage girls:

'The hair on a girl's head should be long, thick and well-styled. She should have long eyelashes and narrow eyebrows that are plucked so that they form a shapely arch over the eyes. Any other hair on the face, such as the odd wisp on the chin, the forehead or the upper lip must be removed. This applies as well to hair under the arms and on the legs. The line where the panties end (the so-called bikini-line) has to be shaved smooth as well. The forearms should preferably be smooth, although a fine, fair down is acceptable.'

Deviating from the norm involves loss of the sensual potential of one's hair or even the loss of one's femininity. Refraining from controlling the extent of one's hirsuteness excites revulsion. In many instances direct comparisons are drawn between having hair in the 'wrong' place and being a lesbian. 'Other rules apply to a guy. The hair on his head should be short, not long, but not too short either. He shouldn't pluck the hair on his face, even though it wouldn't hurt for his eyebrows to appear even and regular. He shouldn't shave his body hair either, neither under the arms nor on his legs ... it is vitally important ... that he doesn't look as though he's been shaved baby-smooth.'[2]

'I crave your mouth, your voice, your hair', Pablo Neruda wrote in a poem. Touching hair discretely or in a one to one situation is an intimate action, as is twirling a curl round your finger. A child's hair can be touched by strangers but to have a colleague at work or a teacher running a hand through a co-worker or a student's hair would not only be unexpected but also inappropriate. Hair is as intimate as your skin. In painting and in fairytale illustrations women combing their hair in solitude is a favoured motif. Often the depicted sees herself in a mirror or her reflection in a lake. It is a private scene where the subject either is engaged and satisfied with herself or to be looked at by a voyeur. Professional haircutting is instead a social activity. For men, paying a visit to the barbers goes back to ancient times, while woman were attended to in the home. The first hair-salon for women was set up in the seventeenth century. In the salons that were subsequently established, it was more a matter of styling hair than cutting it and it was not until the twentieth century that the cutting of women's hair outside the home became more widespread.[3] The first short female hairstyle to catch on was the bob in the nineteen-twenties. The style was controversial and the New York Times commented teasingly that the new hair fashion would mean that poetry and literature would have to be re-written. At a major department store in Chicago, the bob was forbidden for employees. Anyone who had already had it done was supposed to use a hairnet while it grew out and the store kept a check on this with hair inspections.[4]

A clean-shaven head on a woman is even more freighted with meaning than short hair. It often gives rise to feelings of indignation since it is associated with acts of cruelty. Women accused of collaboration with the enemy, prisoners of war and concentration camp victims, internees, soldiers and hospital patients have their heads shaved against their will. Exercising power over someone by depriving them of their hair is to take away the last means they have of expressing their personality. Voluntarily choosing to have your head shaved may indicate repudiation, separation or be a means of creating solidarity.

Women (and sometimes men) strictly obeying certain religions cover their head. Female orthodox Jews and Muslims conceal their hair not to attract attention to their charms or parade them. Within the Christian tradition, Catholic nuns have shaved their hair or, as is still the practice today, hidden it away as a means of eschewing vanity. The Mexican born artist Frida Kahlo is known for her elaborate braided hairstyles and adornments such as necklaces, earrings and embroidered blouses, depicted in her self-portraits. The contrast is great in Kahlo's *Self-Portrait with Cropped Hair* from 1940, where the artist is sitting on a chair dressed in a suit, with her hair cut short and surrounded by strands of her shorn hair. The painting was made in connection with her divorce from Diego Rivera. Ten years earlier she had cut her hair in reaction to an adulterous affair on the part of Riviera. To crop her hair was to divest herself of her femininity and a means as well, perhaps, to rid herself of her vulnerability. On the self-portrait are the lines from a Mexican song:

'If I loved you it was for your hair, now that you are hairless I no longer love you.' (Mira que si te quise fue por el pelo, ahora que estás pelona, ya no te quiero.)

Hair goes on growing for a few hours after death but does not then decompose. Hair that is shed spontaneously is no longer part of the body, but is seen as dirt. When parents save a lock of their child's hair, together perhaps with lost milk-teeth, it functions instead as memory. When we know to whom the hair belongs, it becomes representative of the individual concerned although hair also carries within itself a form of memory that goes beyond what we can know about a person from experience. It is a biological marker that contains the DNA code of an individual, an arrangement of inherited genetic material unique to every person. A single hair-root can provide enough information to identify our DNA.[5] A human hair can reveal how we have lived and what we have eaten. After an analysis was carried out on his hair, the cause of death of the French emperor Napoleon was reinvestigated in 2001. Arsenic was discovered in the strands, which indicated poisoning.[6]

A combination of hair serving both as material and memory can be found in the tradition of weaving and plaiting decorative objects from hair. Examples of this almost exclusively feminine craft can be found in Europe as early as the seventeenth century.[7] The phenomenon of the *hårkulla* (Swedish women who earned a living making and selling 'hair-work', jewellery made from hair) had its primary origins in a single parish in the Swedish province of Dalecarlia during the nineteenth century. After years of crop failures, when more than half the population felt forced to emigrate, mainly to America, these female hair-workers became the economic salvation for an entire rural community. They not only developed techniques to create decorative objects from hair but were also enterprising travelling saleswomen. They would often travel in couples around Sweden and the Nordic countries, also venturing as far afield as Russia, England and America. Most of the men in their district were forced to travel to get temporary work doing bricklaying and carpentry.[8] The *hårkulla* was able, in contrast, to earn up to forty

times as much for her work. While parts of a family emigrated to America, a *hårkulla* and her closest relatives would often be able to remain behind and keep the family farm owing to her relative affluence.[9] Examples of work produced by the Dalecarlian hair-workers comprise rings, bracelets, bridal wreaths and watch-chains made of human hair. Their story dates from a time when hair jewellery was fashionable across several social classes. In America in the eighteen-fifties the leading lady's magazine *Lady Godey's and Petersons* published a series of articles about hair jewellery and how it was made.[10] Hair-work was not the unusual sight it would be today.

Translated from the Swedish by Frank Perry

Notes

1 Karen Stevenson, 'Hairy Business: Organising the gendered self', in *Contested Bodies,* ed. R. Holliday and J. Hassard, London 2001, p. 151.

2 Fanny Ambjörnsson, *I en klass för sig: Genus, klass och sexualitet bland gymnasietjejer,* Stockholm 2004, pp. 143, 147.

3 Stevenson in Holliday and Hassard 2001 (see note 1), pp. 138–139.

4 Ibid., p. 141.

5 DNA-analyser av biologiska spår, (2003), www.polisen.se/inter/mediacache//1688/6544/6545/vad_ar_DNA.pdf.

6 'Napoleons poison theory revived', CNN.com/WORLD, June 1, 2001.

7 Stig Björklund, 'Kring uppkomsten av två unika hantverk – korgmakeri och hårarbete i Ovansiljan', in *Från Bonäs bygdegård: Kulturdagar* 1967, ed. S. Björklund, Uppsala 1967.

8 Fredrik Reinhold Arosenius, 'Beskrifning öfver Mora socken', in *Beskrifning öfver provinsen Dalarne,* Avesta 1978.

9 Anna Sparr, *specialarbete,* Katedralskolan Lund 1997.

10 Mark Campbell, *The Art of Hair Work,* ed. J. and K. Kliot, Berkeley 1994.

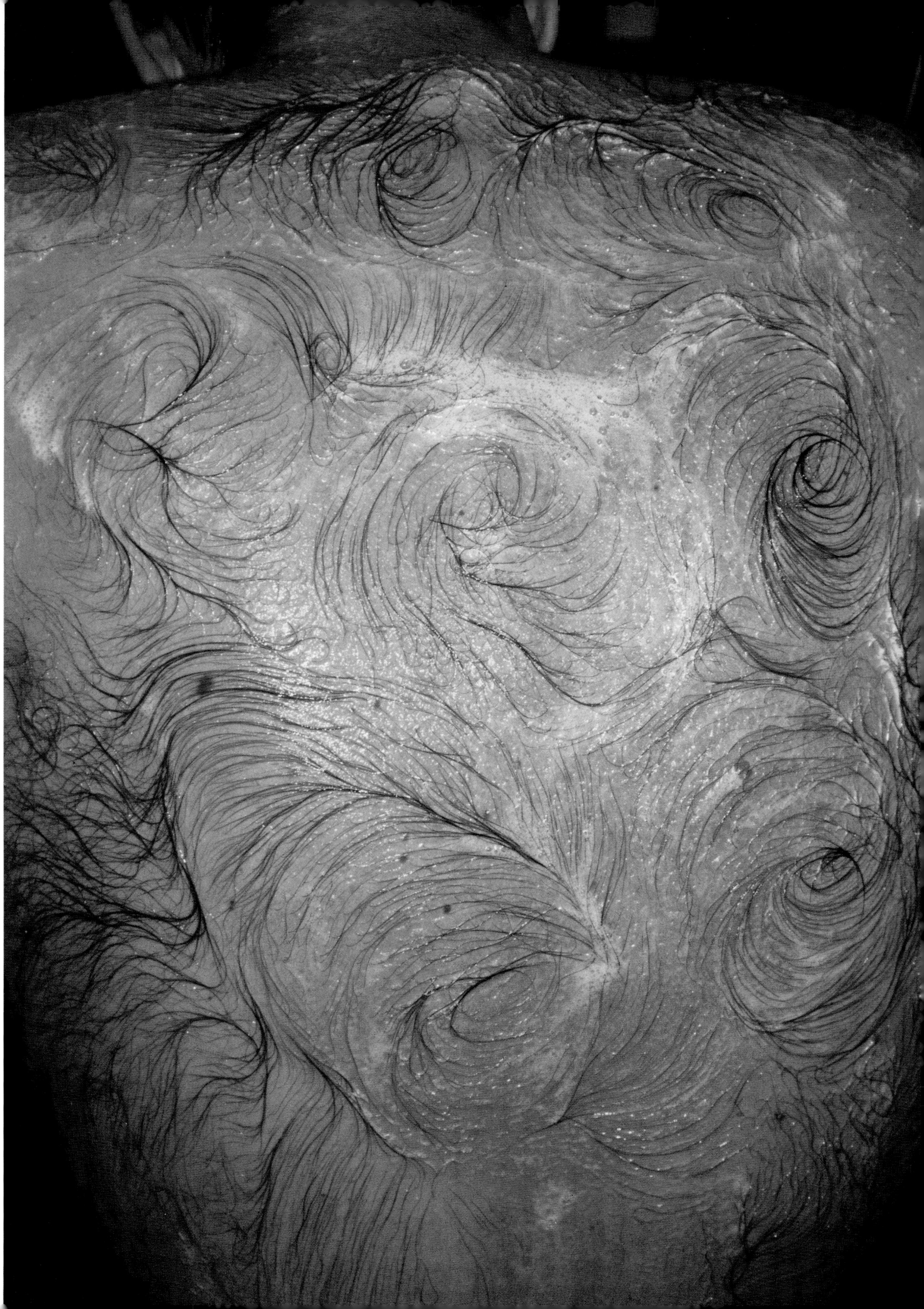

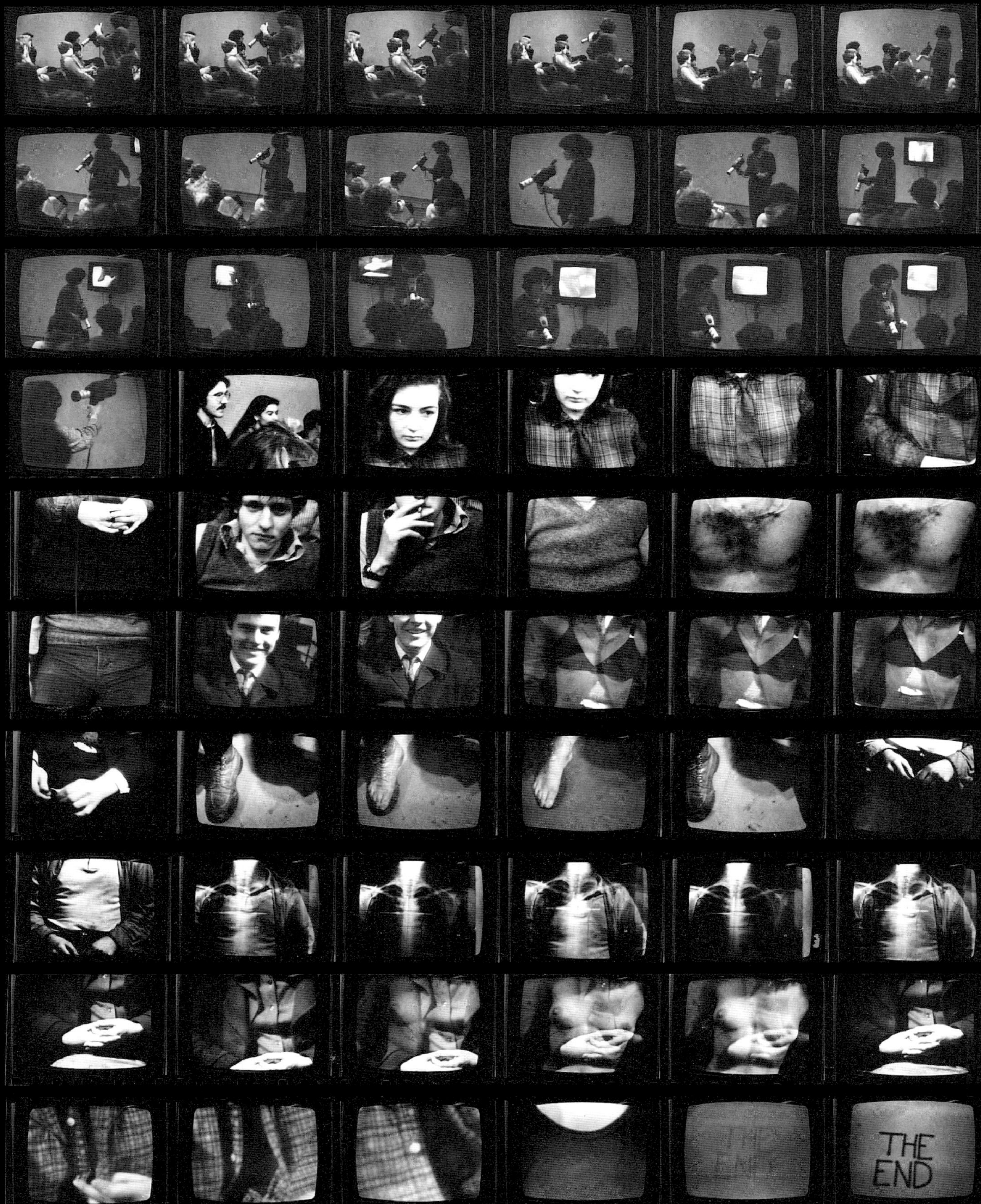
THE
END

Christoph Heinrich

Artist at Work

An Annotated Catalogue Raisonné of the Performances

Mona Hatoum herself has in the past described her performances as installations in disguise. At London's Slade School of Art, where she studied from 1979 to 1981, her experiments with live electric currents were not gladly tolerated and so, 'tired of all the bureaucracy', as she puts it, she began to look for a way of presenting her work to a small audience of invited guests.[1] It was to be many years before Hatoum was able to realise installations using electricity on a grand scale,
fig. p. 15 in such pieces as *The Light at the End* and
pp. 20–21 more recently *Homebound*. In the meantime, she built up a vocabulary of thematic and formal possibilities upon which to draw in many of her later sculptures, installations and videos. In this respect, Hatoum's work traced a trajectory of development that began with installations, passing through a phase devoted almost entirely to performances and culminating in the use of many different media – an approach whose strength lies in the carefully considered application of each respective material. Hatoum's later works follow on from her performances in the sense that they are aimed at the spectator whose relationship to the work – in terms of both space and content – constitutes a major part of its reception.

'Performance was very attractive to me because I saw it as a revolutionary medium, setting itself apart from the gallery system and the art establishment. It fitted exactly the kind of issue-based work I was beginning to make.'[2]

In performances, Hatoum discovered a means that gave her the freedom to respond to topical themes while at the same time allowing her to interact directly with the spectator. Last, but not least, performance was a medium that the young artist's limited means could accommodate.

Mona Hatoum undertook some thirty-five performances between 1980 and 1988,[3] twenty-six of which are documented in this publication. The others are regarded by the artist herself as too peripheral for inclusion in her oeuvre as a whole. It is not easy to find a common denominator for her performances. Painstakingly prepared sequences of action alternate with improvisations, solo performances with tableaux vivants and participatory experiments with carefully calculated arrangements of electronic media.

If there is any common denominator at all, then it is the relationship to the audience, for Hatoum's performances were aimed at direct communication: none of them were made for the camera or the video. The photographic records that exist are of uneven quality and were created more by chance than by design. Communication with the spectator might take on very different forms, and Hatoum's relationship to her audience is widely varied. In her early performances, she took the role of an authority dominating the audience (1, 2, 5, 6). The spectators became the unwitting object of the gaze, watching themselves, detached from their own physical perception of self, while the artist took control. In a number of performances which were to become her best known – among them *Under Siege* and *The Negotiating Table* (7, 11) – she inverted the role of controlling authority to take on the role of victim instead. In several instances, Hatoum put herself on display in cage-like cells, signalling a sense of isolation and marginalisation (as in 7, 18, 25). Yet here, too, the artist gave the audience a role that goes beyond that of the detached observer. Hatoum turned the spectators into witnesses forced to face up to their own passiveness and impotence.

In her theatrical performances, a masked Hatoum – part perpetrator and part victim – crawled through the audience, threatening the spectators while being threatened herself (12, 14, 15).

In her street performances in Brixton and Sheffield, she wore overalls, in the latter, declaring herself to be an *Artist at Work*, and approached unsuspecting passers-by, who became spectators by dint of her action (16, 22). She became, as it were, an actor in a 'social sculpture'.

Plumbing the depths of borderline existential experiences in the way that was so central to the aggressive or self-destructive performances of Rudolf Schwarzkogler, Chris Burden and Gina Pane in the sixties and seventies played only a marginal role in Hatoum's work. The self-harming element these artists explored involved presenting the artist as hero while at the same time seeking to create a new body in order to become more receptive to the world and to others.[4]

In fact, in only two of her performances has Hatoum ever risked physical injury (18, 19). She has, however, used self-castigation as

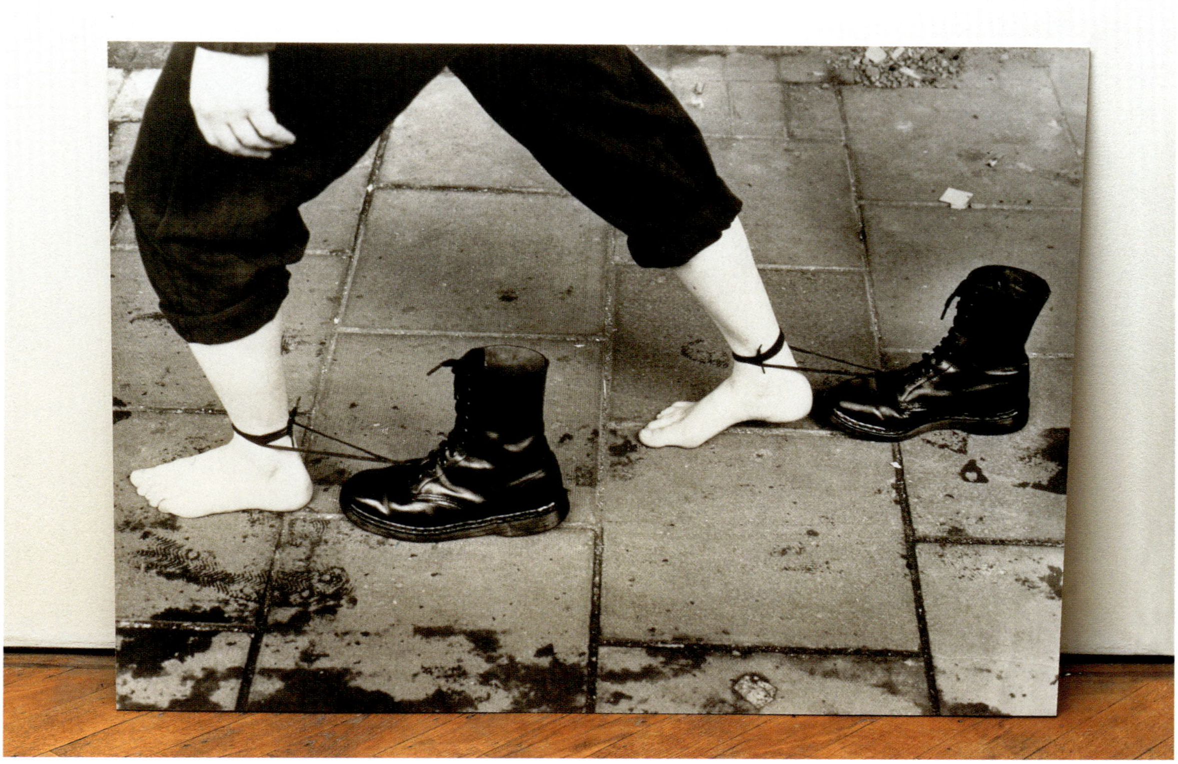

 Performance Still · 1985-95

a dramatic device on several occasions: in *Under Siege*, for instance, when she spent seven hours struggling in a slippery, muddy cell, or in *The Negotiating Table*, where she lay motionless for three hours wrapped in polythene sheeting. These had less to do with exploring a borderline experience than with the visual expression of physically exhausting actions. Other additional elements such as sound, language and lighting made the performance into a complex yet unequivocal statement.

While struggling in slippery clay, lying prone on the negotiating table or carefully picking a way through barbed wire may be seen as universally valid metaphors of the human condition and the futility of all we do, Hatoum's use of sound and image gives these statements a locus that makes many of her performances into profoundly personal reports of her own experience as an Arab woman of Palestinian origins living in exile in London. In spite of this, all her performances have a universal validity. In an interview with Michael Archer, Hatoum stresses the contemporary political relevance of her most famous performance, while at the same time pointing out its broader significance:

'*Under Siege* happened a week before the Israeli invasion and the siege of Beirut; it was almost like a premonition. But in general in my work at that time, I was trying to remind people that wars were still raging in many parts of the world.'[5]

Translated from the German by Ishbel Flett (introduction) and Pauline Cumbers (commentaries)

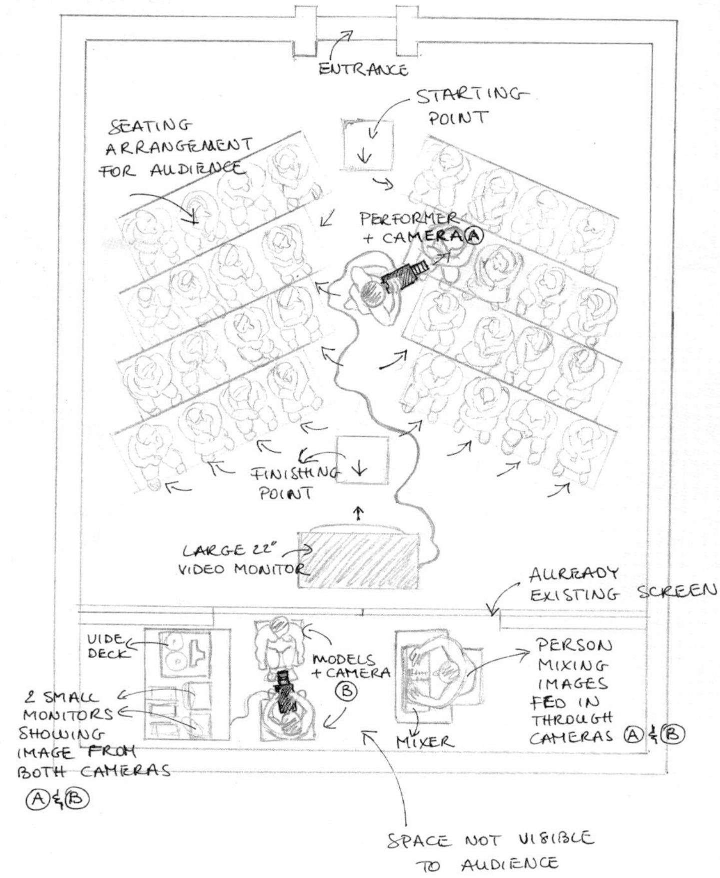

Notes

1 Archer, Brett, de Zegher 1997, p. 9.
2 Archer, Brett, de Zegher 1997, p. 9.
3 In *Pull* (1995) Hatoum followed on from her performances for the last time (26); the work was both installation and performance.
4 See Jindrich Chalupecky, 'Art and Sacrifice', in *Flash Art*, no. 80–81, February/April 1978, pp. 31–35 (here pp. 33 f.).
5 Archer, Brett, de Zegher 1997, p. 13.

The descriptions of the performances are written by Mona Hatoum. They precede the commentaries.

Don't smile, you're on camera! · 1980
(Sketchbook drawing)

1
Don't smile, you're on camera! · 1980

Live action with a video monitor, two live video cameras, a video mixer and various props
In collaboration with Paul Jackson
First performed at 'Five Days at Battersea', Battersea Arts Centre, London, 26 March 1980
Repeated at 'New Contemporaries '81', Institute of Contemporary Arts, London, 3 and 4 March 1981
Duration: 40 minutes

fig. p. 80

The artist points a live video camera directly at the audience, panning up and down the rows, very slowly, sometimes stopping and focusing on parts of a person's body. Faces, torsos, crotches appear on the monitor facing the audience. A shirt slowly fades away and a ghost image of bare breasts appears behind it, creating the illusion that the camera could see through the person's clothes. In the same way a shoe disappears and reveals a bare foot inside it. A man's jacket turns transparent and a hairy chest or a woman's naked torso is seen through. Superimposed on another person's chest is the ghost image of an X-ray of the same part of the body. This performance is made possible with the participation of three assistants who are not visible to the audience. Two assistants use a second live camera to scan their own naked bodies while a third assistant mixes the images fed in by the two live cameras.

fig. p. 83

Lit.: John Roberts in *Art Monthly,* no. 26, May 1980; exh. cat. Paris 1994, p. 52; Archer, Brett, de Zegher 1997, pp. 10-12, 70, 71, 146; Marth 2003, pp. 67-69, 72,188, note 112, fig. 9.

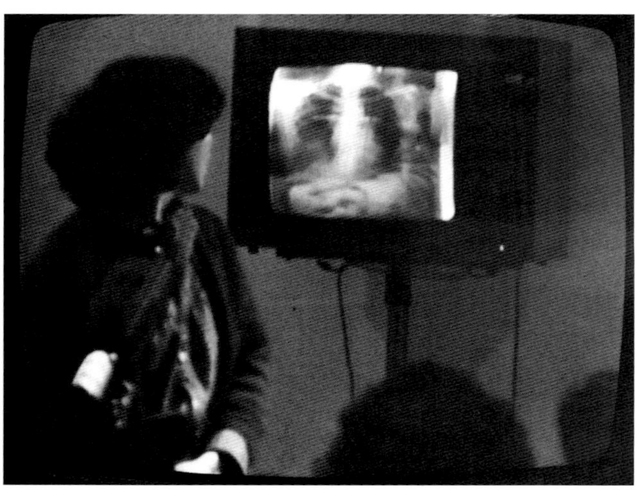

Don't smile, you're on camera! · 1980

2
Video Performance · 1980

Live action with one video monitor, one live video camera, a pre-recorded videotape and video player
Performed at 'Summer Show '80' Film Makers Co-op, London, 11 July 1980
Duration: 30 minutes

During the first part of the performance, the artist points a live video camera directly at the audience and scans up and down a couple of rows in detail. What the camera sees is simultaneously shown on a large monitor facing the audience. The artist then puts the camera down and draws a white chalk circle on the floor. She sits cross-legged in the middle of the circle, with her back to the audience. She picks up the video camera again but this time, unsuspected by the audience, she switches on a pre-recorded tape. Pointing the video camera towards herself she systematically scans her body from head to foot.

The monitor this time shows what the camera would see if the performer were unclothed. It is made to look as though the camera could see through the clothes but not through buttons, buckles, items in pockets, etc. The artist's movements with the camera are synchronised with what is shown on the monitor to create the illusion that the action is taking place in real time.

fig. p. 86

Lit.: Catherine Elwes, 'Notes from a Video Performance by Mona Hatoum', in: *Undercut,* no. 1, March/April 1981, p. 28; exh. cat. Paris 1994, p. 53; Archer, Brett, de Zegher 1997, pp. 135-136; Marth 2003, pp. 67, 68, 188, fig. 10.

In the first two of Mona Hatoum's performances, *Don't smile, you're on camera!* and *Video Performance,* the gaze that breaches the barrier between the audience and the performer played a major role. In the first performance Hatoum turned the camera on her audience, appearing to expose them. In the second performance, she filmed the audience without resorting to any such irritation, but then focused the camera on her own body. In the catalogue to 'Summer Show '80' the artist noted: 'This particular work deals with childhood memories of a scopophilic nature. I imagined that my pair of binoculars were magic and enabled me to see through layers of clothes, skin, flesh, etc. It is the curiosity of a child wanting to see behind the surface and finding, through fantasy, a way out of social restraints.'[1]

The childlike fantasy of magic X-ray glasses, usually associated with nascent sexuality, is linked here with the suggestion of surveillance carried out by some authority. The artist claims a power that goes far beyond the proverbial capacity of an artist to get to the very heart of things. She appears here to be in possession of a technology that pretends to make daydreams and nightmares come true, and at the same time breaches one of the last boundaries between private and public space. This device, however, merely emphasises something that is basically inherent in any situation where the performer films his or her audience.

After *Video Performance*, i.e., the action where the audience was only filmed but not 'exposed', a female member of the audience wrote: 'With a gathering sense of alarm, I realise that I am in the direct line of fire. My mind races around those deep-rooted, repressed fears that the situation is forcing into my conscious mind. Suddenly to become the focus of public attention in a situation that is controlled by another individual fills me with a kind of terror that I find hard to define. Memories of public school humiliation invade my mind. Parental scrutiny, moral judgement and the strictures of Catholic confessionals merge into the single male gaze forever scanning a woman's body, appropriating her sense of self, returning her identity stamped with value X on a scale of desirability. ... I feel trapped. If I get up and move out of the camera's range, I draw attention to myself. If I stay where I am, I become exposed to this electronic voyeurism. The conflicts and contradictions of being a woman and a public spectacle overwhelm any vestige of exhibitionism that may remain and I cover my face with my hands, mimicking rapt concentration.'[2]

Hatoum did not comment throughout this performance, but remained totally silent, something which was bound to increase the oppressive aspect of her actions. The audience was thus suddenly made an object of observation; they could see themselves as if detached from their own perception of their bodies, while at the same time thrown back on themselves, as confirmed by the comments of the eyewitness. The penetrating gaze, mediated by the events on the monitor, becomes a metaphor for an escalating surveillance by some kind of unknown authority that transgresses all barriers.

Closed-circuit installations, i.e., arrangements in which a monitor simultaneously displays what is being filmed by a camera, were used by Bruce Nauman and

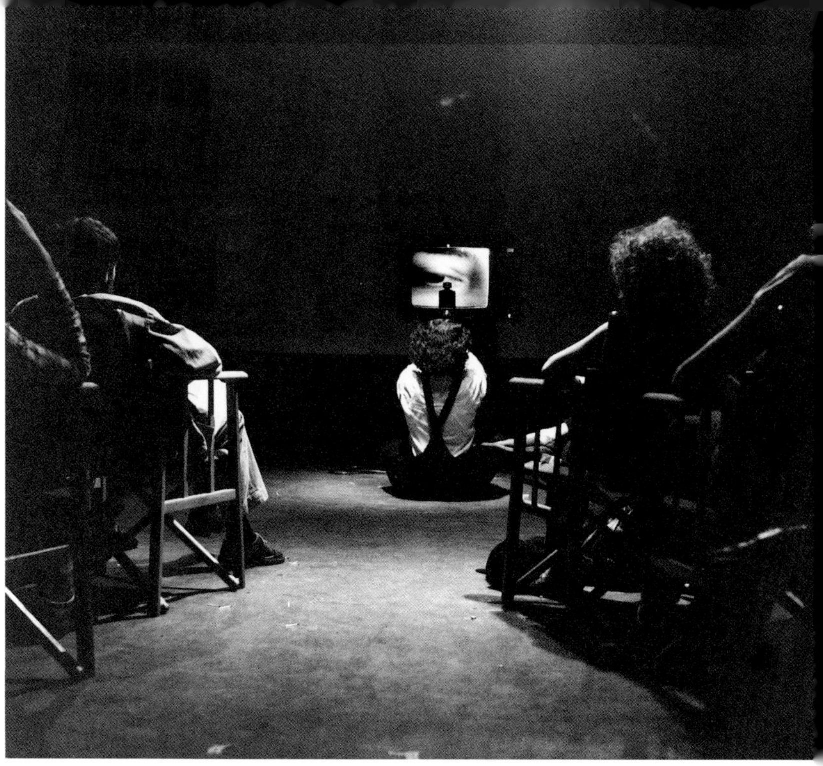

Dan Graham in installations designed to make the viewers observe themselves. It was not difficult to deduce from these early installations allusions to an omnipresent surveillance.[3] The closed-circuit device was regularly used in 'action art' of the seventies in order to actively integrate into the production of art an audience criticised for its passive, consumer-like attitude. In actions by Vito Acconci or Chris Burden the closed-circuit device was used as part of a quasi-experimental set-up which constituted a test situation for the audience and where the latter were forced either to assume responsibility or – expose their own passivity. These early actions were related to the legendary Milgram Experiment, which, using certain fictional methods of punishment, tested the willingness of people either to accept responsibility or else subject themselves unconditionally to the orders of someone with seeming authority.[4]

The test which Hatoum set her audience was more harmless, more playful. After all, the trick was exposed, at the latest when the genders were substituted or when the X-ray image was inserted in *Don't smile, you're on camera!* But the result must still have been one of unease. For the video camera was only supposedly used here for the purposes of self-assurance and documentation; its true essence was that of a controlling presence. The transformation of the passive audience into active participants in these early works already anticipated the later installations, which were not just autonomous artworks, but also situations directed at the viewer, as in the case of *The Light at the End* or *Light Sentence.*[5] It would seem that a direct line leads from the gaze penetrating the private sphere in the early surveillance performances to the video installations *Corps étranger* and *Deep Throat* – the 'scopophilic childhood dreams' have come true thanks to the modern medical technique of the endoscope.

fig. pp. 15–17
fig. pp. 46–49

Notes

1 Statement from the catalogue of *'Summer Show '80',* London Film Makers Co-op, 1980; also cited by Catherine Elwes, 'Notes from a Video Performance by Mona Hatoum', in *Undercut,* no. 1, March/April 1981, p. 29.

2 Catherine Elwes in *Undercut,* no. 1, March/April 1981, p. 28.

3 Bruce Nauman, *Video Surveillance Piece: Public Room, Private Room* (1969/70); Dan Graham, *Video Piece for Two Glass Office Buildings* (1976).

4 Stanley Milgram, *Obedience to Authority,* New York 1974; see also, Thomas Blass, *Obedience to Authority: Current Perspectives on the Milgram Paradigma,* Mahwah, N.J. 2000.

5 Cf. Nina Zimmer's essay, pp. 66-72.

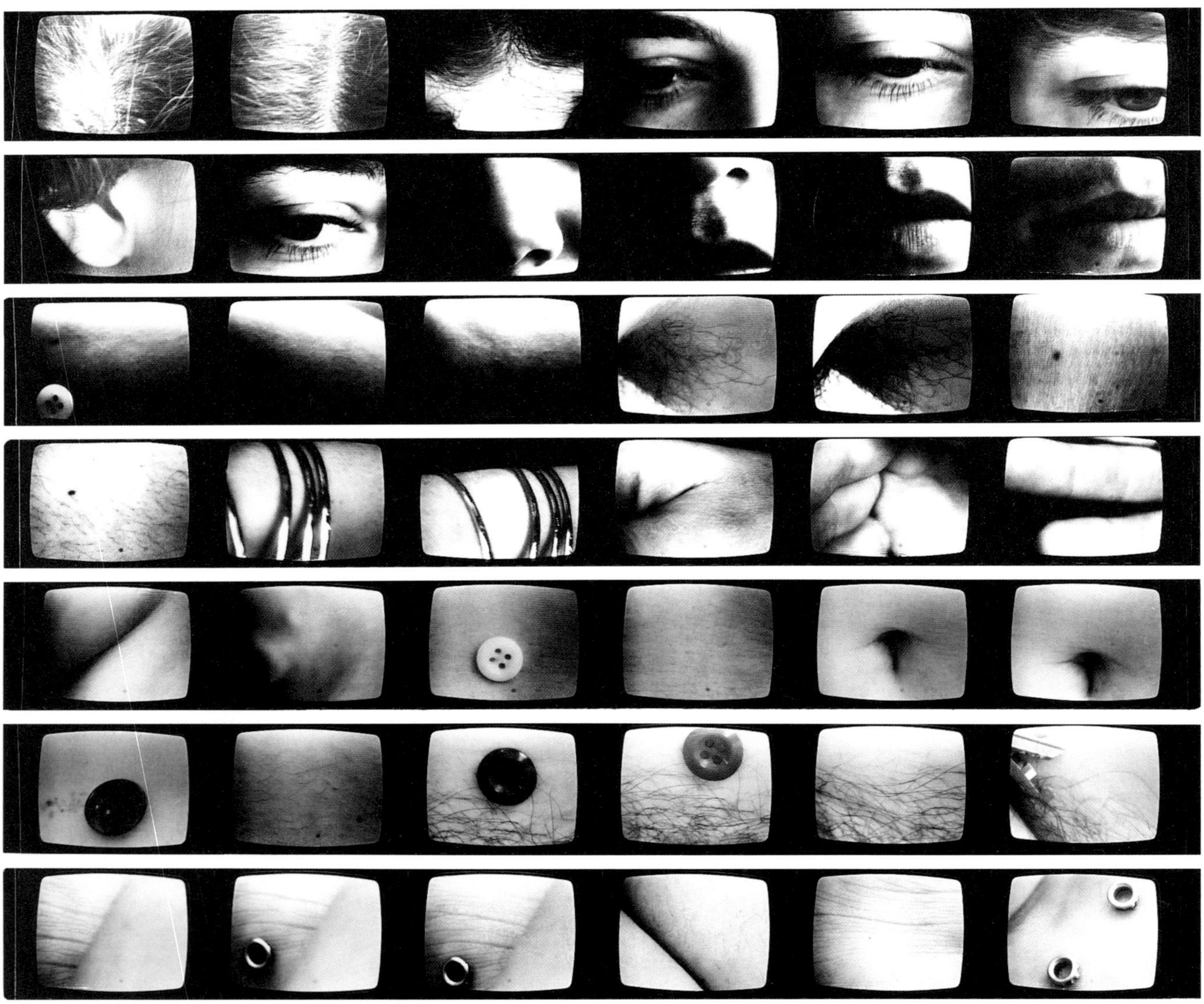

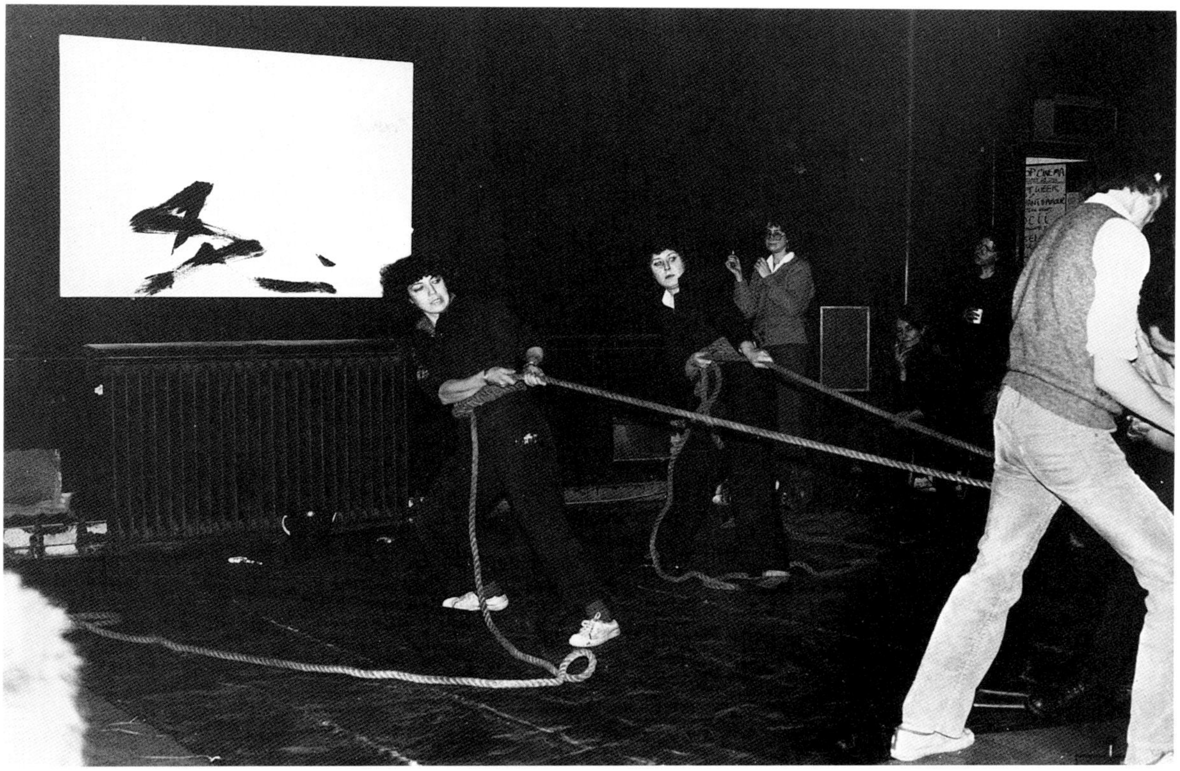

3
Anything you can do ... · 1981

Live action with two performers, sound tape, rope, bucket, black paint, brushes and canvas
In collaboration with Brenda Martin
First performed at 'Gender Views', Film Makers Co-op, London, 4 February 1981
Repeated: Portsmouth Polytechnic, Portsmouth, 11 March 1981
Duration: 30 minutes

Two women tied to each other at the waist with a long length of rope slung around a metal pole held in place by two men. The women compete with each other to reach a blank canvas and leave an 'Abstract Expressionist' mark on it. Throughout the performance the following songs could be heard: 'Sisters, there were never such devoted sisters' (Music by Irving Berlin from the movie *White Christmas*) and 'Anything you can do I can do better' (Music by Irving Berlin from the musical *Annie Get Your Gun*).

Lit.: John Roberts, 'Madness at Home', in *Artscribe*, no. 28, March 1981; exh. cat. Paris 1994, p. 53; Archer, Brett, de Zegher 1997, p. 12.

Mona Hatoum created this allegorical performance in collaboration with Brenda Martin, a friend from her years at the Slade School of Art in London. The performance resulted in an expressive painterly action turning into an exhausting tug of war – literally, a parable.

The idea of Action Painting was born around 1950 with Hans Namuth's famous photographs of Pollock painting in his studio and the response to them by critics like Harold Rosenberg.[1] The reception of these photographs related them immediately to Pollock's expressive paintings, thus advancing a new understanding of the artist: the painting had become an arena, paint a primal force, the artist a torero subjugating that force, or, in the case of Georges Mathieu who first carried out such Action Painting before an audience in the late fifties, a warring samurai capable of advancing to the cosmos through his art. If the performance genre does not derive solely from theatre, then its origins can be seen to lie in such painting actions.

Yet here we are also dealing with the concept of the artist that was a feature of art after 1945: the artist as hero. For Action Painting was an altogether male pleasure; art critics like Rosenberg and Clement Greenberg established the figure of the cultural hero in the distinctly masculine Pollock.[2] Pollock's macho-image, which represented an abstract art defended by men, became a locus of attack for many artists in and around Fluxus as of the sixties, and especially in the work of feminist artists.[3] This background also has relevance for Hatoum: 'At the Slade we used to have these feminist Consciousness Raising Groups. Both, Brenda and I, were critical of this whole idea of "sisterhood", of this assumed mutual support amongst women. For her, it was issues of class, and I always thought that certain issues of Western feminism don't apply to women in the Third World.'[4]

If the men were not holding the post so far from the canvas, the two women could paint their picture together; as things were, they created conditions whereby only one of them at a time had a chance to paint. The men control the goal-posts, as it were, and thus play one woman off against the other, with the result that they get into open competition with each other. This was a feminist performance which also questioned the ideals of feminism, and which to date stands as a unique work in Hatoum's œuvre.

Here, as in only a few of her performances, Hatoum playfully presented an action that can be situated somewhere between vaudeville and women's wrestling. It was accompanied by two popular songs, one of which initially praises female solidarity, only to finally expose it as an ersatz-ideal serving until the right man, the 'real' objective in life, comes along; the second song tells of the ambition of a famous markswoman determined to compete with a Wild West hero (but who in the end misses the target deliberately, this being her only way of winning the man she loves.) Mona Hatoum says: 'Today, I think, the performance was a bit too illustrative, too literal. But I still think the statement was valid. We did this performance twice, and then we never worked together again.'[5]

Notes

1 See *Pollock painting,* ed. Barbara Rose, New York 1978.
2 Ibid, see also Amelia Jones, *Body Art/Performing the Subject,* Minneapolis 1998, pp. 53-102 (The 'Pollockian Performative' and the Revision of the Modernist Subject).
3 For example, Carolee Schneemann, *Eye Body,* 1963; Shigeko Kubota's *Vagina Painting* carried out in 1965 at the Perpetual Fluxus Festival in New York, or Paul McCarthy's *Face Painting – Floor, White Line* of 1972.
4 Mona Hatoum in conversation with the author, Hamburg, 20 December 2003; on the history of the Consciousness Raising Groups, see Mary D. Garrard, 'Feminist Politics: Networks and Organizations', in Norma Broude and Mary Garrard, *The Power of Feminist Art,* New York 1994, pp. 88-103.
5 Mona Hatoum in conversation with the author, Hamburg, 20 December 2003.

4
Live work for the black room · 1981

Live action with chalk and candles
Performed at Reading University, Reading, 11 February 1981
Duration: 45 minutes

The performance takes place in a room where all surfaces are painted black. It begins in complete darkness and for the first few minutes the action of the performer is heard but not seen. The artist repeatedly falls on the floor and draws the outline of her own body in white chalk. She repeats this action several times until the floor becomes entirely covered with overlapping chalk lines. Each time she falls, she lights a small candle and places it inside the body-outline.

Lit.: Exh. cat. Paris 1994, p. 53; Archer, Brett, de Zegher 1997, p. 133; Marth 2003, note 82.

The candle-light in the darkness was deliberately used as a theatrical device – 'just to keep the mystery going for a bit longer in the dark', Mona Hatoum delayed the lighting of the first candle.[1] Before the eyes of the audience, a drawing gradually emerged whose outlines covered the space.

After an almost dance-like action in which the artist used her body to define the space, the viewer must have immediately had the impression of a battle-field, and the mysterious candles must have looked like cemetery lights. The solitary human figure gradually became lost in a confusion of lines which increasingly dominated the space. In a sketchbook drawing Hatoum calls these outlines 'Forensic Chalk Lines', alluding to the outlines marking the position of the victim at the scene of a crime or accident.[2] In the same drawing she had delineated the action with the words: 'DEATH, DISASTER, DOOM & GLOOM'; the artist had also noted down an alternative or sub-title on the drawing, 'The light at the end of the tunnel', an expression to which she would have recourse eight years later in her first large-scale installation.

This action is reminiscent of Yves Klein's *Anthropométries* – large paintings for which the artist used female models' bodies as living paint-brushes, so to speak. In Hatoum's performance, however, there was no such division of roles between active male artist and passive female model: here subject and object are one. Also, instead of a sensual painterly print made with flesh, she drew a thin contour with dry chalk: an objective sign of permanent collapse, of lunging and falling. As in the other early performances, there was no overt reference in this action to political or current affairs. In later performances (7, 8, 16), Hatoum would return to the cyclical action of falling and rising again and again.

Notes

1 Mona Hatoum in conversation with the author, Hamburg, 20 December 2003.

2 Sketchbook drawing for *Live Work for the Black Room/ The lights at the end of the tunnel,* February 1981, unpublished.

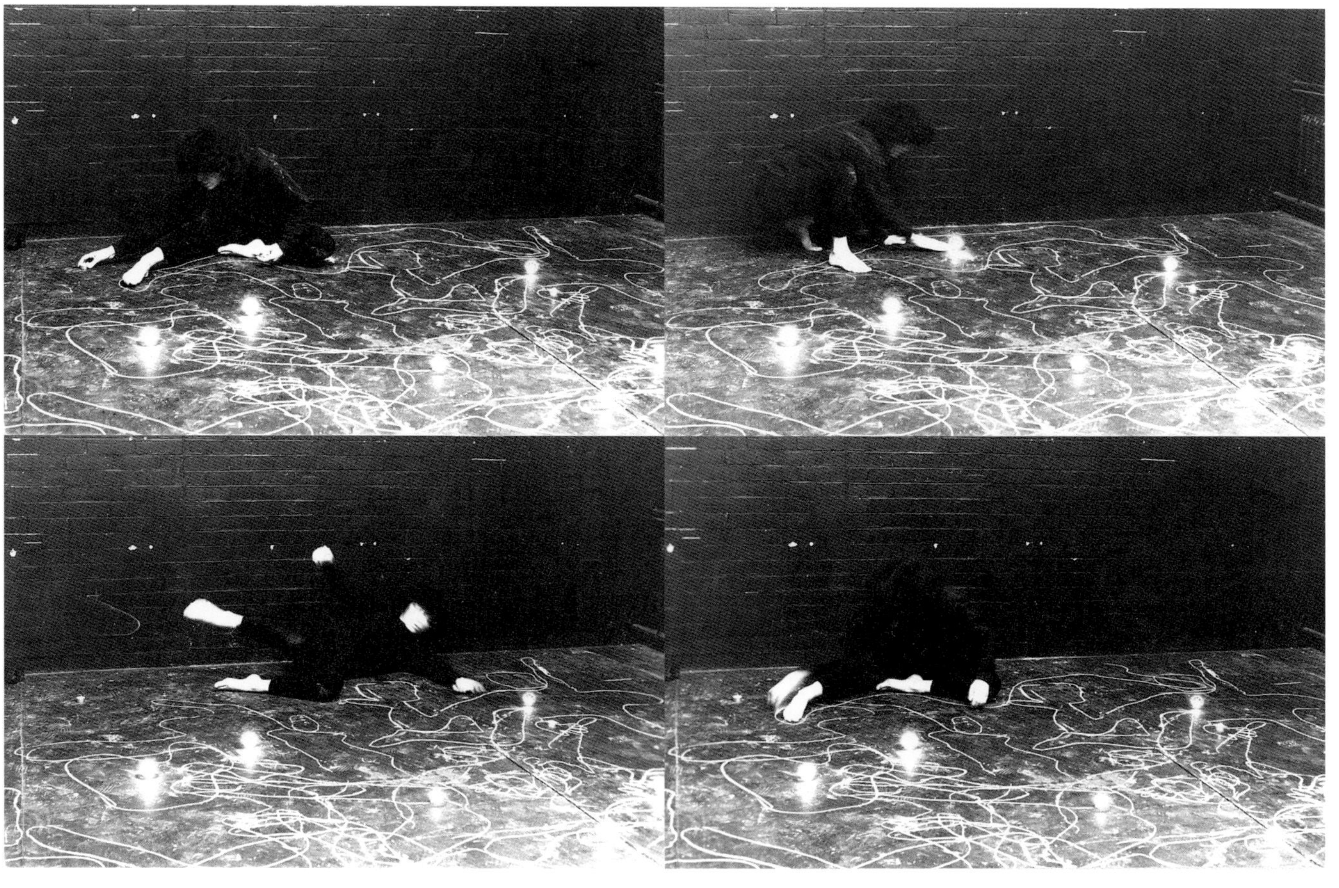

5
Untitled · 1981

Live action with three performers and three large balls of twine
Performed at 'Leeds Events Week', Leeds Polytechnic, 19 March 1981
Duration: 30 minutes

Chairs are placed in a grid formation far enough apart to allow a person to walk between them. The artist starts by pacing up and down between the rows of chairs announcing that within a few minutes an action will be performed in which the audience will be asked to remain still and quiet and inviting those who are not willing to do so to leave the room. A few people get up and leave. The door is then locked and the artist, with her two helpers, each armed with a large ball of twine, proceed to tie up each member of the audience to their chair and to each other, creating an intricate web of twine across the whole space. The artist and her helpers then leave the space, leaving the audience to untangle their way out of the web of twine.

Many performance works of the seventies and eighties were aiming to integrate the audience into the action – however, only a few artists took this as literally as Mona Hatoum. Today, the artist remarks laconically on this particular performance: 'It was the time when there was a lot of hostage taking. Here I was taking the audience hostage.'[1]

The helplessness of the artist in the face of political power is expressed in a provocative action that re-

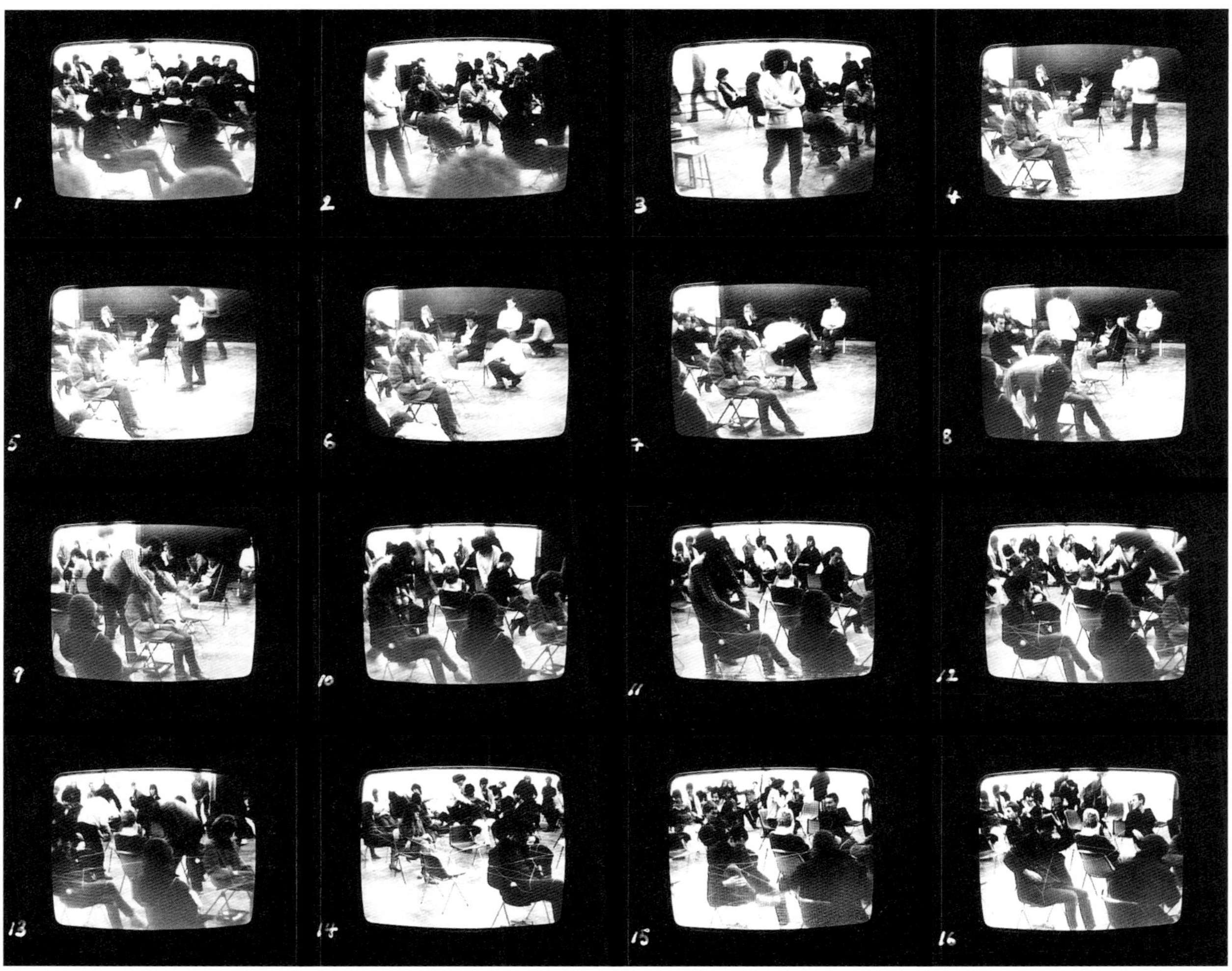

versed the notion of activating the audience, and which assumed a certain seriousness on account of Hatoum's (known) Palestinian origins. Just as in the two early video actions (1, 2), here too the artist acted as a controlling, dominating authority whose repeated announcements to the audience must have made her seem like an orderly or a prison warder.

In a sketchbook drawing for this performance Hatoum notes: 'I would like to be able to immobilize people in their chairs metaphorically, or by emotionally manipulating them. For the moment, I feel I am only capable of doing it physically.'[2]

Of particular interest is the form that she chose, which was extremely pragmatic and yet had a deeper meaning, for Hatoum literally spins a web around her audience. In the world's oldest cultures, the spider is regarded as a creature with a markedly dualist nature. In religions and superstitions it often possesses two characteristics: beneficent and evil, restorative and destructive; it is a soul-creature and totem, divine messenger and a work of Satan. In most cultures, the spider has female connotations and is associated both with the promise of happiness and with aversion and anxiety. 'How can you see a big spider and not go back to childhood curiosity, comfort, terror, indeed, to actively experiencing those feelings?' Mieke Bal asked when confronted with the huge spiders that Louise Bourgeois produced for the Tate Modern in 1997.[3]

The typical divergence in Hatoum's performances – between a dispassionate, minimalist action and implications of various danger and threat, enticement and seduction – holds a clue to her later installations and sculptures: In these, the viewer was also confronted with totally ordered, almost austere structures (the verticals in *The Light at the End*, the wire lockers in *Light Sentence*, but also her outline kitchen appliances) which opened up a conceptual space with a huge range of symbolic, psychological and poetic possibilities, without being in the least bit narrative.

Notes

1 Mona Hatoum in conversation with the author, Hamburg, 20 December 2003.

2 Notes and drawing for a performance in Leeds, March 1981, unpublished.

3 Mieke Bal, 'Narrative Inside Out: Louise Bourgeois' Spider as Theoretical Object', *Oxford Art Journal*, vol. 22, 1999, pp. 101-126, here p. 104.

6
Look No Body! · 1981

Live action with video monitor, sound tape, water hose and a stack of plastic cups
Performed at The Basement Gallery, Newcastle-upon-Tyne, 28 March 1981
Duration: 40 minutes

The artist repeatedly performs the task of filling a cup with water, drinking it and offering every other cup to a different member of the audience. Behind her a video monitor is placed, showing a view from a high angle of the toilet just outside the performance space.

Throughout the performance a sound tape is played which consists of a monologue by the artist talking about an obsessive dream and then reading a scientific and detailed description of the act of urinating and other thoughts, fantasies and questions related to it. Her voice is mixed with the amplified sounds of her heartbeat, breathing and loud stomach rumbles which she had recorded using medical equipment.

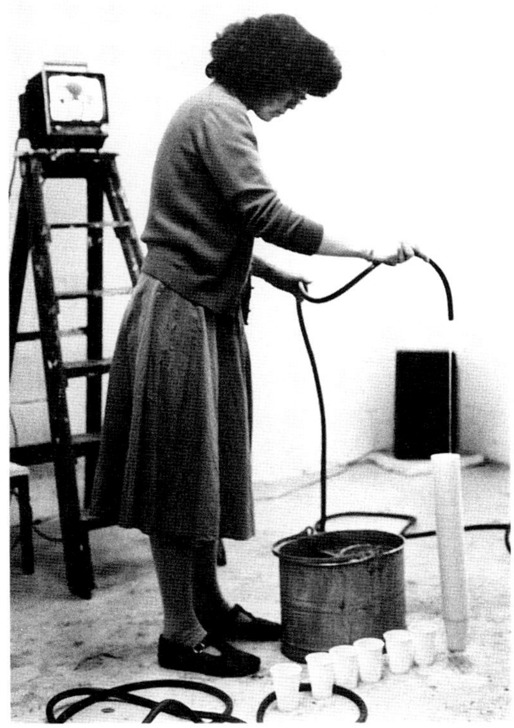

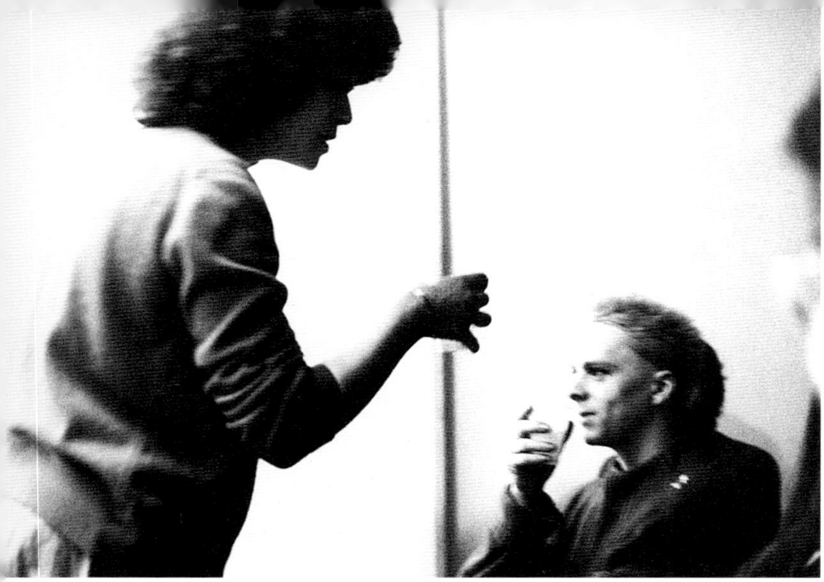

Lit.: Exh. cat. Paris 1994, pp. 13, 54; Archer, Brett, de Zegher 1997, pp. 10, 38, 118-120; Marth 2003, pp. 70-72, 188, fig. 11.

In the first two video performances (1, 2) the principle of the closed-circuit was in a way associated with magic powers; here, it is returned to its essence: the surveillance camera. The boundary between public space and private retreat is shot through soberly and shamelessly, with all the implications adhering to such authoritarian control. The audience was assigned the role of Big Brother.

The key issue for Mona Hatoum in this performance was the exploration of the boundaries of the body. On the accompanying soundtrack there was a passage which has an application to most of Hatoum's performances, as well as to her later video works and installations, and which also could be considered as the motto for many of her works: 'it's just that I often wonder where my body ends ... I mean what my boundaries are ... whether it's the skin ... what about things like hair and nails, and you know, things that come out of the body in the form of urine, faeces, blood ... where does it actually end?'

This exploration of the body's boundaries refers not only to the differences between public and private behaviour, but also to the concrete treatment of taboos, interpreted by Hatoum, on the tape which runs throughout the performance, as gender-specific suppressive mechanisms of Western culture: 'I very often wonder why women's loos are divided into cubicles with doors and locks, when men have large communal open urinals, and the same for showers ... it's like another conspiracy against us women ... it makes us feel as if we've got something to hide, even from each other ...'

This action was followed by *Waterworks* – a project which met with a lot of resistance and censorship. For the exhibition 'New Contemporaries' at the Institute of Contemporary Arts in London, Hatoum proposed installing a surveillance camera in one of the cubicles of both the women's and men's toilets on either side of the ICA bookshop. This would relay the events there on two monitors in the foyer. A sign on the respective cubicle would inform the users about the camera and leave them with the choice of using a different, unobserved toilet. As Hatoum mentioned later, the ICA rejected the project, arguing that visitors to the toilet were in a public space, 'where people have not made a conscious decision to be confronted by art'. Hatoum tried again to realise *Waterworks* for her post-graduate exhibition at the Slade School of Art, where it was also rejected. Instead she finally presented the proposal for this project and the history of its rejection together with a documentation of the performance *Look No Body!*.[1]

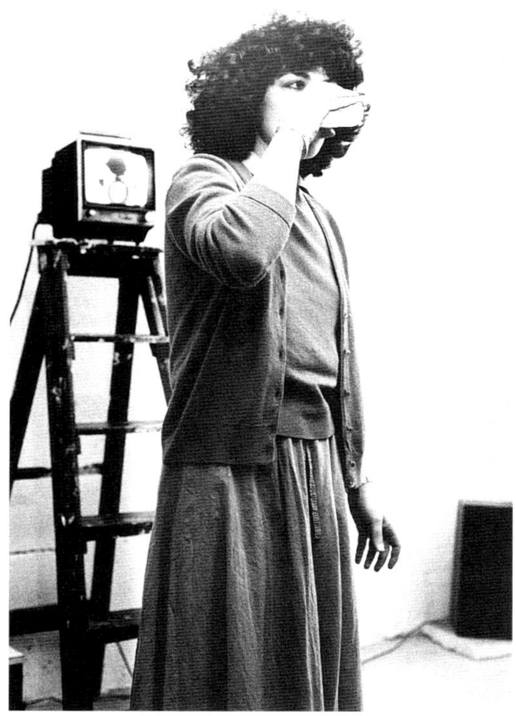

Look No Body! and *Waterworks* can be linked with Michel Foucault's *Discipline and Punish: The Birth of the Prison*, in which surveillance, nowadays almost omnipresent, is depicted as an instrument for imposing a bio-politics of physical norms. The aim is the unconditional adaptation of the individual to an authoritarian society. The exclusion of the theme of excretions, which became evident in the *Waterworks* project, can be seen as linked to such a repressive bio-politics, which even here, in the context of art, thinking about and presenting such a taboo is excluded.[2]

Hatoum continued to use video to explore the boundaries of her body and to question taboos (for example, in *Corps étranger* and *Deep Throat*). Moreover, the transgression of the boundaries between public and private space still remains one of her themes, for example, in the monumental video work conceived in 2004 for the dome of the Hamburger Kunsthalle.

pp. 46–49
pp. 130–133

Notes
1 On the history of the *Waterworks* project see Archer, Brett, de Zegher 1997, pp. 10-12, 116 f. The documentation material on *Look No Body!* is on p. 119 f. The passages from the performance cited here are also from that publication. A small version of *Waterworks* with one camera and monitor was created by Hatoum for the London Film Makers Co-op in 1981.
2 Cf. Marth 2003, p. 72; Michel Foucault, *Discipline and Punish: The Birth of the Prison*, London 1977.

7
Under Siege · 1982

Live action within a structure made of wood and plastic sheeting; sound tape, bucket and liquid clay
First performed at 'Women Live', London Film Makers Co-op, London, 30 May 1982
Duration: 7 hours
Repeated at 'Reflections – 9 Women Artists', Aspex Gallery Portsmouth, 2 October 1982
Duration: 3 hours

The artist's figure, reduced to a form covered in clay, trapped, confined within a small transparent structure, struggles to stand up, slipping and falling again and again. The live action is continuously repeated over a period of 7 hours and is accompanied by 3 different sound tapes (on loop) continuously blasting the space from different directions, creating a collage of sounds: revolutionary songs, news reports and conversations in English, French and Arabic.

Lit.: News reports in the *Daily Telegraph*, London, 1 October 1982; *Daily Star*, London, 1 October, 1982; *Daily Mail*, London, 1 October 1982; *The Sun*, London, 1 October 1982; *The News*, Portsmouth, 29 September, 4 and 8 October 1982; *Performance Magazine*, no. 22, February/March 1983; Desa Philippi, 'Mona Hatoum: The Witness beside Herself', *Parachute*, no. 58, April-June 1990, p. 13; exh. cat. Bristol 1993, pp. 17, 20, fig. p. 17; exh. cat. Paris 1994, pp. 13, 20, 54, fig. p. 37; Archer, Brett, de Zegher 1997, pp. 13, 42, 122-123, 146; exh. cat. Munich 1997-98, pp. 91, 100; exh. cat. Chicago/New York 1997-98, pp. 4, 7, 28, fig. p. 6; exh. cat. Mexico City 2002, pp. 18, 73; Marth 2003, pp. 32, 50-56, 135, 158, 164, 188, fig. 3.

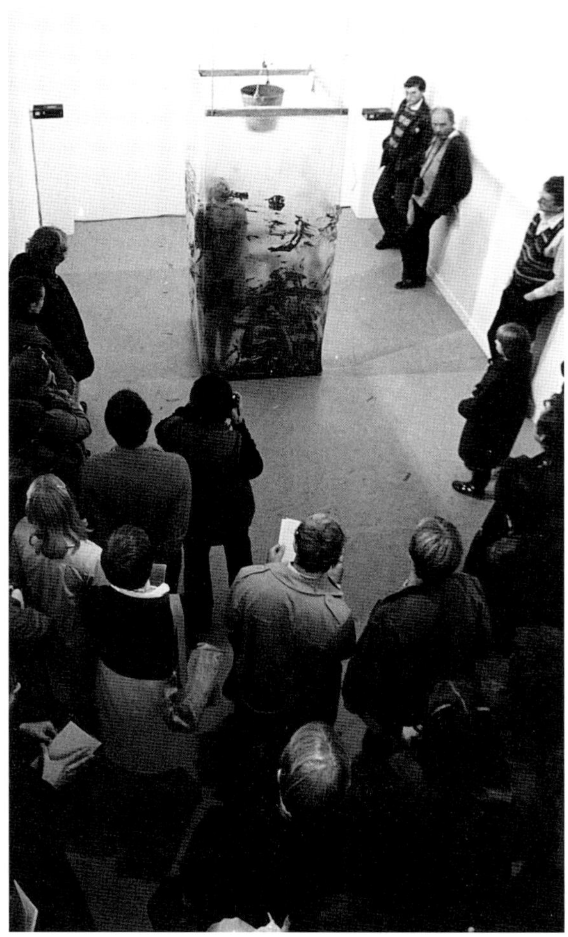

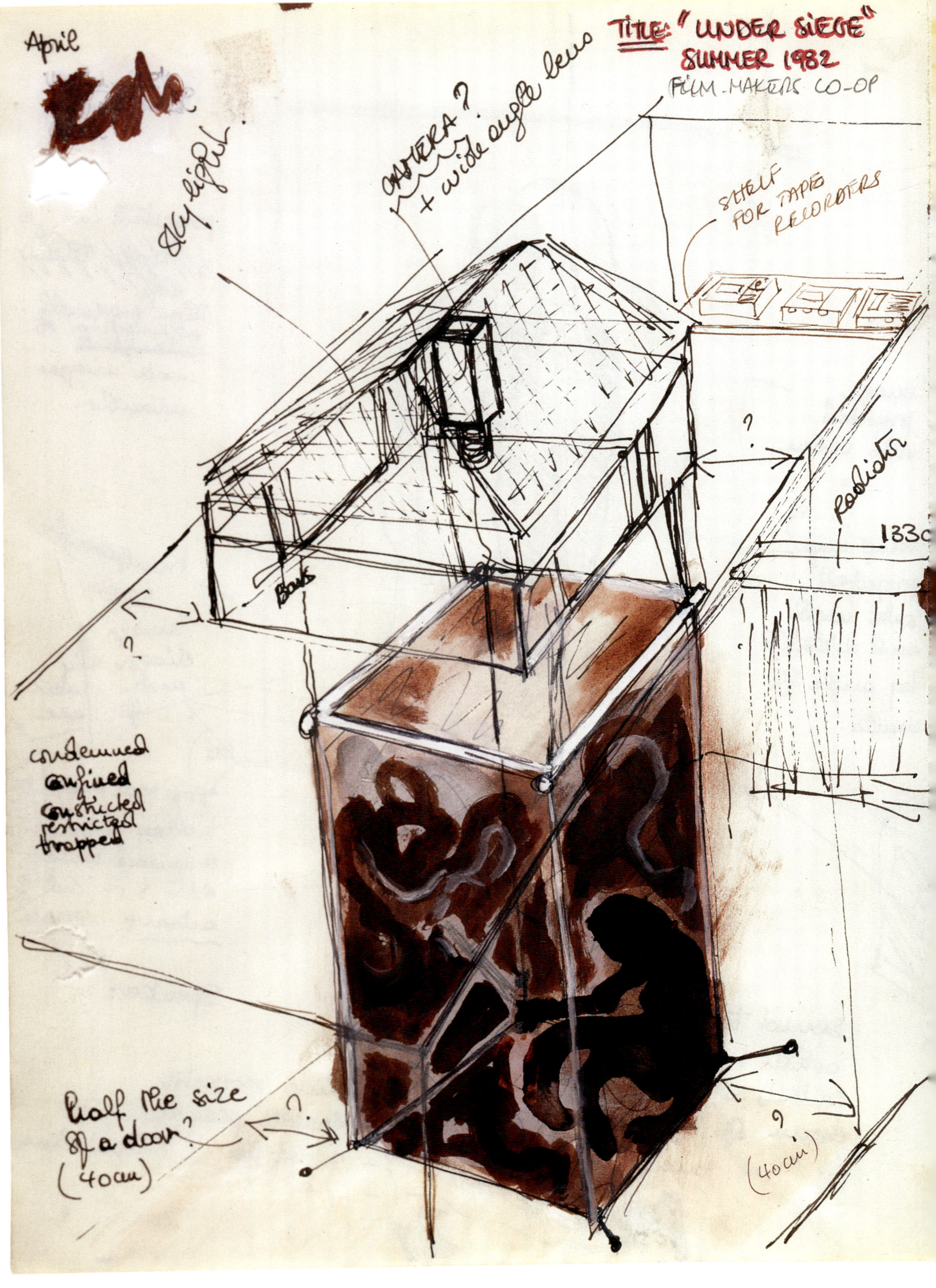

April
TITLE: "UNDER SIEGE"
SUMMER 1982
FILM-MAKERS CO-OP
Sky light
CAMERA ?
+ wide angle lens
SHELF FOR TAPE RECORDERS
Radiator
133c
Back
?
condemned
confined
constricted
restricted
trapped
half the size of a door?
(40cm)
?
(40cm)

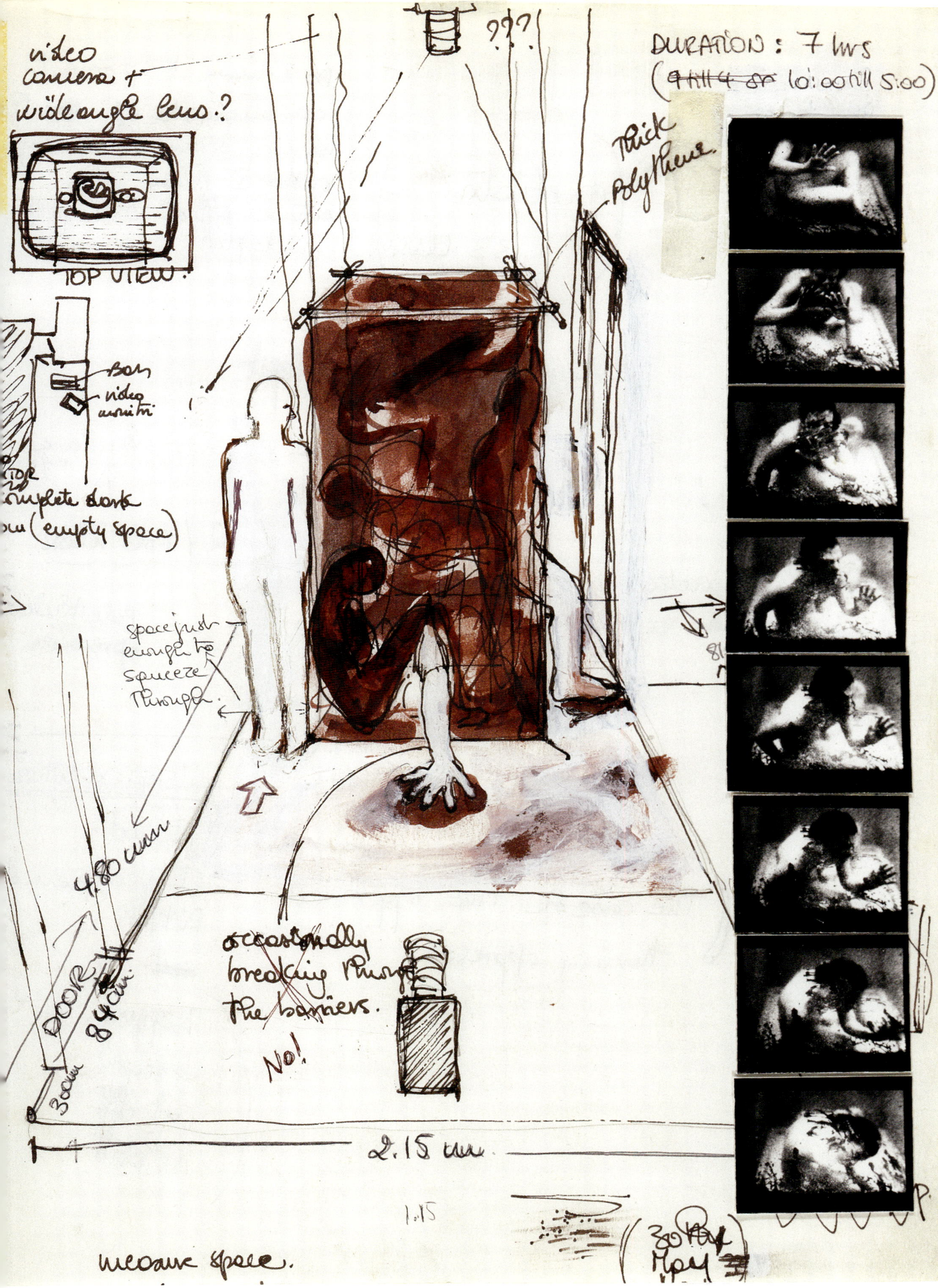

video camera + wideangle lens ?
???
DURATION : 7 hrs
(10:00 till 5:00)
TOP VIEW
Thick Polythene
Box
video monitor
(empty space)
space just enough to squeeze through
4.80 mm
DOOR
84 cm
300 cm
occasionally breaking through the barriers.
No!
2.15 mm
1.15
welcome space.

8
And another summer of ... mourning 1983

Live action with sound tape, slide projection, wooden frame, plastic sheeting and liquid clay
Performed at Bridewell Studios, Liverpool, 26 March 1983
Duration: 45 minutes

Against a backdrop of projected slides showing scenes of war and devastation and a sound tape of snippets of news reporting about invasion and massacre, the artist repeatedly attempts to climb out of a shallow frame filled with liquid clay up the adjacent staircase, only to slip and fall back again and again ...

Lit.: Exh. cat. Paris 1994, p. 54.

From a bucket above the shower-like structure, Mona Hatoum pours red clay which she smeared on the walls of the cubicle so that she herself gradually became invisible to the audience. 'Struggling to stand up again and again ... slipping and falling again and again ...',[1] is how she described the action, which was formally connected to the motif of falling down and getting up again in *Live work for the black room* (4).

'Condemned, confined, constricted, restricted, trapped', the artist had noted on the edge of a preparatory drawing for the action, thus outlining the conceptual framework of the performance in these terms. In her cell she is at once segregated and on display. The drawing initially included a video camera mounted above the cell to document the activity within the structure, but this idea was later abandoned. Accordingly, the notion of surveillance had no role to play in this case.

Instead, Hatoum focused the action exclusively on a direct confrontation with the viewers, who move around someone struggling in complete isolation. This struggle with the primal material, clay, can be seen as a general, and here initially open, metaphor for human existence and behaviour. Reaching for the bucket that holds the clay from which, according to the most diverse creation myths, man was fashioned, may even refer to Promethean, and thus world-creating powers. The artist's struggle with this primal mass, the nature of which can suggest either creation or faeces – for which the performer reaches, with which she shapes, and which ultimately swallows her up, so to speak, by hiding her from view – is a powerful image describing the human condition: struggling for survival, resisting, repeatedly rising up, refusing to surrender even under the most adverse conditions.

Almost a year later, Hatoum once more took up the motif of the individual struggle against opposition in her performance *And another summer of ... mourning* in which she tried in vain to climb out of a shallow tray filled with liquid clay and climb a staircase covered in plastic. *Under Siege* – despite the hopelessness – also alluded to something formative, creative: behind the finger-marks visible from the outside, perhaps there is something of the action-painting of a Jackson Pollock (or the current, existential adaptation by Ana Mendieta, for example).[2] In *And another summer of ... mourning* everything was reduced to the futile activity of a modern-day Sisyphus.

Under Siege was the first in a whole series of performances (7-11) in which Hatoum made some reference to the war in Lebanon and the Israeli siege of Beirut: 'As a Palestinian woman, this work was my first attempt at making a statement about a persistent struggle to survive in a continuous stage of siege. Members of the audience, depending on their own background, spoke of various powerful images of oppression: the Irish hunger-strikers, prisoners in solitary confinement, the Bantustans ... As a person from the "Third World" living in the West, existing on the margin of European society and alienated from my own ... this action represented an act of separation ... stepping out of an acquired frame of reference and into a space which acted as a point of reconnection and reconciliation with my own background and the bloody history of my own people ...'[3]

In these performances, as in the ones that followed, Hatoum's actions were linked for the first time with a concrete historical context by means of a second level of sound, or sound and image projection. This coupling of documentary sound and visual material with an action is reminiscent of Erwin Piscator's political theatre and its later influence on Brecht's theory of epic theatre: the slide or film projections situate the action of the struggling individual within a concrete socio-political context; and vice versa, the concrete individual action gives an emotional charge to the political documentation. Piscator describes this principle with reference to his legendary production of *Trotz alledem!*: '*In Trotz alledem!* the film used was a docu-

◀ Under Siege (Sketchbook drawing) · 1983

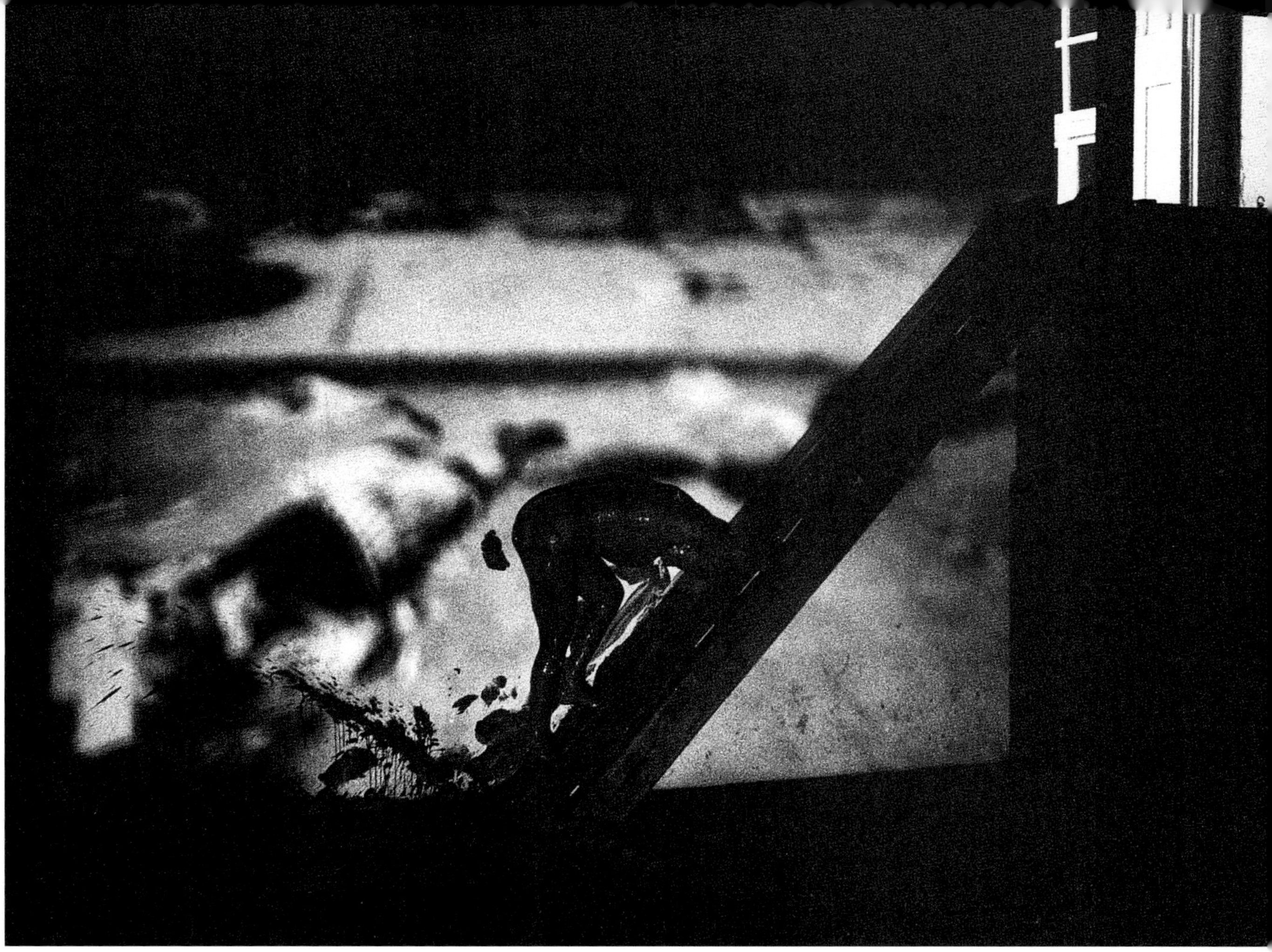

ment. From the material in the Reich archives ... we used mainly footage of the war, of demobilisation, of a parade of all Europe's leaders, etc. The takes showed the brutality of war: attacks with flame-throwers, heaps of torn bodies, burning cities ... The surprise element created by the alternation of film and acted sequences was very effective. Even stronger was the dramatic tension with which the film and the acted sequences mutually imbued one another, heightening each other to such an extent that at certain points a veritable furioso was achieved the likes of which I have only seldom experienced at the theatre. For example, when the vote of the Social Democrats on the war loans (acted scene) was followed by the footage of a military assault and the first dead bodies, this not only underscored the political character of the procedure, but also brought about human distress, i.e., created art. It transpired that the strongest politico-propagandist impact was along the same line as the most potent artistic creation.'[4]

For Hatoum, too, the aim of this coupling was to create a tension between the action and the documentary material in order to communicate something of her own sense of shock to the audience. Yet the performances did not come across as agitation or propaganda, because the artist's subjectivity was clearly identifiable each time. Hatoum's works did not provide generalized directions, but reflected her position, which she perceived as isolated, in the face of both mass and power.

Two years later, Hatoum incorporated scenes from *Under Siege*, filmed before the admission of the audience, in her video work *Changing Parts*. Reproduced fig. p. 14 there in close-up and in slow motion, these images, which are reminiscent of shots taken underwater, suggest both the struggle to give birth or someone in the throws of death.

Notes
1 Archer, Brett, de Zegher 1997, p. 122.
2 Cf. Ana Mendieta, *Body Tracks* (1974), University of Iowa, Iowa City; in his performance *Doru ni idomu* (Fighting with mud, 1955) the Japanese artist Kazuo Shiraga, a member of the Gutai artists association, used his body to produce the painting, so that the genesis was also a component of the work; see *Out of actions: Zwischen Performance und Objekt 1949-1979,* exh. cat., MAK Österreichisches Museum für angewandte Kunst, Vienna 1998, p. 27.
3 From a brochure published on the occasion of Mona Hatoum's first performance tour in Canada. Extracts reprinted in Archer, Brett, de Zegher 1997, p. 122; quoted here from the original.
4 Erwin Piscator, 'Das Politische Theater', in Piscator, *Zeittheater: 'Das Politische Theater' und weitere Schriften von 1915 bis 1966,* ed. Manfred Brauneck and Peter Stertz, Reinbek/Hamburg 1986, pp. 64 f. (trans. Pauline Cumbers).

9
Untitled · 1983

Live action with sound tape, slides and leather travel bag
Performed at The Radiator, Manchester, 30 March 1983
Duration: 20 minutes

The audience is led into the dilapidated basement of a theatre. The artist walks in holding a leather travel bag out of which she removes a small cassette player, a slide projector and a bag containing an untidy heap of tapes and slides. She announces that she will be playing some music and showing holiday snaps from a recent trip home, instead every tape she plays seems to be of air raids, shelling, or news reports about war. Every slide she shows depicts scenes of war and devastation. She apologises each time for playing the wrong tape or showing the wrong images and attempts in vain to search amongst the jumble of tapes and slides. She eventually gives up in exasperation, apologises again and walks out.

Lit.: Exh. cat. Paris 1994, p. 54.

Many of Mona Hatoum's performances were conceived in such a way that they could be enacted in their respective form in any 'neutral' gallery or other such space. Some of her performances were conceived in response to a given situation: for example in *And another summer of … mourning* her action was designed to make use of the existing steep staircase. In the untitled performance for *The Radiator* theatre in Manchester she used the dilapidated basement because of its atmosphere, which she later characterised as 'looking like a run-down shelter, very damp and dank and cold'.[1]

Hatoum emphasised this bunker atmosphere by using a single light bulb which made the surrounding jumble cast long shadows on the mouldy walls, creating an oppressive, ghostly backdrop for the action, in which she presented a struggle for 'normality': the supposedly well-meaning attempt to present holiday slides and music from her home country ended in frustration. The artist's origins and her country's recent history did not allow normality.

Here Hatoum played the role of the failed entertainer. The situation is a familiar one: Everything is supposed to be so pleasant, somewhat bourgeois perhaps, but altogether well-intentioned. However, this intention is thwarted by events, the perversity of fate causes everything to go awry – and end up in anger and despair.

The image and sound material, which Hatoum had been using in her actions since *Under Siege,* was determined for the first time here by the action itself. A similar spatial situation, this time in a disused lift shaft, later inspired Hatoum to make another site-specific performance: *Forced Flight* (24).

Note
1 Mona Hatoum in conversation with the author, Hamburg, 20 December 2003.

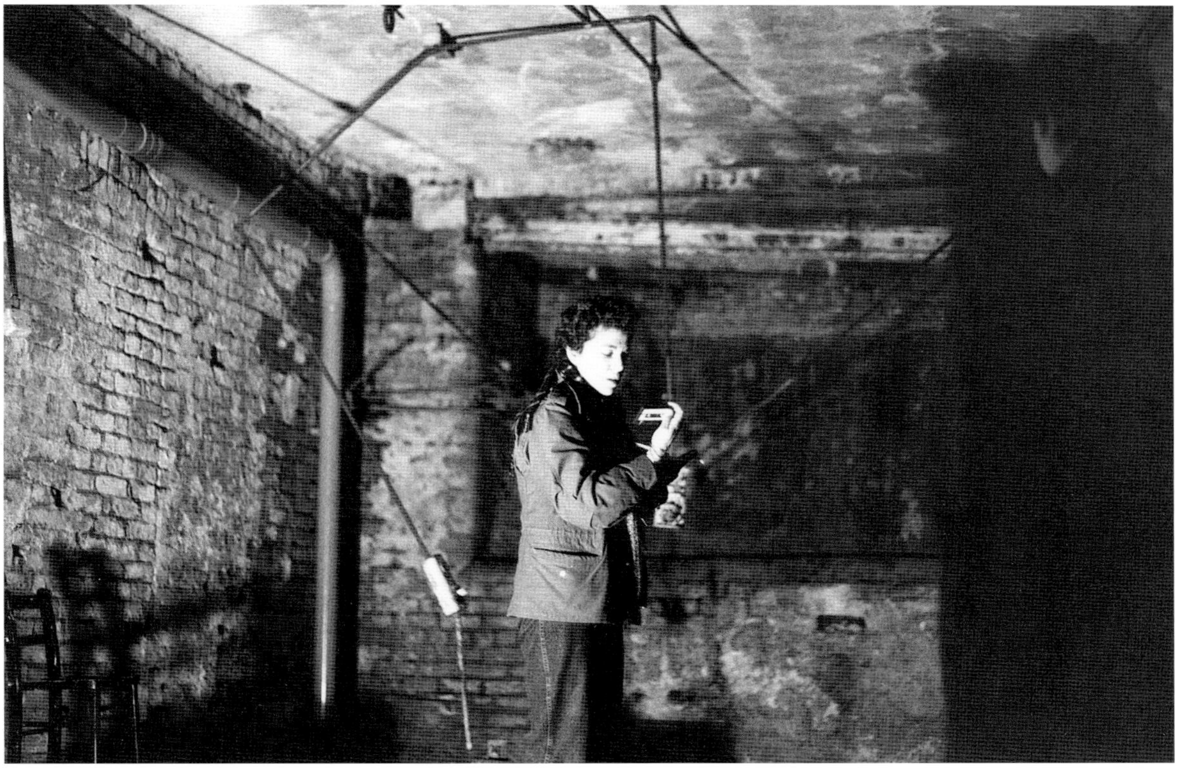

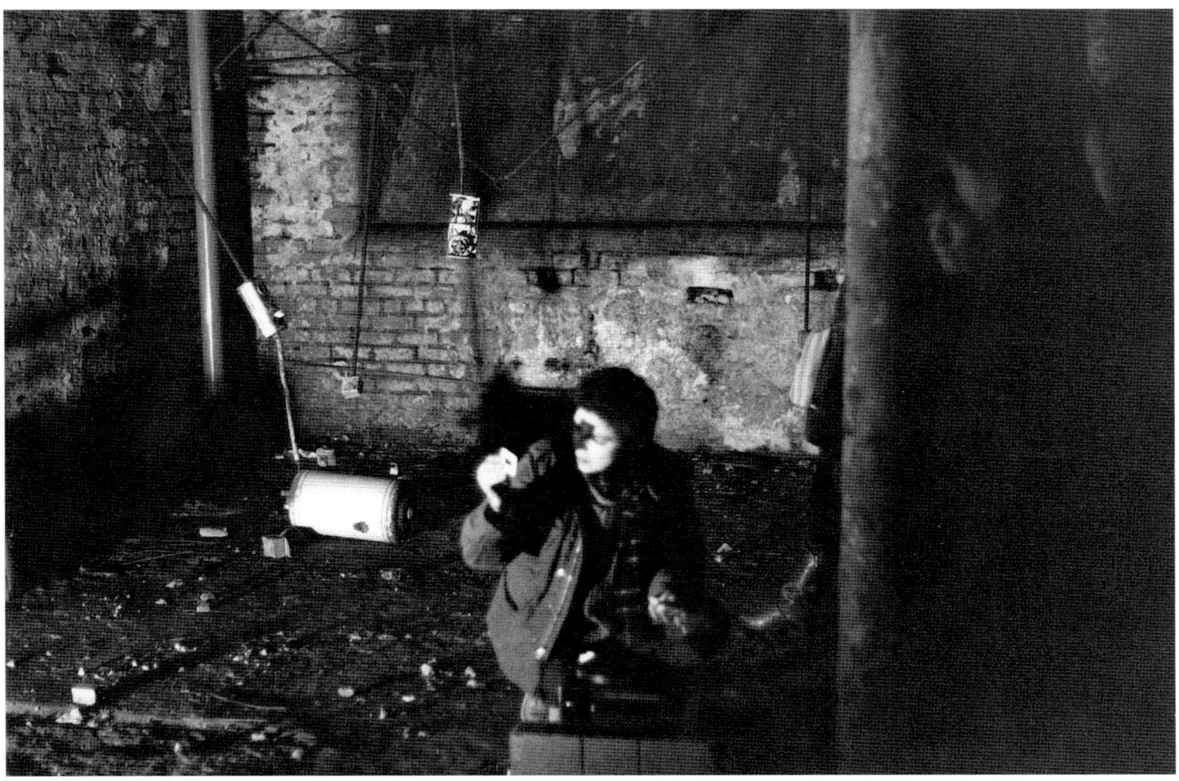

Untitled · 1983

10
An hour in a day of another bloody year · 1983

Live action with sound tape, live amplified phone, and a stack of newspapers
Performed at 'Blind dates', The Blackie, Liverpool, 18 June 1983
Duration: 40 minutes

Lit.: Exh. cat. Paris 1994, p. 54; Archer, Brett, de Zegher 1997, p. 146.

The artist paces between a table with a radio on the left side of the stage and a chair and table with a phone and a stack of newspapers on the right side of the stage. She turns the radio on and for a few minutes the searching of the short wave band with static sounds and Morse code signals interrupted by snippets of news, can be heard. She sits in the chair, picks up a newspaper from the stack, looks at it briefly before throwing it around the stage. She repeatedly attempts to dial a long distance call but never gets through. The sounds of dialling and telephone communication signals are amplified and resonate throughout the space.

The artist had included three links to the outside world: newspaper and radio are one-way forms of communication that made her a passive recipient, and the telephone, a more interactive form of communication. However, her many attempts to connect with the outside world failed.

As in previous performances, the outside world took on the concrete form of a soundtrack, and here too bits of news about the war in Lebanon could be heard. The isolation is the result of the artist's personal history and that of her country: 'Basically I was trying to dial home. I kept dialling, but it was always giving an engaged tone or a recording saying, "Lines to the country you are calling are engaged. Please try later." I just never got through.'[1]

This performance belongs to a small group of works in which Hatoum, with just a few props, sets herself up for a short space of time in a small stage-scenario of the kind familiar to us from conversation pieces or Beckett plays. This group of works could be

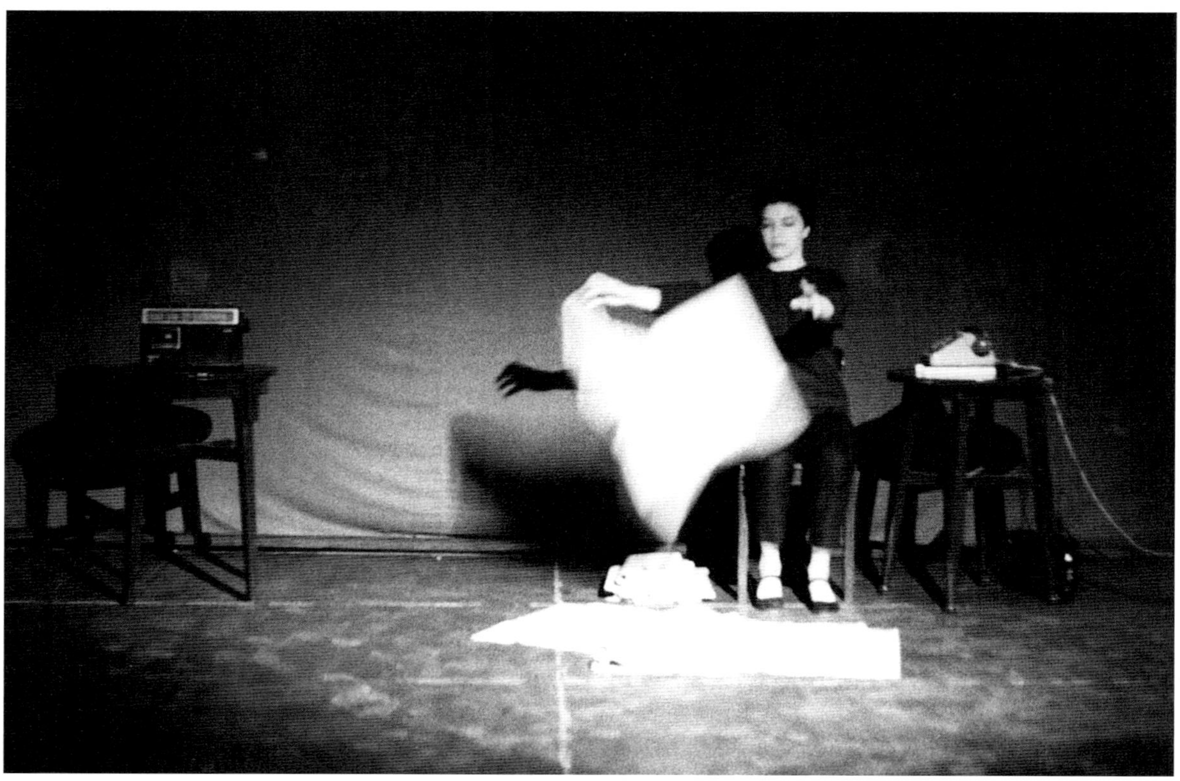

called Mona Hatoum's existential studio-plays; in addition to this one, the group also includes performances 9 and 13.

Note
1 Mona Hatoum in conversation with the author, Hamburg, 20 December 2003.

11
The Negotiating Table · 1983

Live work with table, three chairs, a hanging light, sound tape, plastic sheet, raw beef kidneys, surgical gauze and red paint
First performed at SAW Gallery, Ottawa, 23 November 1983
Duration: 3 hours
Repeated: N.A.C. St. Catherine's, Canada, 24 November 1983; The Western Front, Vancouver, 5 December 1983; '2nd International Festival of Performance', South Hill Park Arts Centre, Bracknell, Berkshire, 23 June 1984; Franklin Furnace Gallery, New York, 29 November 1984

The room is dark, lit only by a light bulb lowered over a table on which the artist lies motionless. Empty chairs surround the table. Her body is bloodstained, covered with entrails, wrapped in plastic, and her head is firmly covered in surgical gauze. On the soundtrack, news reports about civil war and speeches by Western leaders talking about peace can be heard.

Lit.: Evelyn Erskine, *The Citizen,* Ottawa, 24 November 1983; Desa Philippi, 'Mona Hatoum. The Witness beside Herself', in *Parachute,* no. 58, April-June 1990, p. 13, fig. p. 10, 13; exh. cat. Bristol 1993, p. 17, fig. p. 19; exh. cat. Paris 1994, pp. 20, 39, 41, 55, fig. p. 38; Archer, Brett, de Zegher 1997, pp. 43 f, 127-129, 146; *The Artist's Body,* ed. Tracey Warr, London 2000, p. 150; Marth 2003, pp. 32, 54-59, 64, 67, 92, 93, 165, 188, fig. 5.

As in the previous actions, an existential metaphor was set against a concrete historical background by means of a sound-collage. In an interview, Mona Hatoum refers the two elements of the action to the reality of the situation in the Middle East and the representation of the events there from a 'Western' point of view: 'It was basically a juxtaposition of two elements, one referring to the physical reality and brutality of the situation, and the other to the way it is represented and dealt with in the West. This piece was the most direct reference I had ever made to the war in Lebanon. I made this work right after the Israeli invasion and the massacres in the camps, which for me was the most shattering experience of my life.'[1]

The Negotiating Table was not so much a performance as a *tableau vivant:* the only, barely perceptible movement must have been the artist's breathing. She herself calls *The Negotiating Table* a 'live work' as distinct from performances called 'live actions'. In it, Hatoum assigned a role to the audience that went beyond that of the uninvolved observer. One person who attended the action describes the changes that occurred in the audience during the performance:

'At first they crowded around the victim on the table, examining it on an impulse not unlike the ghoulish curiosity of those who stop to look at a car accident. The horror of it soon translated into silent repulsion as everyone moved back. They kept moving back slowly until most were as far away as possible, sitting along the room's walls. It was a distance which most closely approximated the safety of following the crisis on TV. The mood of the performance was like that of a vigil.'[2]

Later, another audience member summarised: 'The performance had no "development", so that even as spectators standing outside the circle of light we had to face our own inaction and passivity, confronting the gulf between the human reality and the representation of it daily served up for our consumption by politicians and the media.'[3]

This action must have had an atmosphere of paralysing coldness due to the complete absence of movement and the blinding overhead light. Hatoum produced four gouaches in preparation for this performance. While one gouache depicts the planned situation – three chairs, a table with a lamp and the wrapped bloodstained body – in two other drawings, the artist depicts a cannibalistic feast in grotesque savageness. Three men, naked in one drawing, and wearing black suits in the other, are viciously tearing apart the body on the table and gulping down the separate pieces.

fig. pp. 102–103

The harsh expressiveness of the gouaches recalls the kind of depictions of 'lust murders' painted particularly by German artists like Dix, Grosz and Schlichter in the years following World War I. These also portrayed man's unbridled impulses and fantasies of private violence, giving expression to artists' and intellectuals' fear of the so-called *Frauenfrage* (question of women's rights).[4]

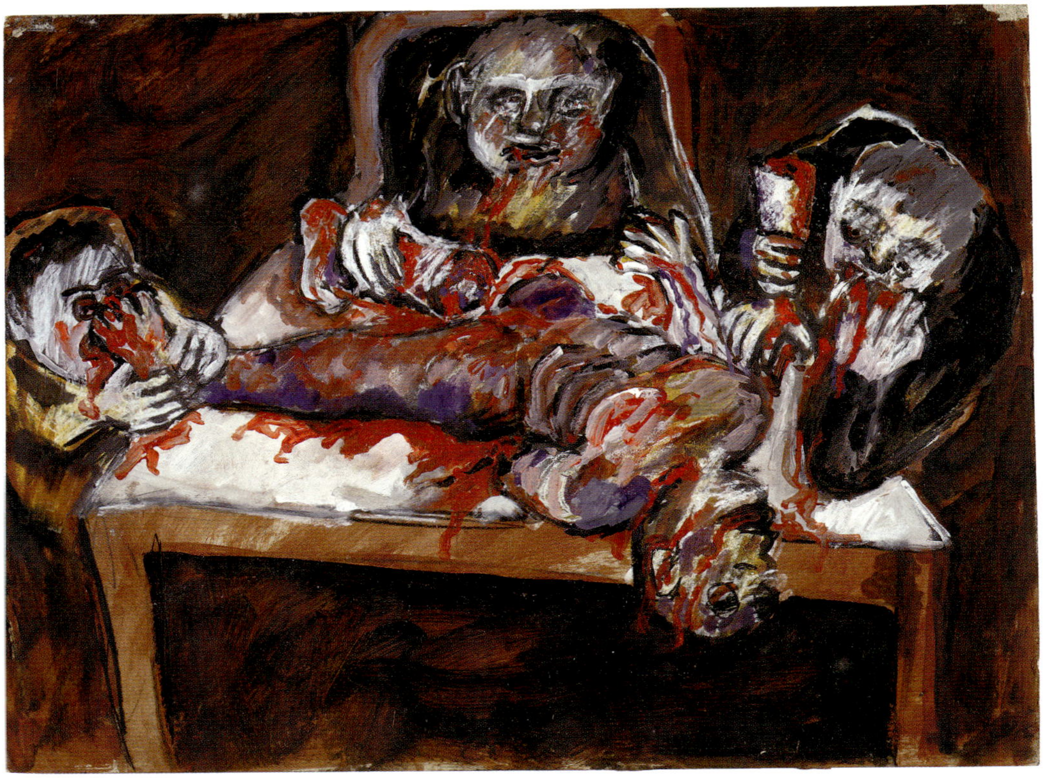

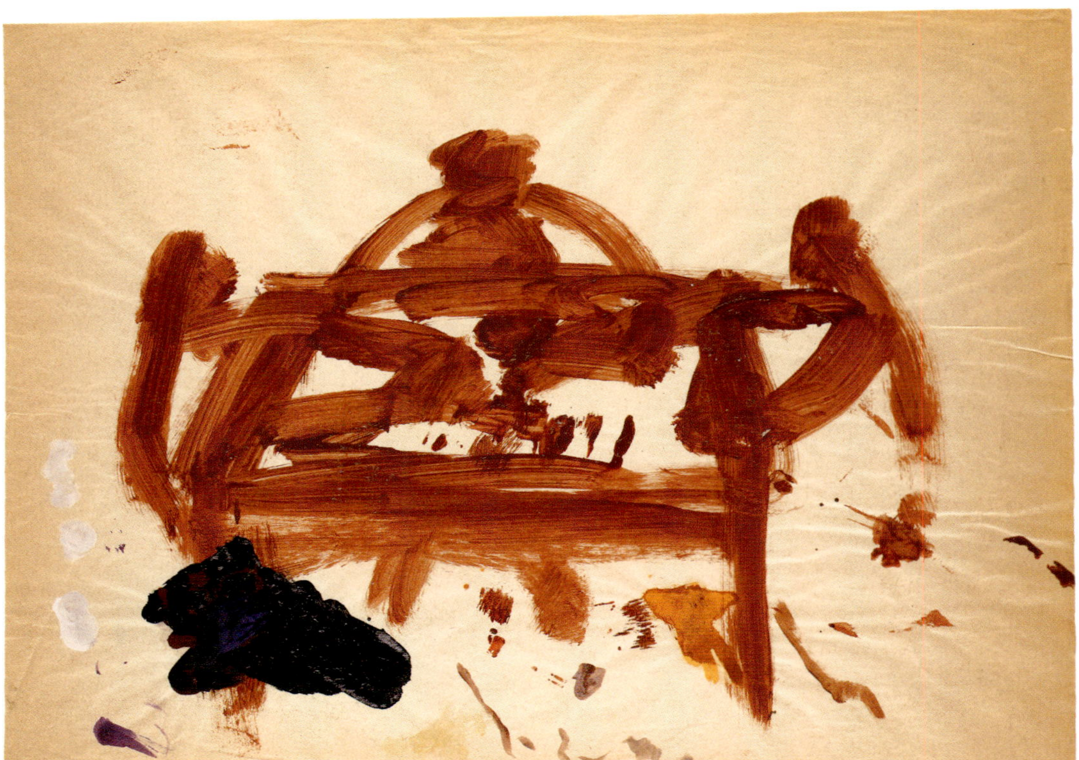

 The Negotiating Table (4 studies) · 1983

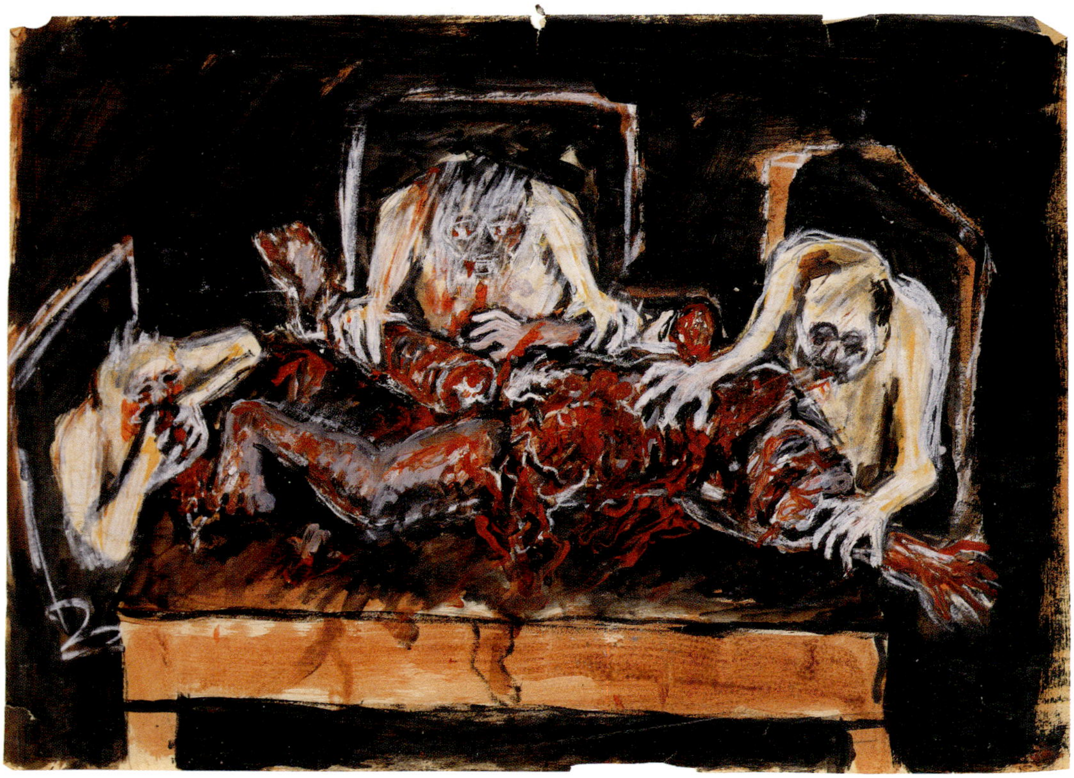

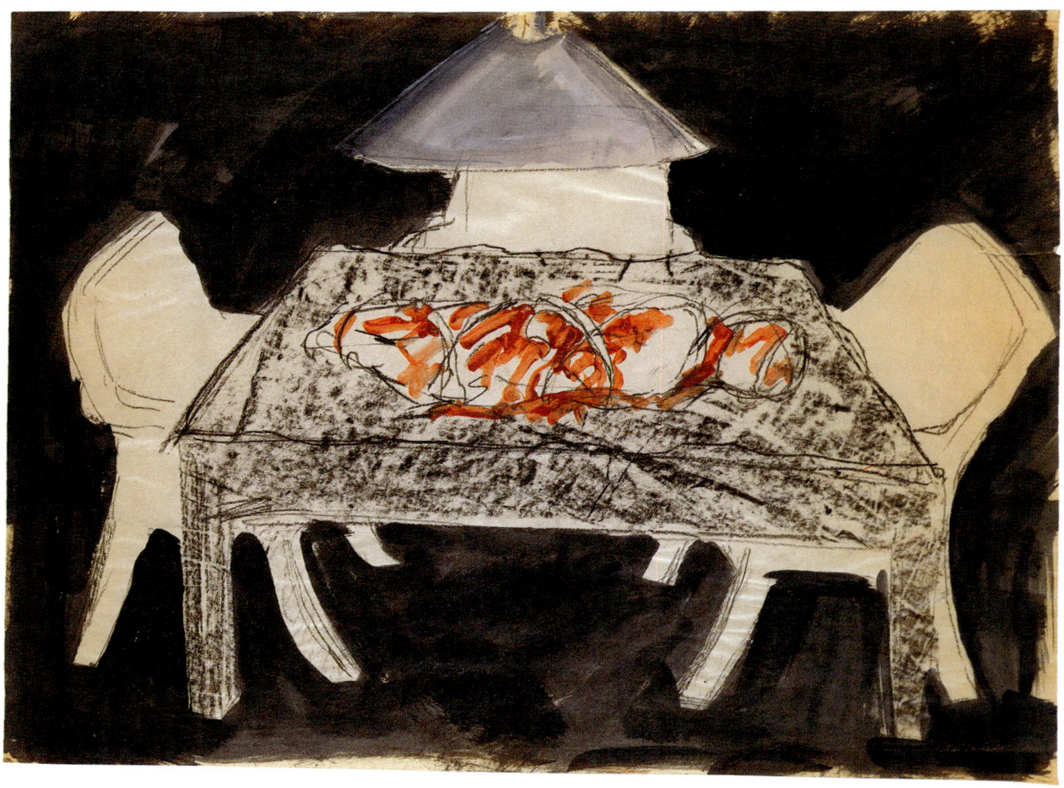

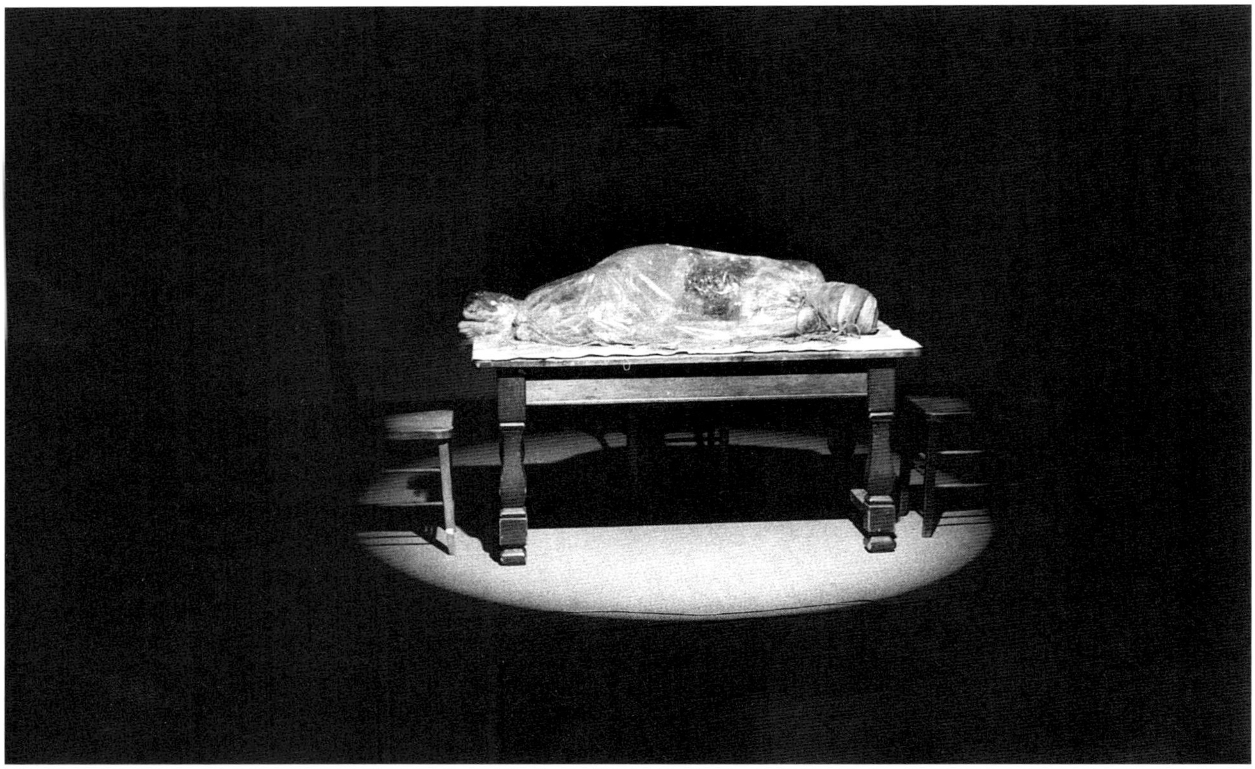

Moreover, individual elements in *The Negotiating Table* were suggestive of the Viennese Actionism of the sixties: the body bound with ropes, for example, evoked early actions by Rudolf Schwarzkogler; the real entrails actions by Otto Mühl's and Hermann Nitsch's so-called 'Orgies-Mysteries-Theatre'. The aim of their extreme sacrificial actions, in which bodies were covered with heaps of flesh and entrails, was to connect with the frenzied cults of archaic religions in order to raise art to a mythical, sacral level again and confirm the artist in his role as martyr. This also had political implications, as for example in the *80th Action of the Orgies-Mysteries Theatre* in Prinzendorf, which took place in the same year as Hatoum's performance. At the end of the various rituals in that action, buckets-full of blood and entrails were poured down over tanks.[5]

Hatoum's 'live work' avoided anything that might associate art with the idea of a cathartic and ultimately healing function, as in Viennese Actionism. Far from the orgiastic rituals of the Viennese artists, *The Negotiating Table* confronted the audience with Hatoum's body, which she used as a metaphor for silent suffering and personal powerlessness. With no action, but with great intensity, she captured a status quo from which there was no way out, in which she was paralysed, and which she would later formulate in the compelling sculptures ∞ (*Infinity*, 1991-2001) or *No Way* (1996). figs. pp. 60

Notes

1 Archer, Brett, de Zegher 1997, p. 127.
2 Evelyn Erskine, 'Audience feels impact of vigil-like performance', *The Citizen*, Ottawa, 24 November 1983.
3 Archer, Brett, de Zegher 1997, pp. 43 f.
4 Cf. Beth Irwin Lewin, 'Lustmord: Inside the Windows of Metropolis', in Charles W. Haxthausen and Heidrun Suhr (eds.), *Berlin: Culture and Metropolis*, Minneapolis and Oxford 1991. Kathrin Hoffmann-Curtius, *Im Blickfeld: George Grosz: John, der Frauenmörder*, exh. cat., Hamburger Kunsthalle 1993.
5 The Artist's Body, ed. Tracey Warr, London 2000, p. 93.

12
Them and Us ... and Other Divisions 1984

Live action with black hood, bucket, brush, red paint, newspapers, wire mesh
Performed at '2nd International Festival of Performance', South Hill Park Arts Centre, Bracknell, Berkshire, 23 June 1984
Duration: 50 minutes

While people sit out on the terrace during lunch, the artist, hooded and in black overalls, crawls on her belly between the chairs and underneath the tables for the entire length of the 300-foot terrace. As she finally reaches a recess in the garden wall, she begins dipping a brush into a bucket and vigorously scrubbing the stone step, but instead of getting it cleaner, it becomes covered with red paint. At the end, she sets fire to a screen of newspapers that burn away to reveal a wall covered with racist graffiti.

Lit.: Nigel Pollitt, 'Notes', *City Limits,* no. 144, July 1984; David Briers, 'The Search for Performance', *Performance Magazine,* no. 31, September/October 1984; exh. cat. Bristol 1993, p. 17, fig. p. 23; exh. cat. Paris 1994, p. 55; Archer, Brett, de Zegher 1997, pp. 44 f, 147; exh. cat. Chicago/New York 1997/98, p. 31; Marth 2003, pp. 32, 59, 60, 64, 165, 188, fig. 8.

This was Mona Hatoum's first performance outdoors, and also the first in which she had to anticipate that there would be some people in the audience who would be caught off guard. An art critic later described her sudden appearance one Saturday afternoon as follows: 'I went outside in search of Mona Hatoum's performance, but thinking that it had been postponed, I sat in the sun on the terrace, and suddenly noticed Hatoum, covered head to foot in boiler suit and mask, crawling from one end of the long terrace to the other. Families from the adjacent estate were taking the sun with glasses of iced lager from the terrace bar. As Hatoum crawled in a straight line between their tables, the usual deprecatory remarks about modern art were made ... The "piece" for me was not Hatoum alone, but Hatoum plus the bemused family, who played their part well. They did not follow Hatoum to her niche with us initiates, who watched her cover its step with red tile paint, and set fire to hanging newspapers revealing a wall covered in racist graffiti, before starting the long crawl back ...'[1]

With his description of the way this particular work by Hatoum was determined, not by herself alone, but also by the somewhat irritated customers, on the restaurant terrace, the eyewitness expresses the situational character of this performance. Hatoum was to expand this aspect in later works, such as *Roadworks*, which will be dealt with in more detail below (see 16, 22).

Another fundamental change in the dramaturgy of the performances could also be seen for the first time here: Hatoum's linking of several independent actions. In the context of the later performance *Variation on Discord and Divisions*, she herself speaks of 'a series of vignettes'. In English this term is used to designate, among other things, a sketch or a scene in a play or movie.

'Vignettes' could also serve to describe the individual actions assembled in *Them and Us ... and Other Divisions:* Whereas the performances to date presented a particular state and focused, in principle, on one situation (for example, filming the audience, offering water, falling, fighting, waiting, lying down), here Hatoum for the first time combined three different actions into a dramatic sequence, a mini-drama, so to speak. Though not necessarily related to one another, separate actions could thus be condensed into an action with a scenario creating a stronger narrative impact than they would have individually. Yet Hatoum did not forego the ambiguity of her images as a result: In crawling across the stone floor on her belly she expressed both humiliation and danger, and being masked even added to this subversion. Instead of cleaning the steps, she made them dirtier. And the burning newspapers only revealed further potential conflict by

Them and Us ... and Other Divisions · 1984

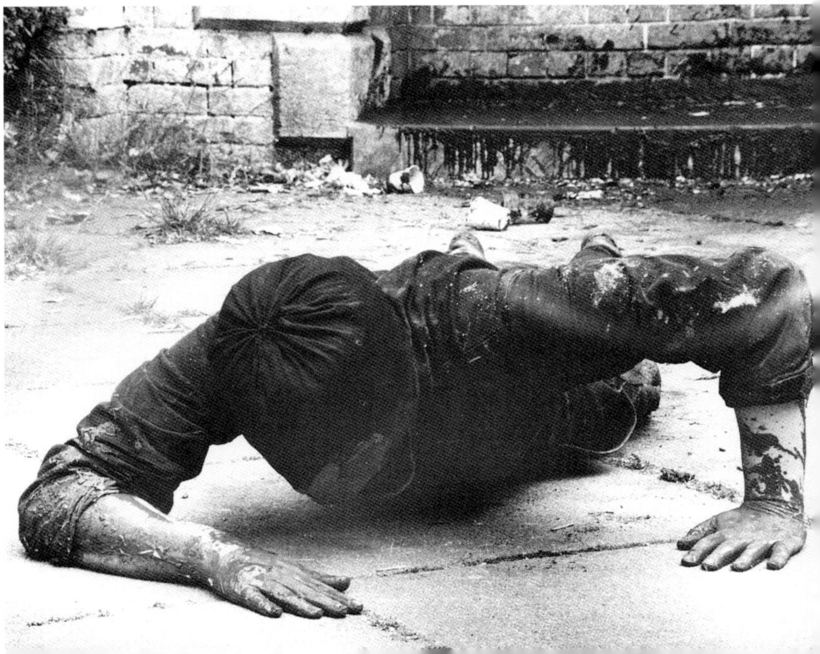

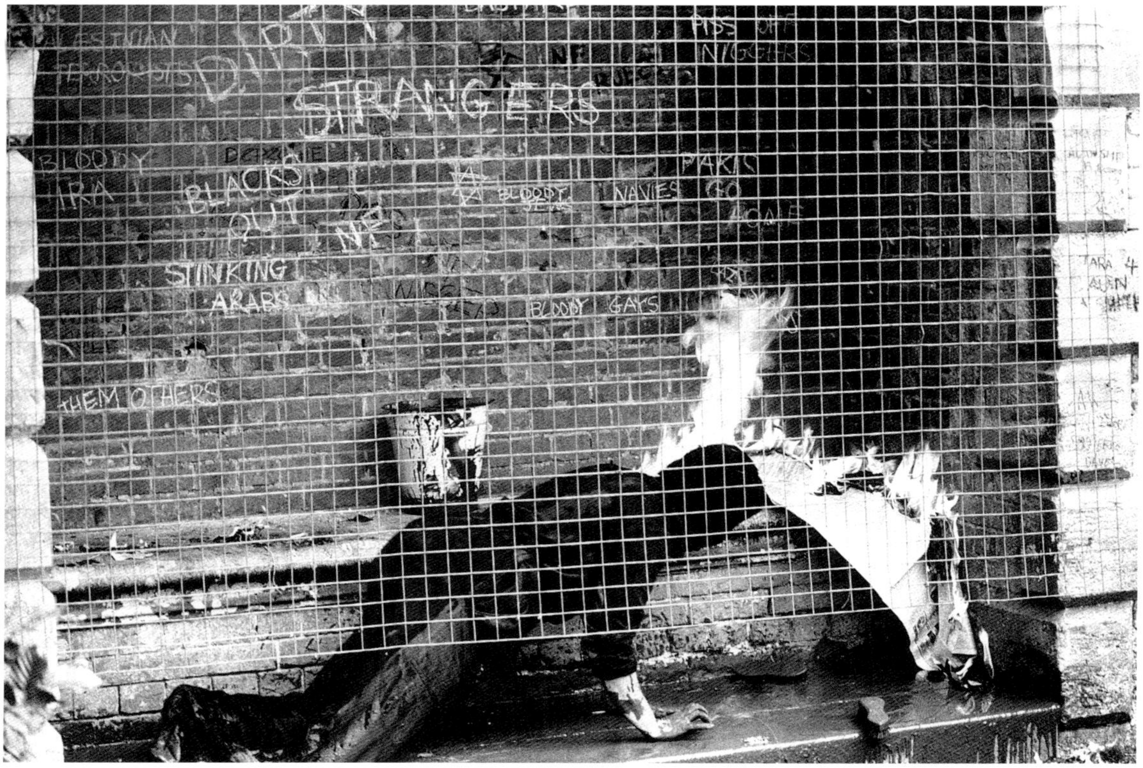

exposing the xenophobic graffiti.[2] Again Hatoum turned the image of victimisation into powerful images of resistance and fighting.

In *Variation on Discord and Divisions* (14) and *Mind the Gap* (23) Hatoum adopted the strategy of linking 'vignettes' together and extended it further.

Notes

1 David Briers, 'The Search for Performance', *Performance Magazine,* no. 31, September/October 1984.

2 Some of the graffiti was already there, others were added by the artist before the performance began, according to information provided by the artist, 9 January 2004.

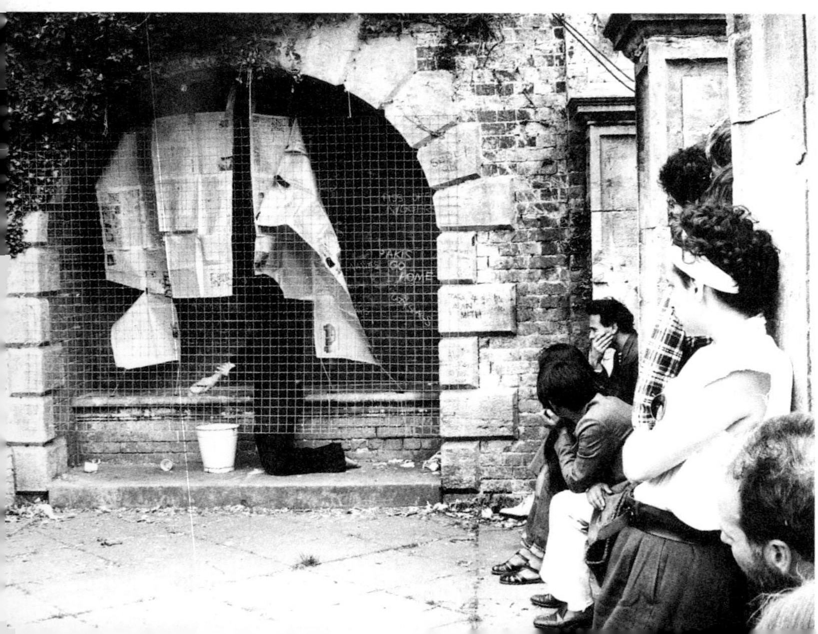

Them and Us ... and Other Divisions · 1984

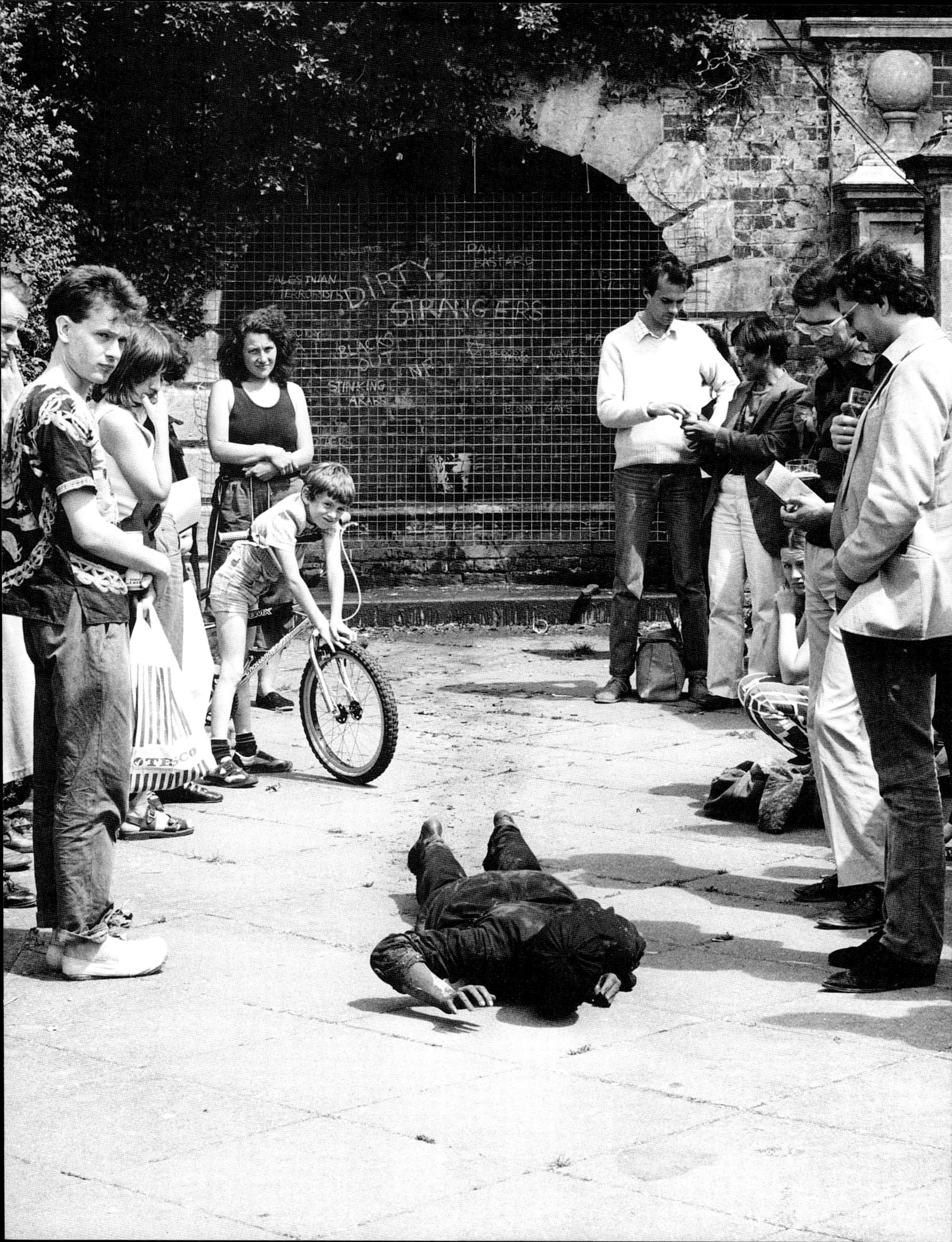
PAKI BASTARD
PALESTINIAN TERRORISTS
DIRTY STRANGERS
BLACKS OUT
NF
STINKING ARABS
BMX
TESCO

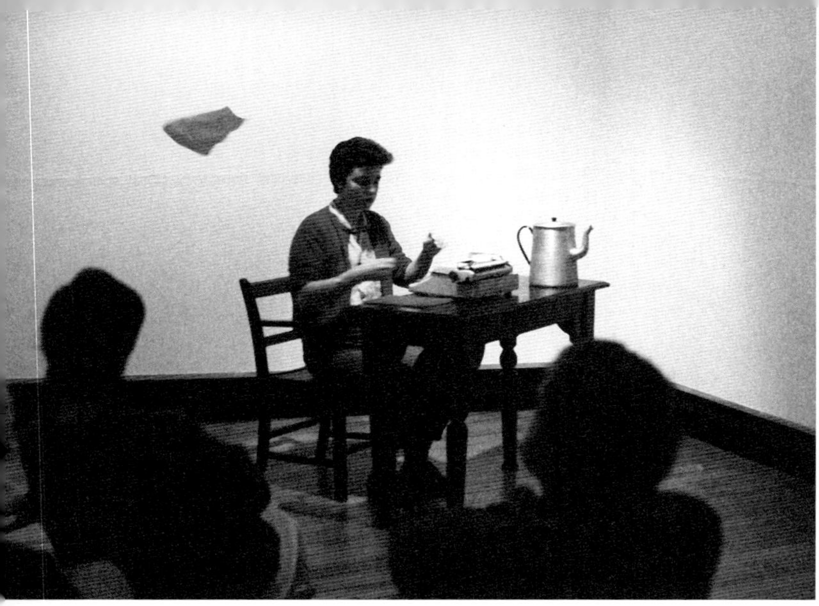

13
Worlds Apart · 1984

Live action with sound tape, typewriter, red tissue paper and large teapot
Performed at 'Women's Performance', Rochdale Art Gallery, Rochdale, UK, 17 November 1984
Duration: 20 minutes

The artist sits in front of the audience at a table with a typewriter and a large teapot. She types various notes on red tissue paper throwing them onto the floor or into the teapot. Occasionally she hands the notes to individual members of the audience. Simultaneously, a sound recording can be heard with the voices of foreigners from different countries speaking English. Each person has a very distinctive accent and gives their biased and sometimes humorous views of how they perceive the English and their culture. The scraps of red tissue paper contain fragments of the artist's personal experience of living in London.

Lit.: Exh. cat. Paris 1994, p. 55; Archer, Brett, de Zegher 1997, p. 147.

'Oh, is that how people really see us?' Mona Hatoum recalls the reaction of some members of the audience.[1] As in the previous performance (12), prejudice towards foreigners is at play here. The 'foreign' voices in this case are extracts from the BBC produced training record *English with an Accent* (1979). This record sought to familiarise speakers and actors, in a humourous way, with the accents of people from different cultures.[2] The smug amusement which might be expressed by Britons on hearing these different accents is balanced by the whole range of prejudices with which they themselves are often confronted.

An accent is not merely indicative of a person's origins, in Anglo-Saxon society – and not only there – it helps to pigeonhole people in social and ethnic categories. Judgements about someone's general abilities and intelligence are often made on the basis of their accent. At the latest since the seventies, a debate has been going on under the heading 'The Politics of Language' in which these mechanisms of social discrimination are reflected upon and attempts made to re-evaluate 'standard pronunciation' and accent/dialect.[3]

The linguist Rosina Lippi-Green summarises this from a contemporary viewpoint: 'A person's accent (the bundle of distinctive intonation and phonological features) is fixed or hard-wired in the mind, and once past a certain age it can only be very laboriously changed, to a very limited degree, regardless of commitment, intelligence, and resources. Thus the constant public debate on good English, on the one right English, is as fruitless an exercise as the hypothetical congressional debate on the ideal height and weight for all adults. We cannot purge language of variation linked to social difference, but more important than that undeniable fact: *it should not matter.*'[4]

This particular acoustic accompaniment situated Hatoum's performance against the backdrop of the 'Politics of Language'. On tissue papers, she typed her accounts of the experience of being a foreigner, a theme which runs through many of her works, with the result that this poetic performance represented a particular act of individual and collective reflection.

Like performances 9 and 10, this too is one of her brief, studio-style improvisations.

Notes
1 Mona Hatoum in conversation with the author, Hamburg, 20 December 2003.
2 *English with an Accent,* 1979, BBC Records 166.
3 Cf. Tony Crowley, *Standard English and the Politics of Language,* Urbana 1989; John Honey, *Language is Power,* London 1997; Geoffrey Sampson, *Educating Eve: The 'Language Instinct' Debate,* London and New York, 1997.
4 Rosina Lippi-Green, *English with an Accent,* London and New York 1997, p. 241.

14
Variation on Discord and Divisions 1984

Live action with hood, knife, bucket, scrubbing brush, red paint, table, chairs, plates, raw beef kidneys, newspapers
First performed at ABC No Rio, New York, 2 December 1984
Repeated: A.K.A. Saskatoon, Canada, 7 December 1984; The Western Front, Vancouver, 14 December 1984; Articule, Montreal, 17 January 1984; 'Dazzling Phrases: Six Performance Artists', Forest City Gallery, London, Canada, 29 January 1985, and Art Gallery of Windsor, Canada, 30 January 1985
Duration: 40 to 50 minutes

The floor and walls of the performance space are lined with newspapers. The performance consists of a series of vignettes: the artist, dressed in black overalls, an opaque stocking masking her face, slithers with some difficulty on the floor along the aisle between the rows of spectators into the performing space; she tries to scrub the floor but smears it with red-stained water; she tries to unmask her face by slitting eyeholes through the stretched out stocking with a long-bladed knife; she circles a long table and chairs, and trying to sit down, she falls; she sets the table with plates, then, removing raw kidneys from under her clothes, cuts them up, puts them on the plates, and serves them, one by one, to the audience.

Lit.: *Dazzling Phrases: Six Performance Artists,* exh. cat., Forest City Gallery, London, Canada; Petra Rigby Watson, 'Mona Hatoum Western Front', *Vanguard,* no. 2, vol. 14, March 1985, p. 32; Roger Lee, 'Mona Hatoum. A review', *Parallelogramme,* no. 4, vol. 10, April/May 1985; Goldie Rans, 'Review', *Vanguard,* October 1985; exh. cat. Bristol 1993, fig. p. 26; Colette Tougas, 'Mona Hatoum', *Parachute,* no. 75, July-Sept. 1994, s. p.; exh. cat. Paris 1994, p. 56; Archer, Brett, de Zegher 1997, pp. 124-127, 147.

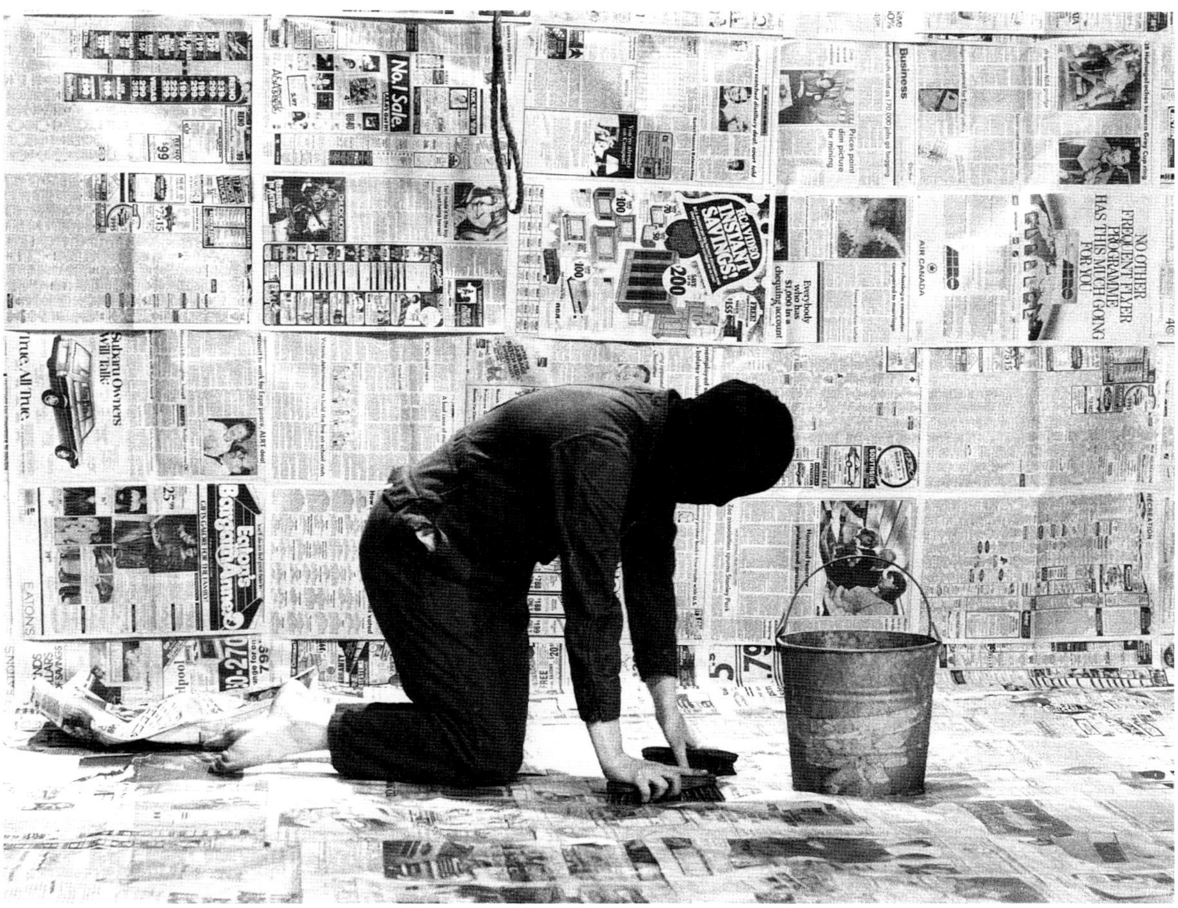

Several independent actions, which Mona Hatoum herself calls 'a series of vignettes', were again combined into a sequence. Some of the actions and props refer to earlier performances: for example, the mask (11, 12), the red liquid in the bucket (12), the newspapers (10, 12), the innards (11); others were new: the artist used a knife to cut eyeholes in the hood, set the table and handed around sliced-up kidneys. All these actions could be read as metaphors for social comment. One Canadian critic wrote of her scrubbing the ground: 'This action refers to the plight of the lower class or recent immigrants. How they, as a group, seem to be hired for lowly and menial jobs. Immigrants and the poor sweat blood, and clean with their blood, our middle class environment.'[1]

Even if this direct interpretation neglects the more poetic and intriguing aspects also inherent in Hatoum's actions, it would still seem to comply with the artist's intention. Hatoum has repeatedly claimed a moral purpose for her performances: 'My work often refers to hostile realities, war, destruction, but it is not localized, it refers to conflicts all over the world while hopefully pointing out the forces of oppression and resistance to these forces – cultural, historical, economic and social forces.'[2]

The performance concluded with a gesture which was akin to the Viennese Orgies-Mysteries-Theatre, or perhaps to Carolee Schneemann's *Meat Joy*, though in Hatoum's case it was stripped of all ecstatic energy, shaped by her individual and political experiences, and performed without turning a hair, so to speak: Having tried in vain to take her place at the table, Hatoum produced kidneys from under her clothes, cut them up and offered them to the audience. This was the immigrant as seen by the Canadian critic, literally offering her flesh and blood, yet it was also the artist, turning

fig. pp. 46–47

herself inside out: once again it would seem that *Corps étranger* – that marvellous, scientifically rational yet cosmically mysterious major work by Hatoum – was also anticipated here. The organ torn from the body was treated as an alien object. In a gesture alluding to the Last Supper, it functioned as a mediator between herself and the audience: between foreign bodies.

Notes

1 Roger Lee in *Parallelogramme*, no. 4, vol. 10, April/May 1985.
2 Mona Hatoum in an interview with Sara Diamond, *Fuse*, Toronto, April 1987, pp. 46-52, reprinted in Archer, Brett, de Zegher 1997, pp. 124 f.

15
Eyes Skinned · 1985

Live action with black hood and knife
Performed at 'Real Time' at the ICA, London, 18 March 1985[1]
Duration: 5 minutes

The artist walks into the performance space wearing black overalls with a black hood covering her face. She kneels down and pulls a large kitchen knife from her pocket and proceeds to circle her eyes with the sharp blade, until holes for her eyes are cut out in the black hood.

Lit.: Exh. cat. Bristol 1993, fig. p. 23; Archer, Brett, de Zegher 1997, pp. 57 f.

Hatoum isolated one of the 'vignettes' from the large sequence used in *Variation on Discord and Divisions*. In this dangerous game with the knife circling her eyes, the menacing mask is reinterpreted as a kind of pupation: female features – identity – literally emerge into view from the anonymous mask.

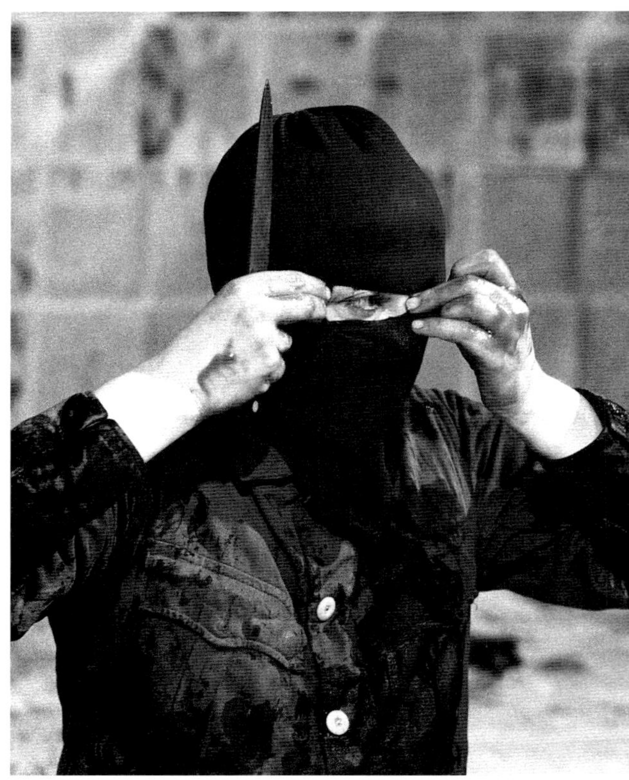

Since Luis Buñuel and Salvador Dalí's *Un Chien andalou* (1929), a knife approaching an eye has become a defining symbol of modernism. In the opening sequence of the film a casually dressed man (Buñuel himself) sharpens a razor-blade and applies it to the eye of a young woman. In a series of short cuts – the man opens the woman's eye, a thin cloud drifts past the moon, the eye of an animal is sliced through – this film stages a disturbing act of extreme violence, chauvinistically brutal and yet intriguing.

Each scene in the film seems random, with no connection to the next – or if there is one, then it is encoded, following a logic that is psychological. Hatoum's sequence of 'vignettes' certainly has an affinity with the dramaturgical indeterminateness of the Surrealist masterpiece, however, in her performances the individual scenes, and thus also *Eyes Skinned*, are more focused, always oriented around the political and social circumstances of the artist's life. Against the backdrop of the poignant fear of terrorism in the eighties, *Eyes Skinned* combines both images of threat and being threatened in a compelling way.

Hatoum returned to this performance once again in her video production *Eyes Skinned* (1988).[2] In the video however, she repeatedly projected slides of the armed conflict in Lebanon onto the back of her hands she held them protectively in front of her eyes. On the soundtrack, we hear alternately loud breathing, snippets of news and sounds of fighting. On the video, in contrast to the performance, she does not cut out the holes in the hood, but instead uses the knife to encircle the eye sockets protruding from the black fabric, completing several times the outline of the figure of eight on its side – the symbol of infinity – which she also uses as a symbol for an unending spiral of military violence in the sculpture ∞ (*Infinity*, 1991-2001). The hood in *Eyes Skinned* turns an image of vulnerability and invincibility of the faceless immigrant into that of the militant freedom fighter.

fig. p. 60

Notes

1 The ICA originally intended to use the short performances put on that evening for a television production; the production never took place.

2 *Eyes Skinned*, 1988, A Western Front Video Production, Vancouver, 4:04 min.

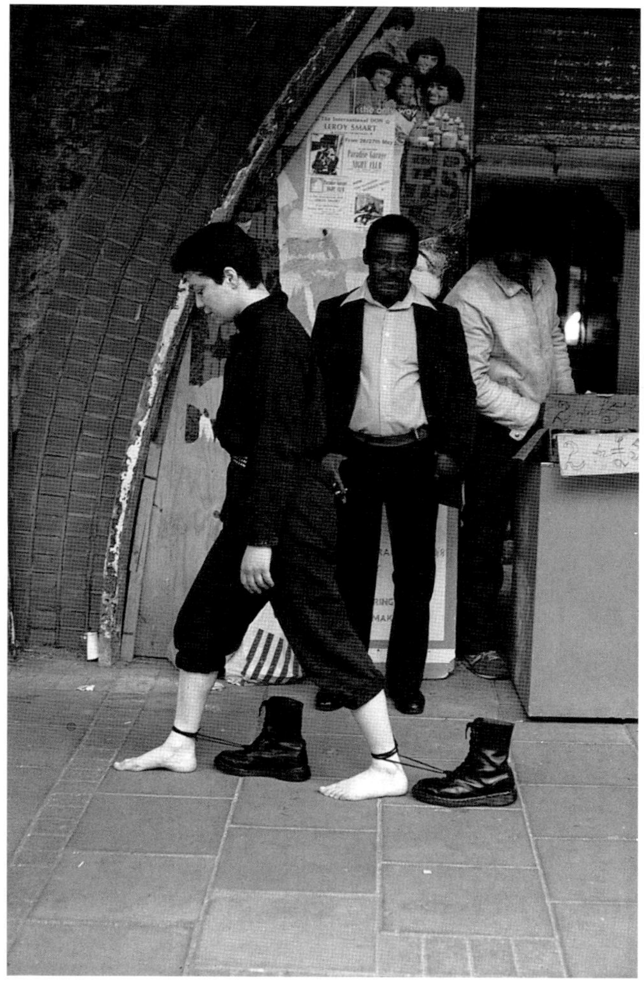

16
Three Street Performances · 1985

Three street performances for 'Roadworks' exhibition, Brixton, London, 18 May – 8 June 1985

16 a
Roadworks, 1985

Live action with Doc Martens boots
First performed in Brixton on 21 May 1985
Repeated for 'Streets Alive', Sheffield, 13 August 1986
Duration: 50 to 60 minutes

The artist walks barefoot through the streets of Brixton dragging behind her a pair of large boots attached to her ankles by their laces.

16 b
Untitled · 1985

Live action with two performers, black overalls and white chalk
Performed with Stefan Szczelkun
Performed in Brixton on 23 May 1985
Duration: 40 to 50 minutes

Two figures dressed in black overalls walk barefoot on the pavement. One figure falls to the ground while the other draws their body outline in chalk. In turn this figure is pulled to the ground by the other and their outline drawn. An endless process of rise and fall is repeated around the block leaving a chain of fallen body outlines on the pavement.

16 c
Untitled · 1985

Live action within enclosure of newspapers, mini bucket, red paint and circular mirror
Performed in Brixton on 24 May 1985
Duration: 20 minutes

The artist stretches various newspapers around both sides of two iron pillars, creating a small enclosure about one meter wide by half a meter deep. She stands in the middle of the paper enclosure but only her feet can be seen. She performs various actions using a small bucket filled with red paint, a scrubbing brush and a small circular mirror. At the end she slowly tears a hole in the newspaper smearing it with red paint until her entire figure emerges.

Lit.: Exh. cat. Bristol 1993, p. 18, fig. pp. 20, 21; exh. cat. Paris 1994, p. 56; *Roadworks,* exh. cat., Brixton Art Gallery, London 1985; *Artscribe,* no. 53, July/August 1985; Archer, Brett, de Zegher 1997, pp. 28 f., 48-52, 131, 147; exh. cat. Chicago/New York 1997-98, p. 28.

Ten artists were invited to participate in a group exhibition entitled *Roadworks* at the Brixton Art Gallery. They were to carry out performances and actions on the streets of Brixton in London. Mona Hatoum performed several improvised actions, including the three documented here.

After the performance *Them and Us ... and Other Divisions* (12),which Hatoum gave in the previous

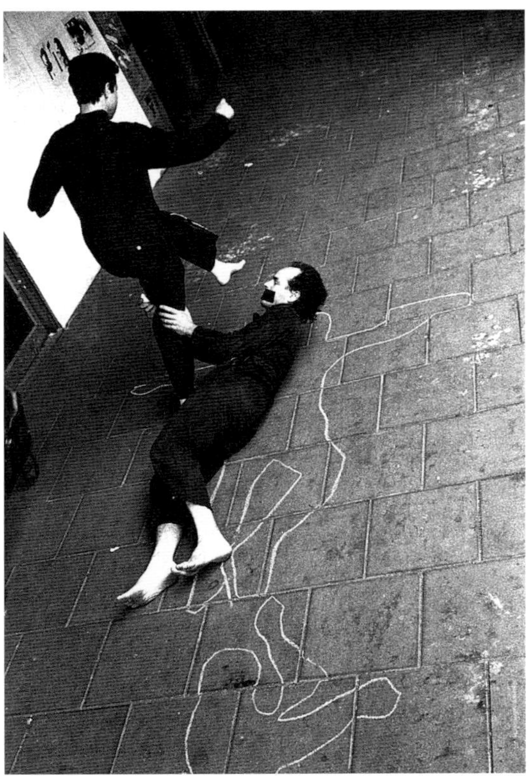

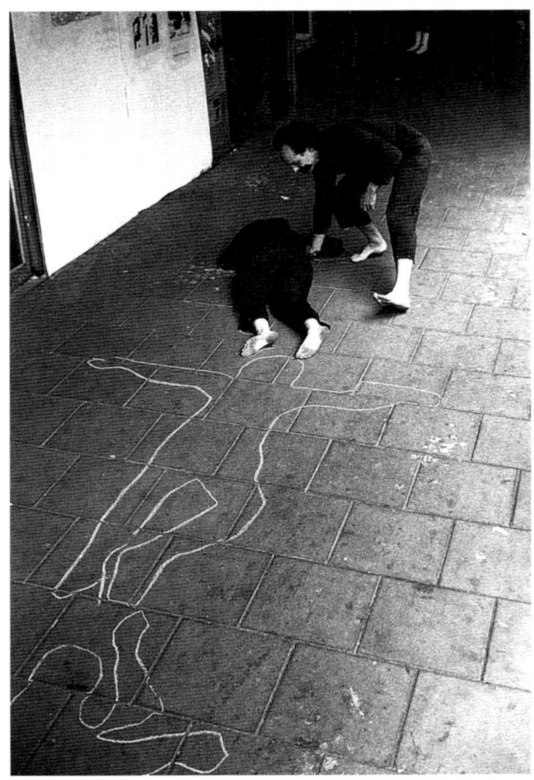

year, *Roadworks* offered her the opportunity of working in a public space again, and for an audience that was unprepared for the action, and unfamiliar with the art scene.

In the catalogue to the exhibition Mona Hatoum explains: 'The aspect I found most interesting about *Roadworks*, apart from the freedom of working outside the confines of an isolating gallery environment and all that it entails, was the very different nature of the audience. The fact that the audience was basically all the other people on the street, a non-specialised, chance audience experiencing casually the artists' actions while passing by, gave the work a more ephemeral, immediate and less precious character. But more important and relevant to me is the nature of the Brixton community being a predominantly black community with which I feel a lot of affinities. I found myself in this rare situation of creating work which although personal/autobiographical, had immediate relevance to the community of people it was addressing. I also found that I was working for the people in the streets of Brixton rather than against the indifferent, often hostile audiences I usually encounter.'[1]

The first performance (16 a), in which Hatoum walked through the streets of Brixton barefoot, a pair of boots tied to her ankles, takes up the theme of the vulnerability of the body facing a hostile environment. Hatoum herself reports on the audience's reactions: 'One comment I really liked was when a group of builders, standing having their lunch break, said, "What the hell is happening here? What is she up to?" And this black woman, passing by with her shopping, said to them, "Well, it's obvious. She's being followed by the police." Very cool, and just went off. One guy came up to me and said, "Excuse me. Do you know you're being followed?" And old people with their shopping, stopping and watching as I went past, would suddenly burst out laughing, or people would come and look inside the boots to see what was in there.'[2]

fig. p. 82 As a result of the edition *Performance Still* (1985-95) published ten years later, the *Roadworks* performance became a synonym for Mona Hatoum's work.

Hatoum developed the second performance from the previous work *Live work for the black room* (4). Whereas for that work the subject and object were one, this time, she included another person, and therefore a mutual relationship could be built up in which the roles of subject and object were constantly exchanged.

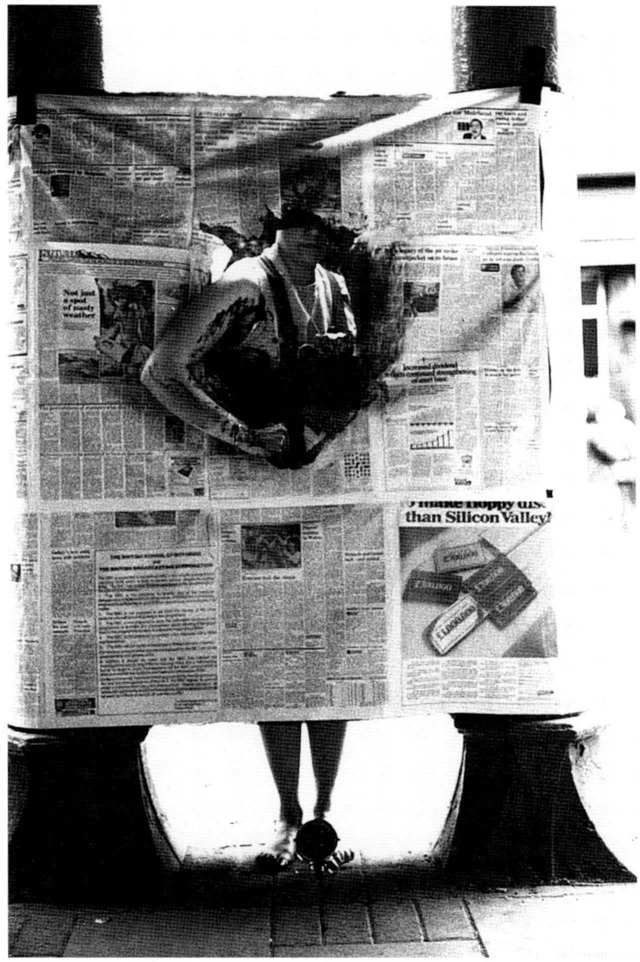

The isolated struggle of the individual in the early work is now developed into an interlinking mechanism which visually renders power and powerlessness, defeat and victory as being mutually dependent. The 'forensic chalk lines' from *Live work for the black room* are now drawn on the pavement, in a public space, and therefore returned to their place of origin. The interlinking of the signs standing for the body is also a reference to the interlinking in her later sculptures, for example, ∞ *(Infinity)*, (1991–2002), *Horizon* (1998), *Vicious Circle* (1999) or *Chain* (1999). fig. pp. 58–63

The first two *Roadworks* performances used the body as a sign carrier communicating with an unsuspecting public. Here Hatoum availed herself of a form that had been tried out on the international performance scene in the sixties.[3] A mention could be made, as a paradigm, of the actions by Valie Export and Peter Weibel in Vienna, for example *Aus der Mappe der*

Untitled · 1985

Hundigkeit (1968), in which Export walks Weibel, on all fours on a leash behind her, through the inner city of Vienna. In such actions, the body functioned as a hinge between art and life, by means of which social conditioning and gender-specific determinations were fundamentally questioned.

For the third performance, Hatoum created an enclosure out of newspaper inside which she performed. This performance could be seen as a study for the performance that followed a week later, *Between the Lines* (17), which was a reworking of and an elaboration on various elements from *Roadworks*.

Notes

1 *Roadworks*, exh. cat., Brixton Art Gallery, London 1985.
2 Mona Hatoum in Archer, Brett de Zegher 1997, p. 131.
3 On this form, as practised in particular in large Latin American cities, see Guy Brett, 'Lebensstrategien: Überblick und Auswahl', in *Out of actions: Zwischen Performance und Objekt 1949-1979*, exh. cat., MAK Österreichisches Museum für angewandte Kunst, Vienna 1998, pp. 197-225.

17
Between the Lines · 1985

Live action within enclosure of newspapers, gravel, a pair of Doc Martens boots, red paint
Performed at The Orchard Gallery, Derry, Northern Ireland, 1 June 1985
Duration: one hour

The artist stretches a curtain of newspapers around two pillars that dominate the space and are situated about five metres apart. The curtain creates a narrow enclosure with a twenty-five-centimetre gap at the bottom showing the artist's bare feet. Attached to her ankles is a pair of large boots that she drags behind her. On the floor, gravel is laid which makes a crunching sound as she paces back and forth within the enclosure. Each time she reaches one end, she makes a line of red paint with her finger on the pillar in the same fashion as prisoners record the days and weeks they have spent in prison. The performance ends with the artist breaking through the wall of paper, and crawling out.

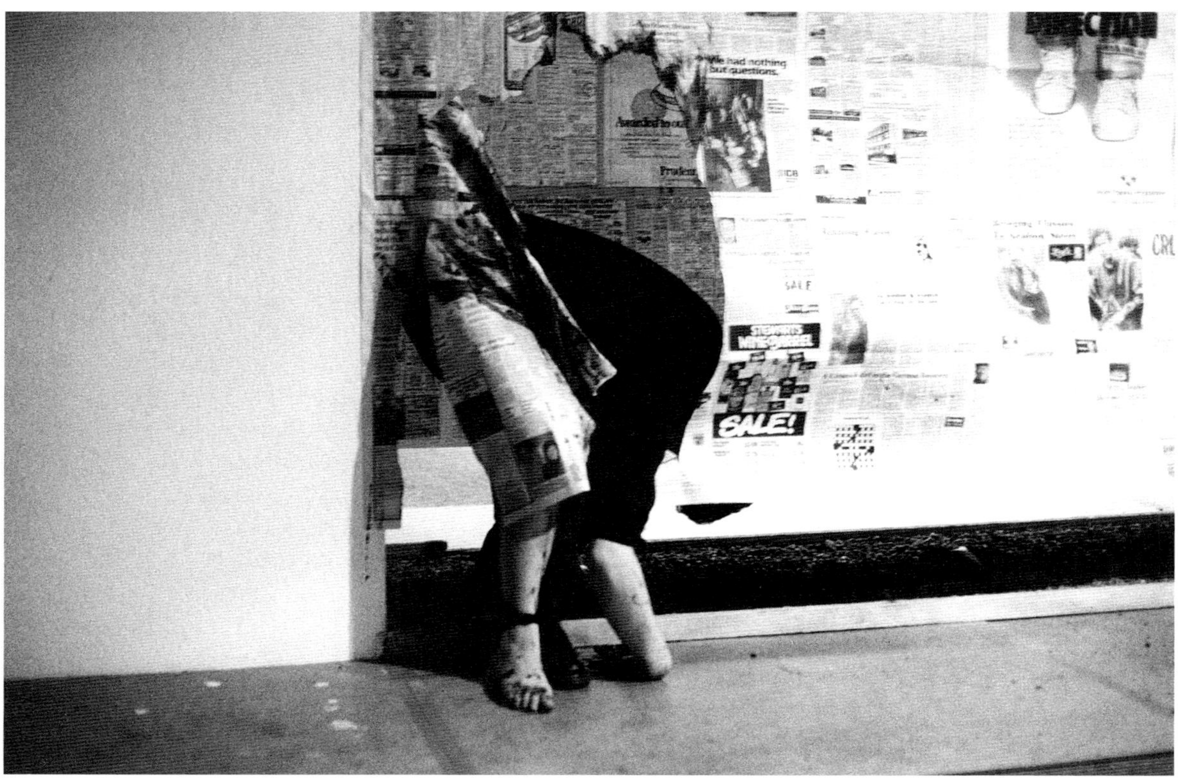

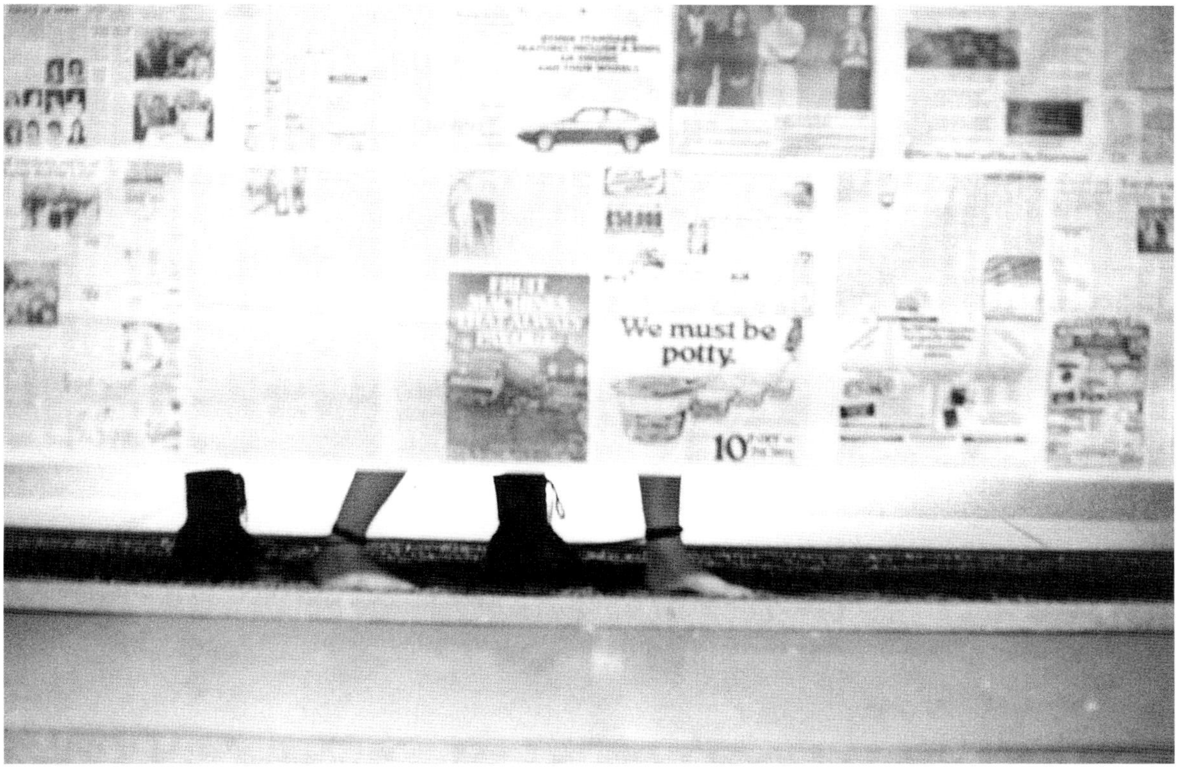

Lit.: Exh. cat. Paris 1994, p. 56; Archer, Brett, de Zegher 1997, p. 147.

Mona Hatoum was invited to Northern Ireland at short notice and responded by combining various elements from earlier actions. She enlarged the newspaper enclosure (16 c) into a continuous wall sheltering her from view, which like the polyethylene-cubicle in *Under Siege* (7), segregated and isolated her from the audience. The boots tied to her ankles (16 a) became a symbol of this incarceration, yet Hatoum managed to escape and finally leave her prison.

18
Position: Suspended 1986

Live action within a structure of wood, corrugated steel and chicken wire; rusty tools, bowl and liquid clay
Performed at 'New Work Newcastle '86', Performance Festival organised by Projects UK, Laing Art Gallery, Newcastle-upon-Tyne, 28 February 1986
Duration: 5 hours

The artist constructs a wedge-shaped structure obstructing the entrance between two galleries. Two sides of the structure are built out of wood and corrugated steel, the third side is screened with chicken wire. Inside, a variety of rusty hand tools are suspended. Covered in mud, the artist paces back and forth within the confined space brushing past the instruments. In doing so, a clanging metal sound can be heard and bits of mud get transferred onto the instruments.

The audience is forced to walk very close to the structure along the chicken wire screen coming into close contact with the artist trapped inside.

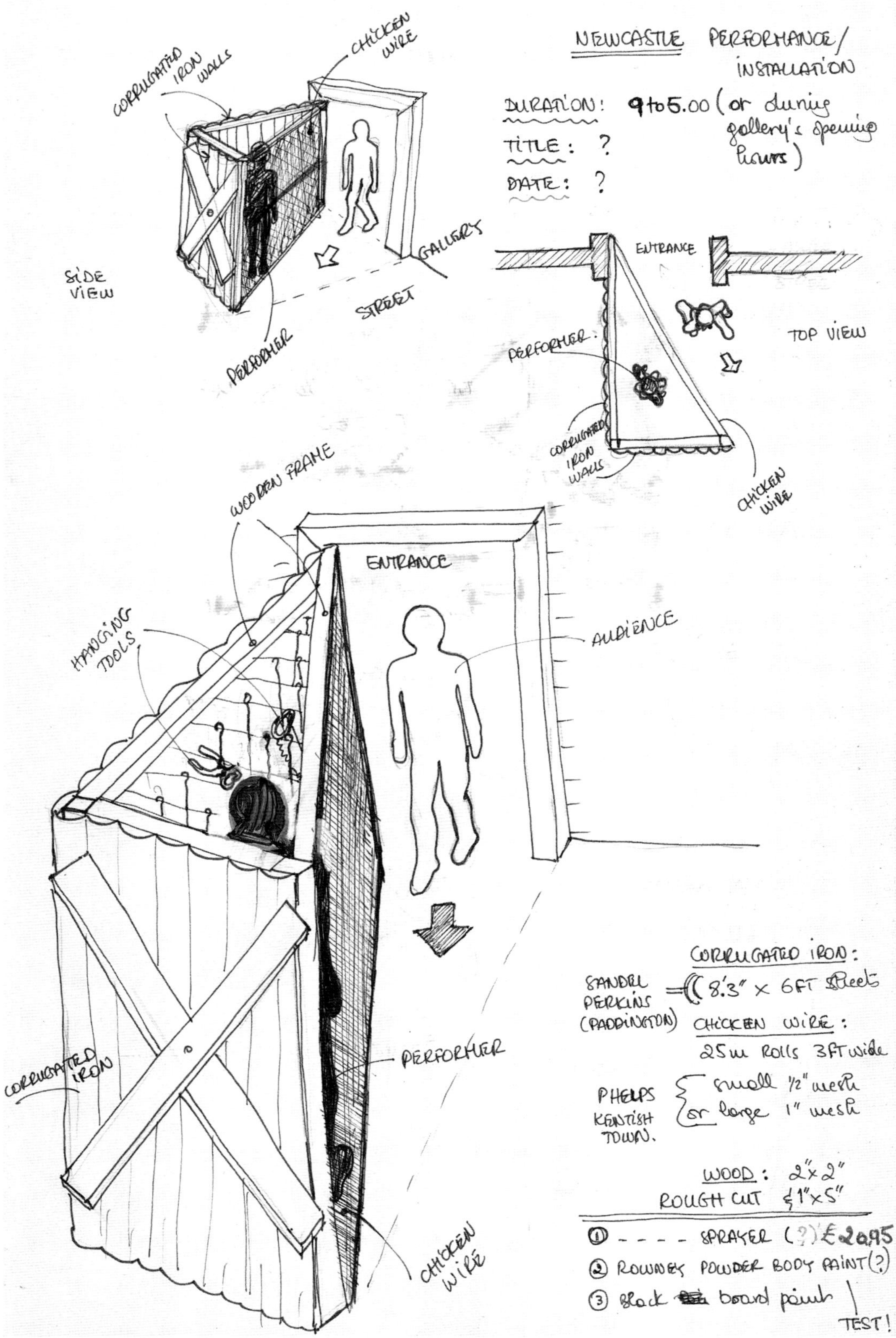

 Position: Suspended · 1986 (Sketchbook drawing)

Lit.: Exh. cat. Bristol 1993, p. 17, fig. p. 27; exh. cat. Paris 1994, p. 57; Archer, Brett, de Zegher 1997, pp. 46 f, 147.

As already in *Under Siege* (7) and again later in *Matters of Gravity* (25), Hatoum built a special space for this performance, which lasted for several hours and addressed the themes of isolation and exposure. In this case, the structure resembles a primitive animal pen.

Chopper, hatchet, hammer, pliers, machete and meat hook: the tools hung at regular intervals from the ceiling of the pen are commonly associated with skilled trade.[1] The hand tools are within graspable reach, but they hang there inactively, robbed of their utilitarian value. In the course of the performance, these tools become threatening as they repeatedly scrub the protective layer of clay covering the artist's bare torso, scraping it off.

Position: Suspended, like just a few Hatoum's performances, possessed something of the self-destructive energy that marked many performances in the seventies, for example, those by Gina Pane, Marina Abramović or Chris Burden. In various actions Gina Pane cut her belly and face with a razor, producing tattoo-like marks on her body which played both with Christian symbolism and with taboos relating to the body. At the same time she reflected on the effect of her actions on the audience.[2] This was also at the heart of Abramović's legendary action *Rhythm 0* (1974), which attempted to gather experience with passive aggression: for over six hours the artist literally submitted to the audience, who were invited to try out every kind of implement on her motionless body. And in *Through the Night Softly* (1973), Chris Burden, wearing only underpants, his hands tied behind his back, crawled across a floor covered in splinters of glass. Through their risky actions, all these artists exposed not only their own psyche, but also that of the audience.

However, in Hatoum's performance, the exposure of the body to danger was only an indirect theme. The tools rubbed against her body, stripping it of its protective coating, yet here, there was no suggestion of any intervention by the viewer to rescue the imprisoned performer from her exclusion. The total isolation in which this metaphor-rich action took place, points to the immobility and confinement an unemployed person may feel. Guy Brett on *Position: Suspended:* 'References to imprisonment, poverty, unemployment and wasted creative energies were combined with the considerable physical dignity with which the artist occupied this marginal and debased corner of the city museum.'[3]

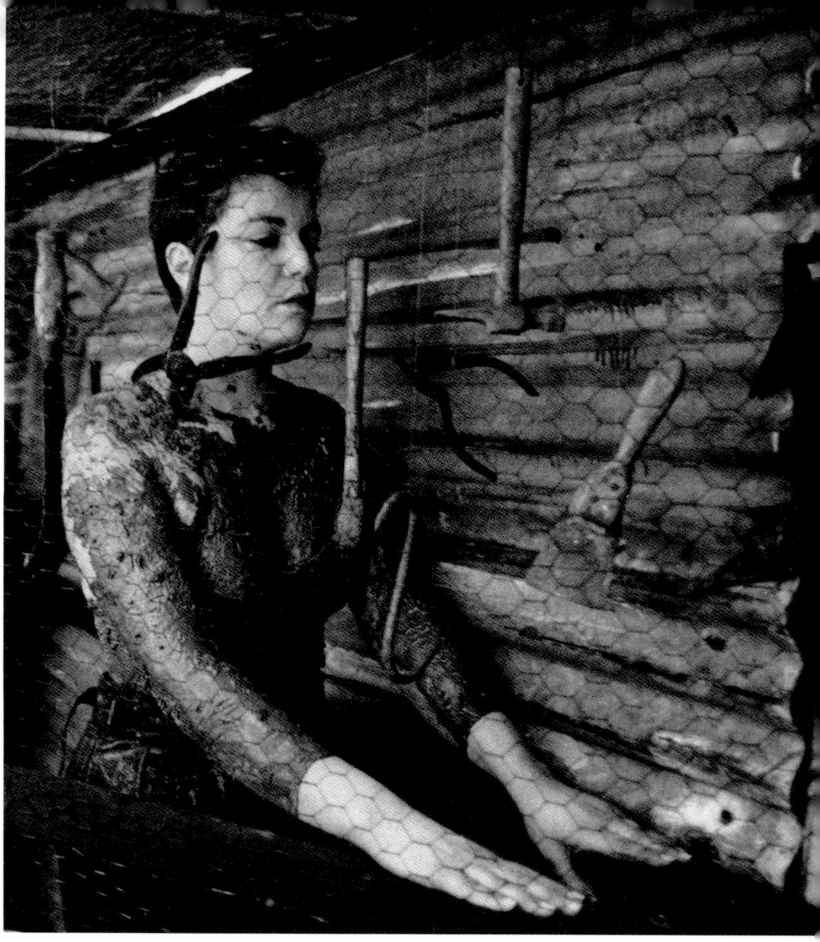

Notes

1 A preparatory drawing for the performance (the property of the artist, unpublished) lists: 'large machete, large hatchet, large chopper and four different pliers'.

2 For example, Gina Pane, *White Doesn't Exist* (1972), *Psyché* (1974), *Le corps pressenti* (1975).

3 Archer, Brett, de Zegher 1997, pp. 44 f.

19
Untitled · 1986

Live action with barbed wire, wooden signs, contact pick-up, amplifier and speakers
Performed at 'Strategies for Survival: State of the Arts/ the Art of Alternatives', International artists conference, Vancouver, 11 June 1986
Duration: 3 hours

A tangle of barbed wire coils covers the whole floor of the performance area. Old-fashioned wooden country signs are placed haphazardly between the coils. The barefooted artist attempts to step over the barbed wire coils, occasionally getting her skirt caught up by the wire, or her legs scratched. The barbed wire is connected to a contact pick-up, so the slightest movement produces a thunderous sound, that reverberates through the entire conference space.

Lit.: Archer, Brett, de Zegher 1997, p. 148.

Mona Hatoum on the circumstances surrounding the performance: '*Strategies of Survival* was the title of a conference that took place at the same time as the 1986 Expo in Vancouver. I was invited to do a performance in the context of the conference. During that time, I was staying at the Western Front, which is housed in a building that used to be a Masonic lodge.[1] In the basement I found all these old-fashioned wooden country signs which is what inspired the idea for the work. Expo is this big international exhibition trying to convey the idea that the world is one big family, one big village. To counteract this image, I did this action which was a reminder of the reality of the existence of borders, of people who are trying to cross borders, illegal immigrants, the sectioning of the world.'[2]

In this performance, Hatoum alluded to an old children's game, which in Germany is called *Heaven and Hell*, but which presumably goes by other names elsewhere in the world. The rules of the game, however, are probably the same everywhere: whoever touches, loses. The game teaches children at an early stage that there are certain borders which they should avoid crossing. This particular performance functions as a vigil because of the barbed wire and the small cuts, but perhaps even more so because of the thunderous noise from the loud-speakers whenever the wire is touched.

Hatoum often used threatening wires in her installations and sculptures, in the most varied of forms, be that as glowing heating rods in *The Light at the End* fig. p. 15 (1989), knife-edged steel wire in *Untitled* (1992, installation at the Mario Flecha Gallery, London), or else in unexpectedly menacing furniture, as in *Incommunicado* fig. p. 6 (1993), or in the electrified metal implements in *Homebound* (2000). In each case: whoever touches, fig. pp. 20– loses.

Notes
1 Western Front Art Centre, Vancouver, offers an Artist's Residency programme, where Mona Hatoum also made video productions for *Changing Parts* (1984) and *Measures of Distance* (1988).
2 Mona Hatoum in conversation with the author, Hamburg, 20 December 2003.

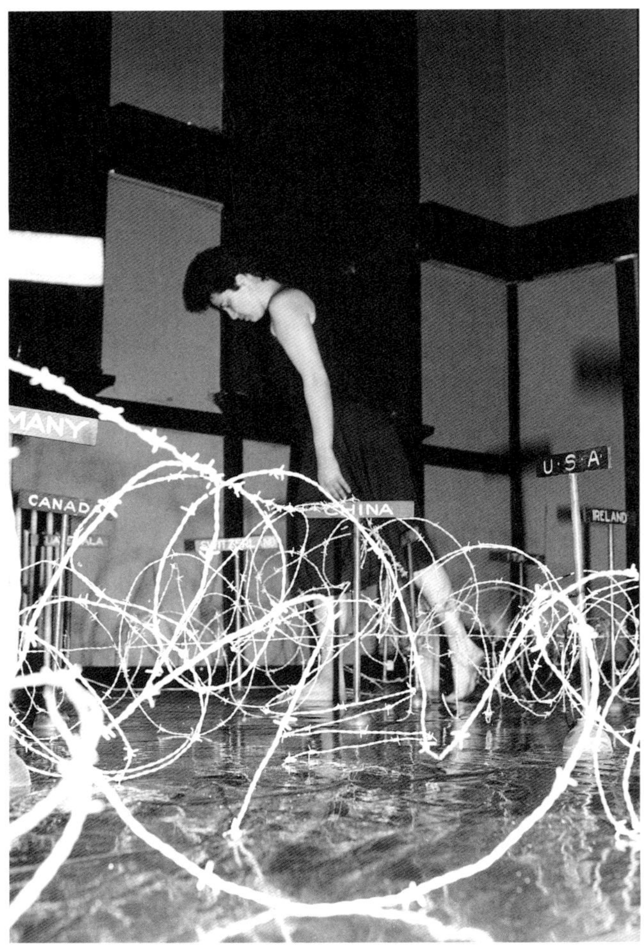

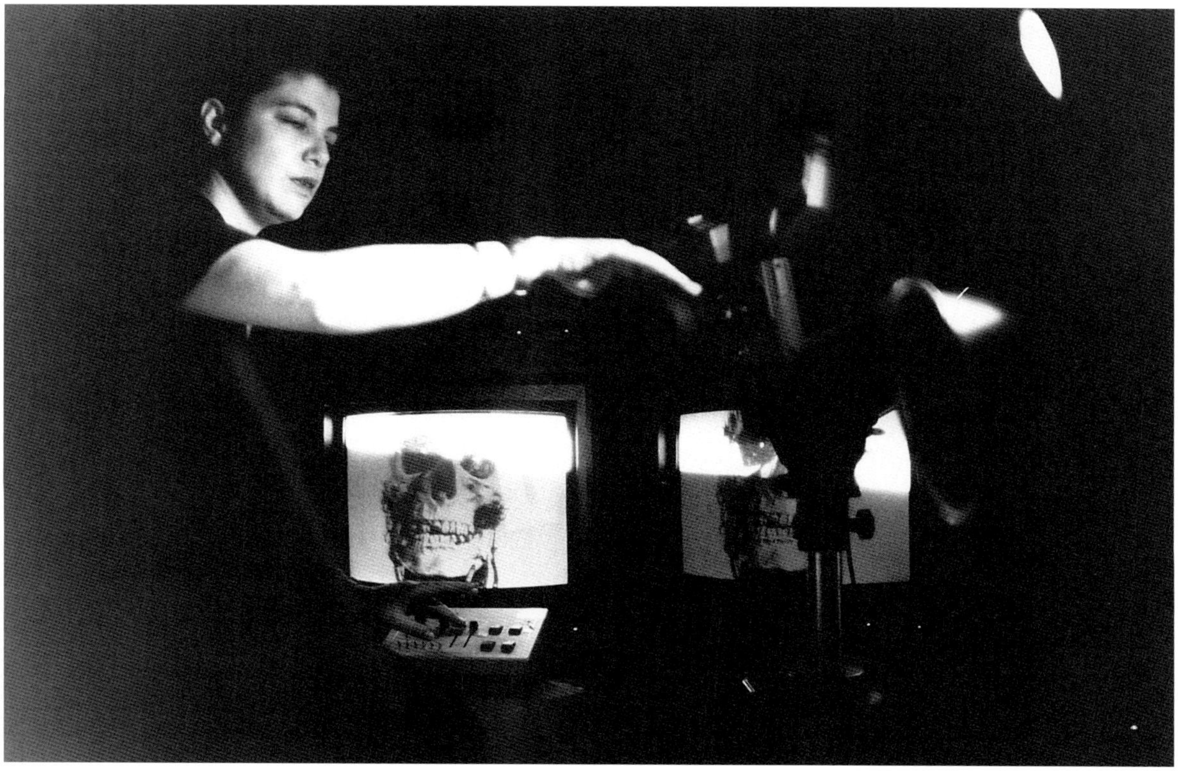

20
On target · 1986

Live action with two live cameras, one monitor, video mixer and various props
Performed with Claudio Goulart
Performed at 'Live video', Amsterdam Summer Festival, Time Based Arts, Amsterdam, 16 July 1986
Duration: 30 min.

A performance that consists of using a live camera to scan members of the audience. The resulting images can be seen on a monitor mixed in with images of shooting targets and various symbols signifying surveillance and close observation.

Lit.: Archer, Brett, de Zegher 1997, p. 148.

A closed-circuit situation similar to that Mona Hatoum had already used in her first performance was further developed here, drawing from a different repertoire of images. In this case, the artist withdrew into the background, not even holding the camera which was filming the audience, but worked behind the scenes at the mixer, controlling the seemingly live recording. It was the audience that had now moved centre-stage, seeing itself as being under surveillance and threat.

21
Crosstalk · 1986

Live action with two performers, two chairs and two old saws bolted together
Performed with Stefan Szczelkun
First performed at 'Streets Alive', Performance Festival in the Streets of Sheffield, 13 August 1986
Repeated at Battersea Arts Centre, London, 2 November 1986; Chisenhale Dance Space, London, 21 November 1986
Duration: 20 to 30 minutes

The performers stand on chairs facing each other. Each performer holds on to the handle of one of the two old and rusty saws that pivot around a bolt which holds them together. The action consists of repeatedly see-sawing forward and back, as if the saws were an extension of a handshake.

Lit.: Exh. cat. Bristol 1993, pp. 20, 22, fig. p. 22; exh. cat. Paris 1994, p. 57; Archer, Brett, de Zegher 1997, pp. 130-131.

As early as the sixties, in the context of Happening and Body Art, artists produced a series of objects which were intended to influence the behaviour of their user. These included James Lee Byars' performative clothes, prosthetic body extensions such as Rebecca Horn's *Fingerhandschuhe* (1972), Hélio Oiticica's cloaks *Parangolés*, or the *Relational Objects* by Brazilian artist Lygia Clark. The latter wanted, with purposely simple objects, to encourage people to explore the language of their own bodies, for example, by joining two arms together with a Möbius strip to form a living sculpture, thus promoting an interaction that was open to the kind of experiences contained within the body's memories at a non-verbal or pre-verbal level.[1] A recurring theme in Lygia Clark's works was the breaching of the borders between the I and the Other, between individual and collective space. Clark was later to successfully use the therapeutic potential of these objects in the treatment of people with psychological problems.

In *Crosstalk* Hatoum seems to be harking back to objects arranged in this kind of relationship to the body: a simple item re-defined by duplication only yielded up its meaning with the introduction of the two actors, whose actions it then would determine. This object, however, contradicts the optimism of its predecessors of the sixties: the double saw, robbed of its original function by having the blades pointing in two different directions, is completely obstructed, as it were, and represents communication that is utterly frustrated. In this case, any approach to each other would involve danger – retreat is impossible. It is a situation of complete stalemate. *Crosstalk* raised fundamental questions about the very possibility of communication.

Note

1 Cf. Guy Brett, 'Lebensstrategien: Überblick und Auswahl', in *Out of actions: Zwischen Performance und Objekt 1949-1979*, exh. cat., MAK Österreichisches Museum für angewandte Kunst, Vienna 1998-99, p. 206; Yves-Alain Bois et al., 'Lygia Clark: Nostalgia of the Body', *October*, no. 69, summer 1994, pp. 85-109.

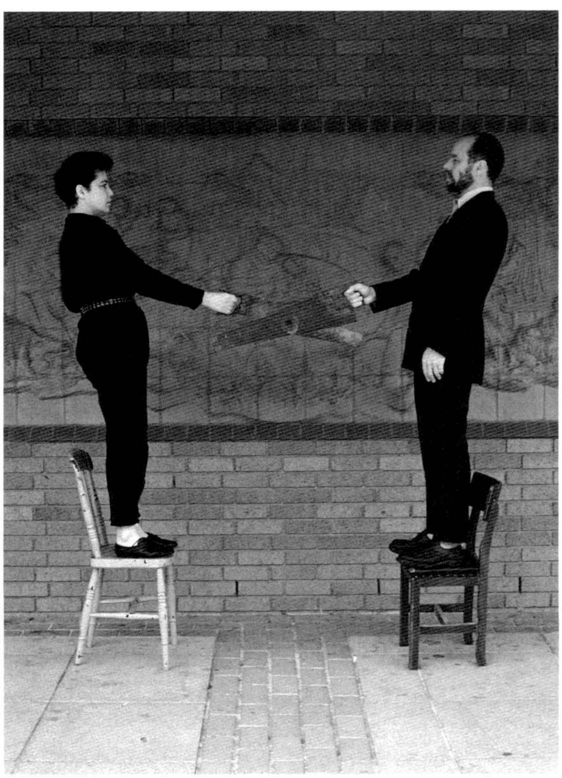

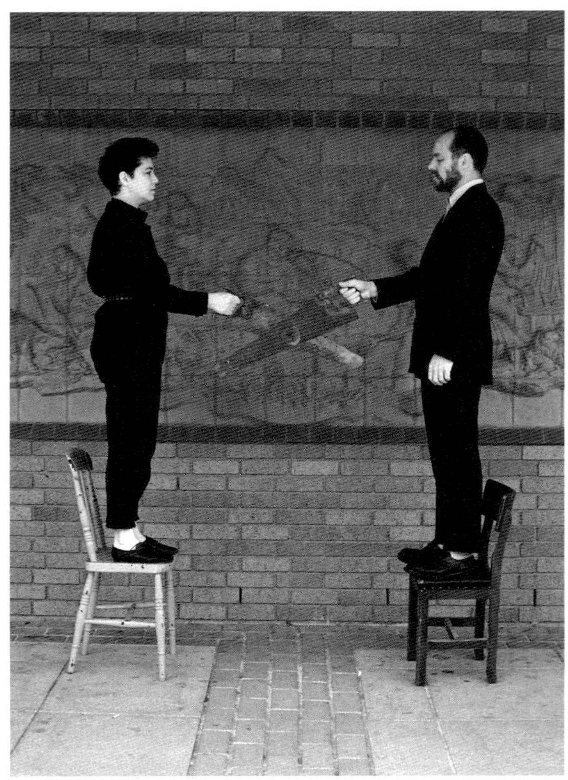

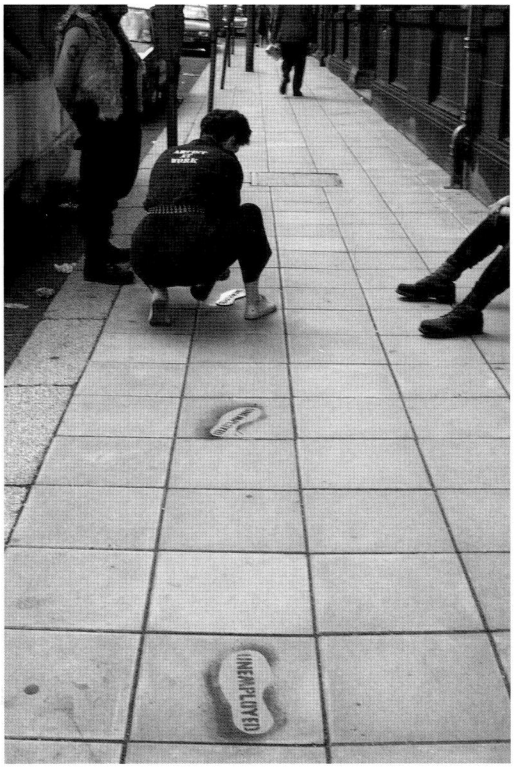

South Yorkshire coalfield. As a result of competition, mainly from the so-called cheap labour countries, and various political changes, the city was badly hit by recession in the early eighties, and in 1986, the year of Hatoum's performance, had the highest unemployment rate in Great Britain (at sixteen per cent it was four per cent higher than the national average).[1]

With her deliberately pragmatic action, Hatoum was reacting to that economic situation: Her specially-made overall proclaimed 'artist at work' while at the same time validating her as a craftswoman reflecting on the role of the artist in a changing society.

Hatoum had originally intended having a stamp attached to the sole of her shoe that would print directly onto the pavement, but since the paint could not be evenly distributed this way, she decided to work with a stencil and spray-paint.

Note
1 Unemployment figures, see http://panizzi.shef.ac.uk/trends/topic/localeco/unemploy.htm.

22
Unemployed · 1986

Live action with black overalls, stencil and spray-paint
Performed for 'Streets Alive', performance festival in the streets of Sheffield, 14 August 1986
Duration: one hour

The artist, dressed in black overalls with the words ARTIST AT WORK stencilled in white on her back, walks from the Sheffield city centre to the unemployment office, stopping every few steps to spray the word UNEMPLOYED on the pavement, using a stencil in the shape of a foot and spray paint. A clearly visible trail of UNEMPLOYED footsteps is left on the pavement behind her.

Lit.: Archer, Brett, de Zegher 1997, pp. 48, 148.

Here Hatoum was once again working in the public domain, this time in the streets of Sheffield. Up until the seventies, Sheffield was an important industrial centre in the steel industry thanks to the large deposits of iron-ore locally and the coal from the neighbouring

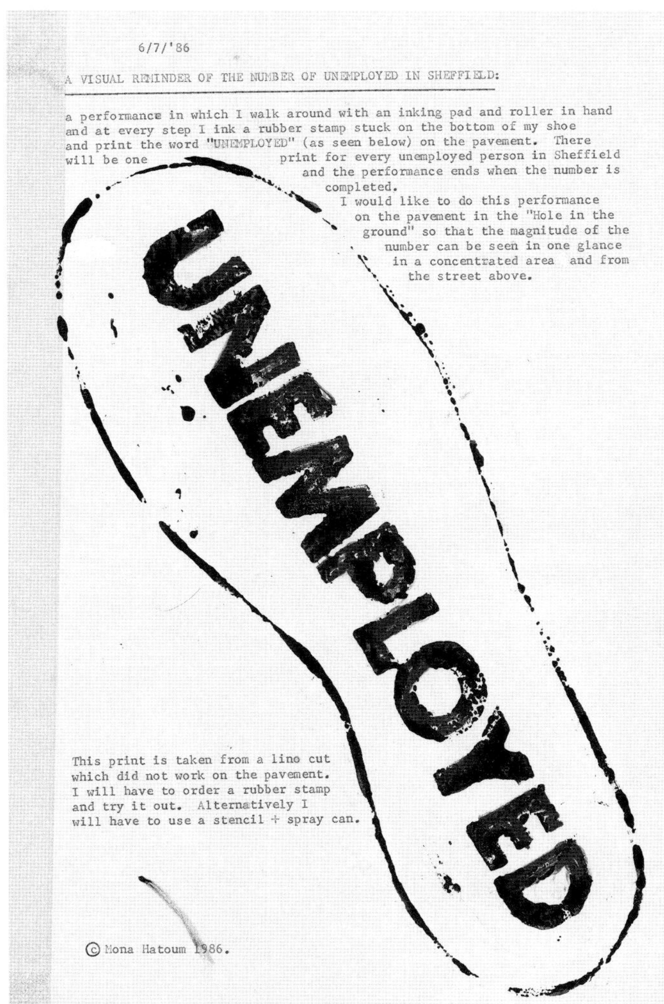

6/7/'86

A VISUAL REMINDER OF THE NUMBER OF UNEMPLOYED IN SHEFFIELD:

a performance in which I walk around with an inking pad and roller in hand and at every step I ink a rubber stamp stuck on the bottom of my shoe and print the word "UNEMPLOYED" (as seen below) on the pavement. There will be one print for every unemployed person in Sheffield and the performance ends when the number is completed.

I would like to do this performance on the pavement in the "Hole in the ground" so that the magnitude of the number can be seen in one glance in a concentrated area and from the street above.

UNEMPLOYED

This print is taken from a lino cut which did not work on the pavement. I will have to order a rubber stamp and try it out. Alternatively I will have to use a stencil + spray can.

© Mona Hatoum 1986.

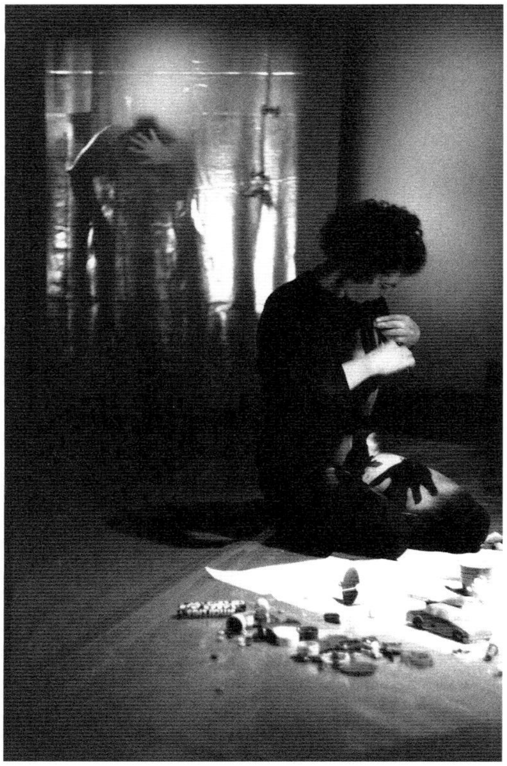

23
Mind the Gap · 1986

Live action with sound tape, slide projection and various props
First performed for 'Identity/Desire, Representing the Body', Collins Gallery, University of Strathclyde, Glasgow, 11 October 1986
Repeated for 'Conceptual Clothing', Ikon Gallery, Birmingham, 11 December 1986; Stoke-on-Trent City Museum and Art Gallery, 16 July 1987; Huddersfield Art Gallery, 24 September 1987 and for 'Figures', Milton Keynes Exhibition Gallery, 25 April 1987; Cambridge Darkroom, 31 May 1987; The Arts Centre, Darlington, 23 October 1987 and for 'Nationalism: Women and the State', A Space, Toronto, 7 and 8 April 1988
Duration: 30 to 40 minutes

The artist sets down a small straw case out of which she takes a variety of toys associated with boys, placing them in front of her. She then pushes them to one side replacing them with dolls and other girls' toys, plays for a little while, then discards them. She dips a brush into a small bucket filled with red paint and tries to paint her fingernails, spilling the red paint onto her lap. A sound recording of 'Mind the Gap' (as heard in the underground stations in London over the archaic sound system) comes on menacingly. She takes a large pair of scissors and cuts out the soiled area of her white skirt and then removes it – she is now wearing a black leotard. Slides come on and are projected onto a semi-transparent plastic shower curtain on which the vague outline of a female figure under the shower can just be seen. A sound recording of the artist reading an English translation of her mother's letters mixed with Arabic conversation between the artist and her mother comes on. The artist circles around the shower curtain, occasionally putting her hand on the screen and spraying it with white powder, leaving a trace of her hand on the plastic. As the curtain gets covered with more and more imprints of hands, the image of her mother becomes more and more clear.

Lit.: *Identity/Desire: Representing the Body,* exh. cat. (booklet), Scottish Arts Council, Collins Gallery, University of Strathclyde, Glasgow1986; exh. cat. Bristol 1993, p. 22; exh. cat. Paris 1994, p. 57; Archer, Brett, de Zegher 1997, pp. 53, 56, 148 f.

Mind the Gap was a return to the form of the 'series of vignettes' which Hatoum had developed in earlier actions (12, 14). Here, however, the individual actions had clearer links to a narrative logic: Hatoum told the story of a self-discovery. Out of the oblivious preoccupation with the toys she developed a sequence of actions that had an almost somnambulant quality. Following the allusions to early experiences with the female body, Hatoum commenced a dialogue with her absent mother, creating a ritual involving both the forging of her own identity and a mother-daughter identification.

'I was going behind the plastic sheet – a sort of shower curtain, with a barely visible image of my mother projected on it, which was like being there and not there. Then I would put my hand on the image, as if I were trying to touch it. And I would spray around it with this white spray. It gave a kind of powdery deposit on the sheet, around my hand. So it created these silhouettes of hands, that gradually covered the screen. The body of my mother became more and more visible ... the hands were almost like Lascaux paintings, it was quite beautiful ...'[1]

With the title, *Mind the Gap*, borrowed by her from the warning issued in the London underground,

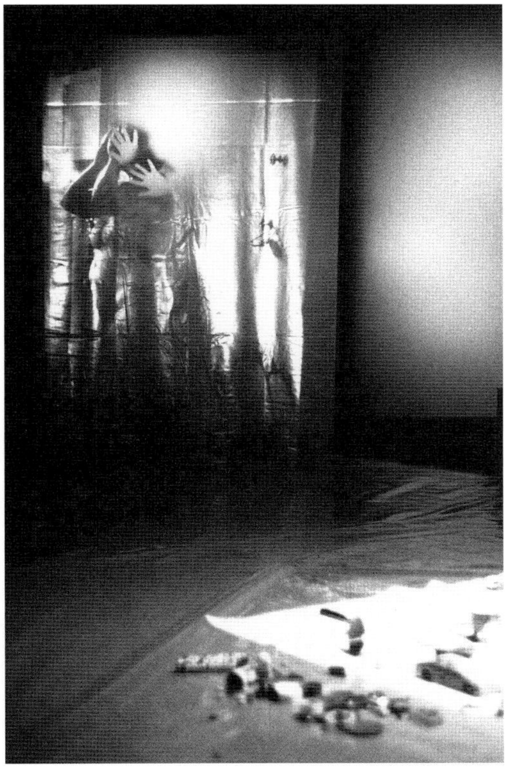

Hatoum was using unknowingly the title of a live performance in 1980 by the British artist Rose Finn-Kelcey. Her *Mind the Gap* action was a famous performance in which the artist did not appear; or to put it more precisely, only appeared after a woman's voice had apologised for her absence and read out a selection of working notes on the unfinished event. Having made her own ambivalence about her performance the theme of the event, Finn-Kelcey introduced the terms substitute-performer and empty performance – a nice deception that enables paradoxical insight into the phenomenon of power.[2]

Though both artists used the same title, in Finn-Kelcey's case it was used for a work in which she dealt with the basic conditions of an artistic performance – artistic work per se – and made her scepticism about the event the central theme. By contrast, Hatoum used the title for a performance in which she presented very personal material about herself, providing an example of female socialisation under very specific conditions. Hatoum's live action thus marked an escape from the blind alley of a self-referential and self-generating system. Herein lies one of the essential features of Hatoum's performances – compared with those of the previous generation – and the narrative, allegorical, always associative quality of her later installation and sculptural works.

With the three autobiographical testimonies – the letters from her mother in Beirut, the recording of the conversations, repeatedly interrupted by happy laughter, between herself and her mother in Arabic, and finally the slides Hatoum took of her mother in the shower – Hatoum used three elements which she reworked into her most famous video: *Measures of Distance*, produced two years later with The Western Front Art Center in Vancouver. fig. p. 45

Notes
1 Mona Hatoum in conversation with the author, Hamburg, 20 December 2003.
2 Guy Brett, 'Lebensstrategien: Überblick und Auswahl', in *Out of actions: Zwischen Performance und Objekt 1949-1979,* exh. cat., MAK Österreichisches Museum für angewandte Kunst, Vienna 1998-99, p. 224.

24
Forced Flight · 1987

Live action with corrugated iron sheet, sound tape, toy soldiers, flashlights and various props
Performed at Chisenhale Gallery, London, 20 March 1987
Duration: 3 hours

The performance takes place in a room at the bottom of the disused elevator shaft littered with old building materials and broken furniture. Three members of the audience are allowed in at one time. Each equipped with a flashlight, they walk into a dark L-shaped corridor where small toy soldiers look like they are crawling out of the cracks in the walls. With their flashlights they follow the trail of toy soldiers that seem to crawl all over the rubble and the broken furniture in the main space, making it look like a war scene. This is reinforced by an audio recording of the sound of air raid sirens and explosions that can be heard in the space. In the main space they encounter a light, projecting through a moving industrial ventilation fan illuminating the derelict surroundings. Suddenly, what looks like a sheet of corrugated metal leaning against the back wall begins to move, creating a startling realisation that someone else is 'inhabiting' the space.

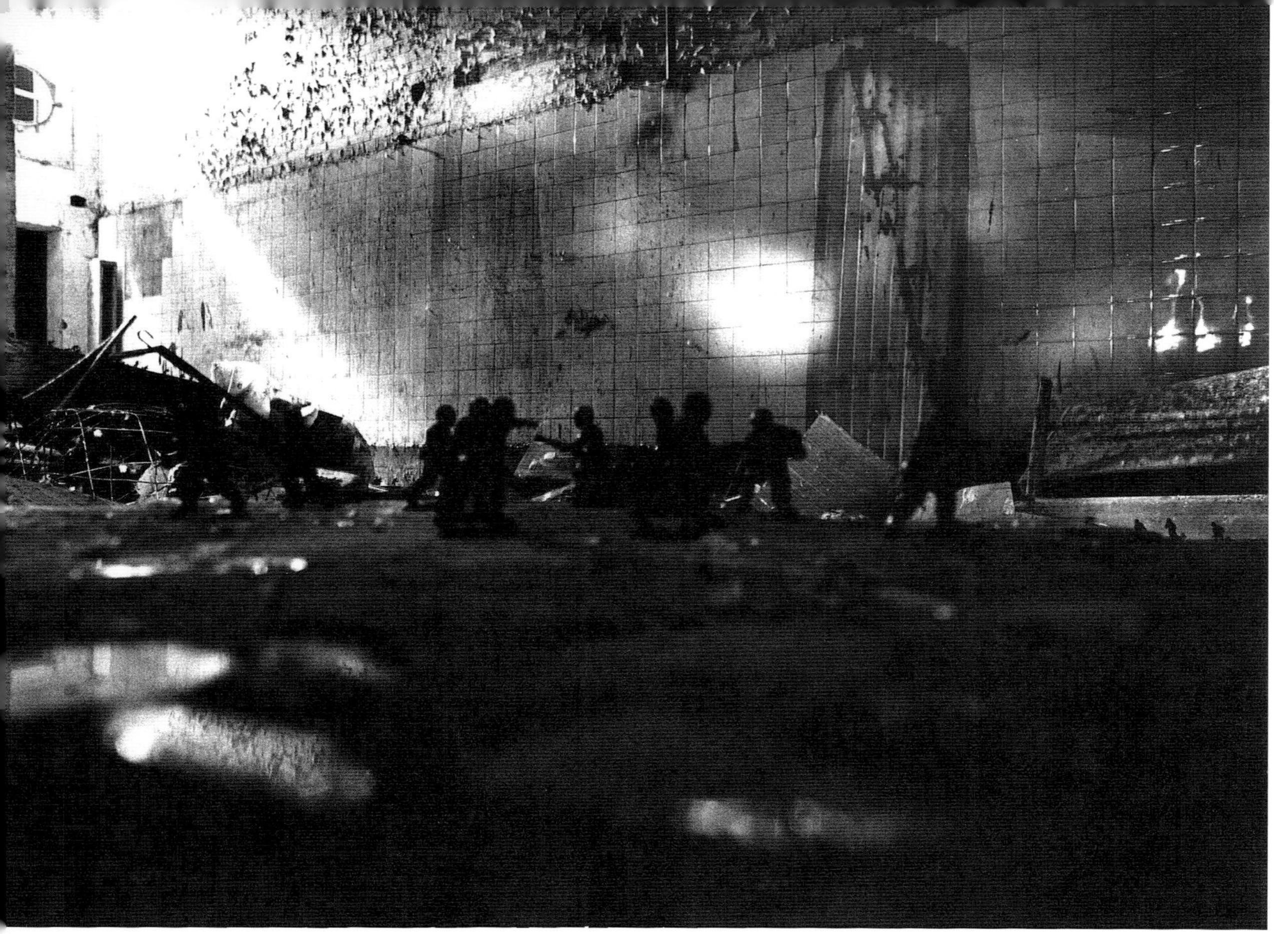

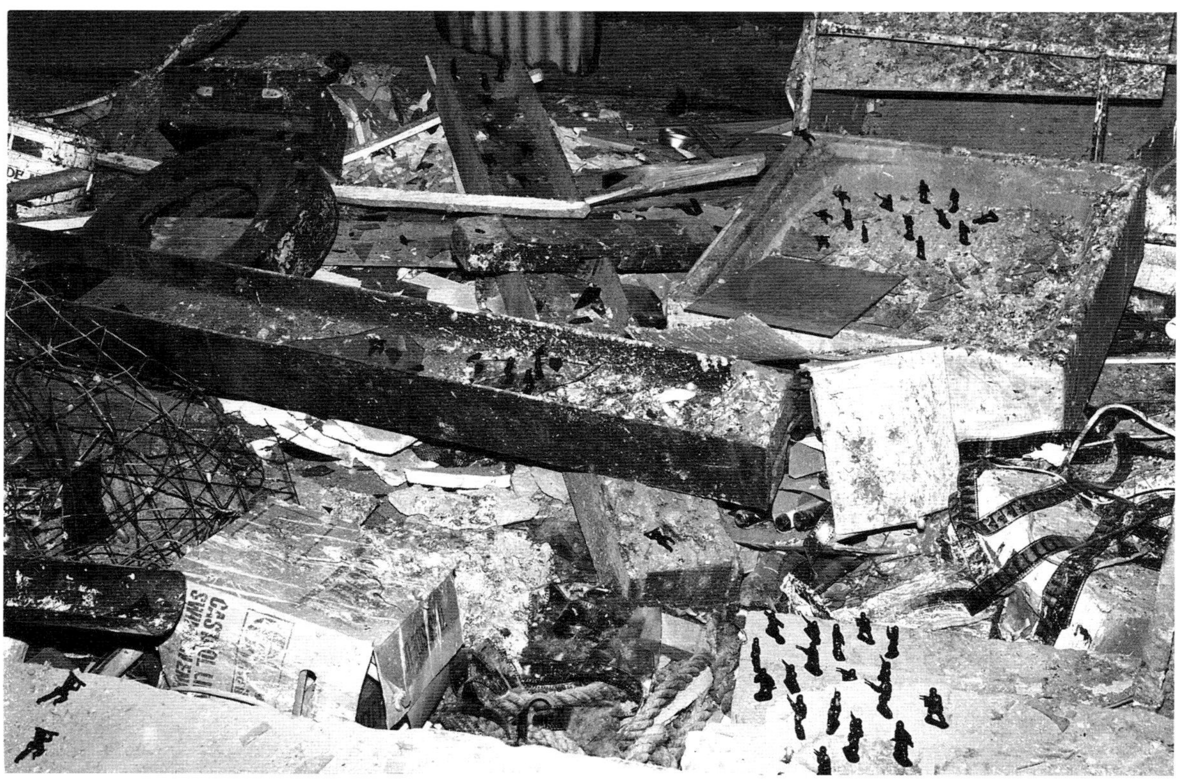

Once again, Hatoum staged this performance for a specific site; the elevator shaft is reminiscent of the run-down basement in which she had performed in Manchester (9). This time, however, she, as the performer, withdrew completely into the background: 'The lift shaft was very old and dilapidated. They actually called it the Black Hole. The pigeons had gone in and made it their home. So there was this sound of pigeons all the time in there – and there was pigeon shit everywhere. The performance was all in the dark. I was hiding behind this sheet of corrugated iron against the back wall, something that nobody suspected. So, every time I saw that some people walked in, I would actually move. So there was the cooing of the pigeons, the sound of air raids and me moving around with the corrugated iron sheet scraping against the wall.'[1]

After *Mind the Gap*, which relied on the artist actually performing, *Forced Flight* was more an installation than an action: by means of light, acoustic effects and the particular atmosphere of the place, which affected both the sense of smell and of touch, Hatoum staged a synaesthetic tableau of threat which was aimed directly at the audience, who were only allowed in three at a time.

Here, Hatoum availed herself of a given situation whose character she emphasised and interpreted. The action was reminiscent of Terry Fox's performance *Cellar* (1970), in which he displayed the dilapidated junk-filled cellar of a New York gallery and persuaded an actual homeless person to live in it.[2] At the heart of the Bowery, Fox confronted the New York art scene with a presentation of the misery to be found everywhere in that city.

In the same year as Hatoum's *Forced Flight* Rebecca Horn created her site-specific installation *Das gegenläufige Konzert*, on the occasion of the *Skulptur Projekte in Münster*. Horn used the atmosphere of a tower in the city's defence walls, where the Gestapo had once executed war prisoners. With her own preference for mechanical things, Horn installed various implements in the tower, including forty mechanical steel hammers whose banging sound accompanied the viewers on their way through the ruin; Horn called this hammering 'knocking sounds from another world'.[3]

In all three works, the experience of a space is transformed into the experience of a specific place. Hatoum, Fox and Horn did not construct artificial spaces for experience, but instead used the aura of an authentic place and, by intervening more or less, underscored its atmosphere, commenting on it with visual and acoustic effects. Fox used his installation to reflect on poverty that is everywhere in New York, for Horn the – specifically German – past of the place played a major role, for Hatoum the concrete history of the place was unimportant; she used its formal aspects and atmospheric qualities to produce a political or contemporary reference by means of the toy soldiers and the sound recording.

With the small plastic soldiers in *Forced Flight* Hatoum constructed a model situation which characterised military engagements as – specifically male – experimental games: laughable and at the same time inescapable. Hatoum used the same toy soldiers again the following year in her billboard *Over my Dead Body* (1988) and again in the works ∞ (*Infinity* 1991-2001) and *Horizon* (1998). This site-specific performance for just a small number of people admitted to a walk-in situation points to the first large installations she produced a little later, *The Light at the End* (1989), *Short Space* (1992) and *Light Sentence* (1992): each a spatial situation that turns the audience into participants whose senses it tries to reach and besiege.

figs. pp. 8, 11
fig. pp. 60–63
figs. pp. 15–17

Notes

1 Mona Hatoum in conversation with the author, Hamburg, 20 December 2003.
2 Terry Fox, *Cellar* (1970), Reese Palley Galerie, New York, in Brenda Richardson, *Terry Fox*, exh. cat., University Art Museum, Berkeley 1973.
3 Rebecca Horn, *Das gegenläufige Konzert* (1987), in Klaus Bussmann and Kasper König, *Skulptur Projekte in Münster 1987*, exh. cat., Westfälisches Landesmuseum Münster 1987, p. 136.

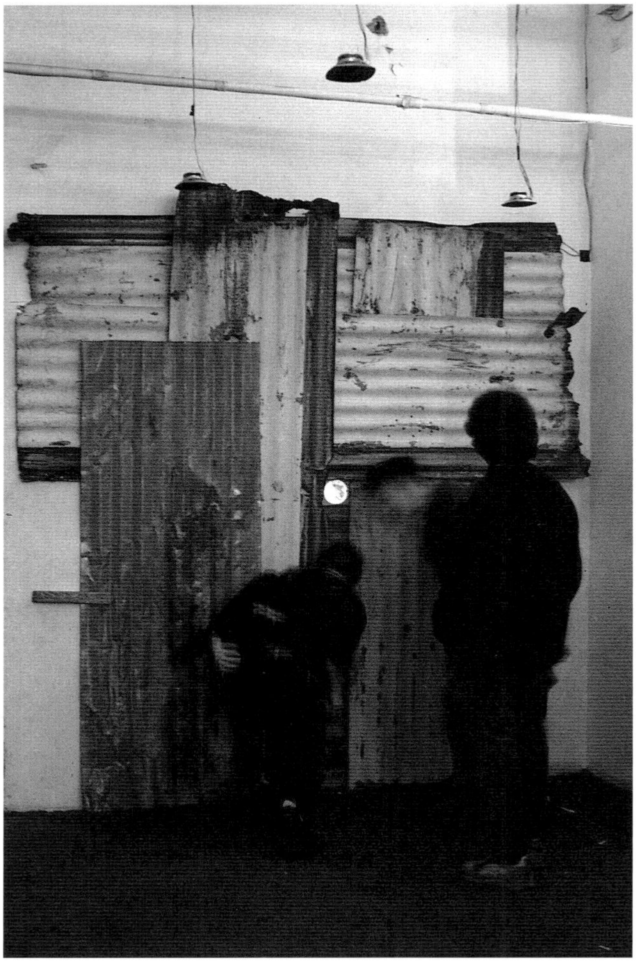

25
Matters of Gravity · 1987

Live action within wood and corrugated iron structure; optical lens, folding bed, two chairs, two sound tapes, eight speaker cones and various props
First performed at 'National Reviews of Live Art', Riverside Studios, London, 8 to 11 October 1987 (Various sessions of 3 hours were performed over a four day period)
Repeated at 'Dislocations', Kettle's Yard, Cambridge, 12 December 1987 and 6 February 1988
Matters of Gravity (a revised version) performed at 'New Work: No Definition', Third Eye Centre, Glasgow, 14 to 16 October 1987

For this performance, an alcove near the restaurant is blocked off with sheets of corrugated iron creating a shack or a bomb-shelter. The artist can only be seen through a lens that not only makes her look remote, but also turns everything upside down making her look as if she is defying gravity. The space appears to be even more illogical because all the contents of this make shift shelter – folding bed, chairs, table, tray with coffee cups etc. – are attached to the opposite wall. Therefore, when the artist seems to lie on the bed, she is actually standing bent over against it and when she appears to be standing, she is in reality lying on the floor and it is as though you are peeping through a hole in the ceiling.

When standing close to the structure you can hear a sound recording of the artist reading extracts from her father's diaries describing a repetitive daily routine of restrictive movement between house and shelter. Eight small speaker cones hang above the tables throughout the restaurant with the continuous sound of aeroplanes flying over head with intermittent air strikes and explosions.

Lit.: *Dislocations*, exh. cat. (booklet), Kettle's Yard, Cambridge 1987; exh. cat. Bristol 1993, p. 18, fig. p. 16; exh. cat. Paris 1994, p. 57; Archer, Brett, de Zegher 1997, p. 47.

Whereas in *Forced Flight* Hatoum was hidden behind a sheet of corrugated iron, in *Matters of Gravity* she literally barricaded herself behind an iron structure. Viewers were kept at a distance. They remained outside the performance space and were only able to look in through a spy-hole – the viewer as Peeping Tom. This questioned the act of looking at something; the viewers were ignored, uninvolved – and only partly understood what they were seeing, for the interior space looked confusing: the lens reversed whatever was to be seen inside, and to make matters even more annoying, the artist had arranged the opposite wall as a floor. This whole place seemed to have its very own spatial laws, its very own force of gravity.

As in *Position: Suspended* Hatoum was again both close to and distant from the viewer. *Matters of Gravity* therefore reflected on both the role of the viewer and that of the artist. One could perhaps see it as a self-portrait which expressed isolation and exclusion, as well as a personal situation of the artist in reference to her home. The artist explains, '*Matters of Gravity* is about the displaced person always feeling at odds with their immediate environment, as if they occupied a different plane of existence. Drawing on diaries her father left behind of ten years of the war in Lebanon, we get a glimpse into a monotonous, repetitive routine of

Matters of Gravity · 1987

Matters of Gravity · 1987
(Sketchbook drawing)

RIVERSIDE

GRAVITY:
Being serious
solemnity
importance
* seriousness
staidness
sobriety

GRAVITY OF ~~CENTRE~~

TITLE → MATTERS OF GRAVITY

A LIFE IN THE DAY...

RESTRICTED VIEW

NOT MATTRESS BUT FOLDING BED

PROPS → ALL FOUR WALLS LINED WITH GREY BLANKETS

- CHAIR
- BOX (FOR TABLE)
- TRAY & COFFEE CUPS

- ~~MATTRESS~~ FOLDING BED
- RADIO
- LIGHT BULB
- DIARIES.

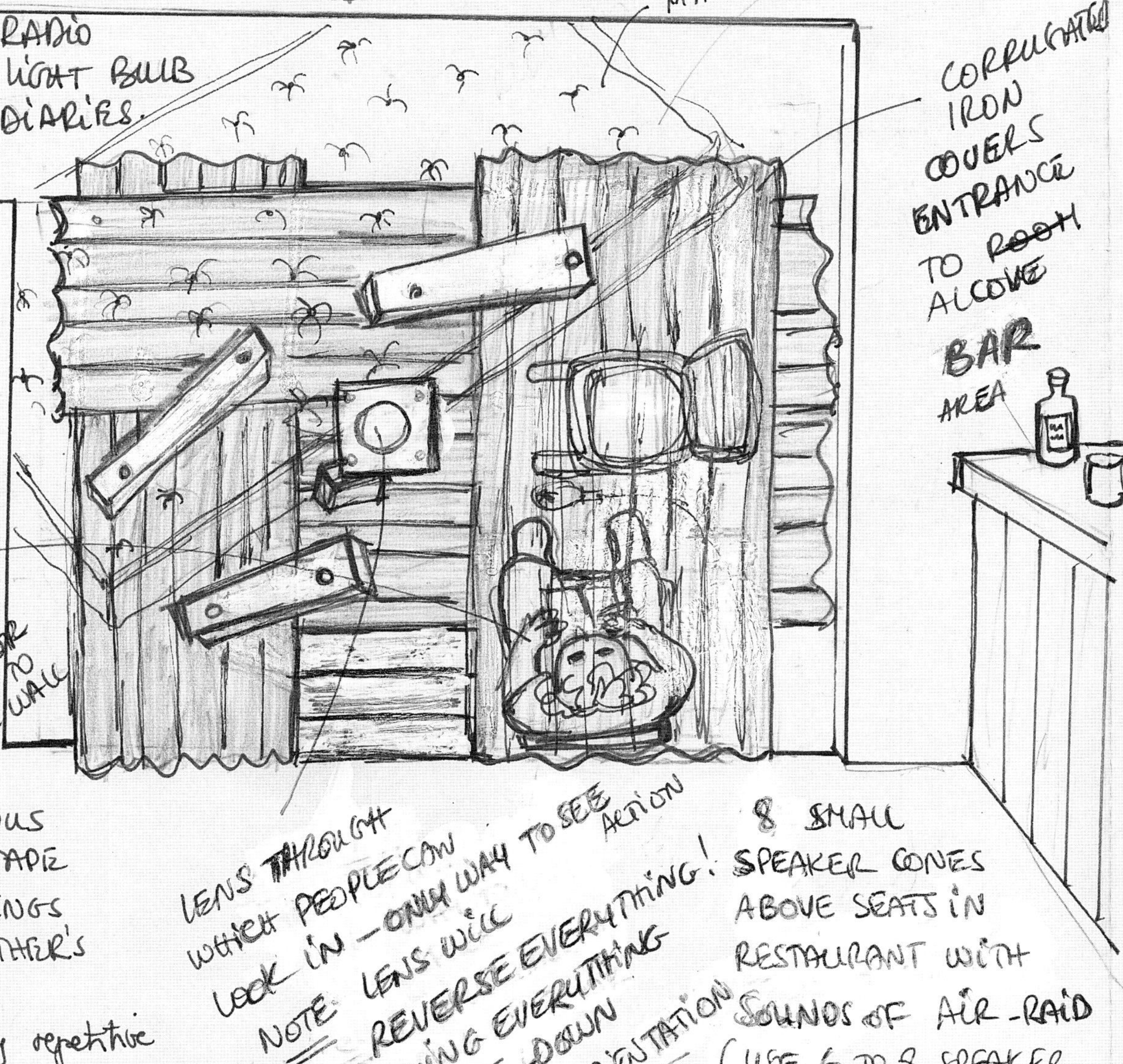

Performer + all objects lie/hang horizontally or ARE ATTACHED TO OPPOSITE WALL

* CONTINUOUS SOUND TAPE OF READINGS FROM FATHER'S DIARIES (describing repetitive day to day restricted movements between house - shelter)

LENS THROUGH WHICH PEOPLE CAN LOOK IN - ONLY WAY TO SEE ACTION

NOTE LENS WILL REVERSE EVERYTHING! REVERSE EVERYTHING SHOWING EVERYTHING UPSIDE DOWN ⇒ DISORIENTATION

8 SMALL SPEAKER CONES ABOVE SEATS IN RESTAURANT WITH SOUNDS OF AIR-RAID (USE 6 TO 8 SPEAKER CONES)

* CONSIDER HANGING PHOTOCOPIES (ON ACETATE) OF PAGES OF FATHER'S DIARIES IN FOYER AREA. (?) NO!

ADDITIONAL EQUIPMENT
- 6 TO 8 SMALL SPEAKER CONES
- TAPE DECK + CONTINUOUS TAPE
- AMPLIFIER.

TO EQUIPMENT
- TAPE DECK WITH AUTO-REVERSE
- AMPLIFIER
- 8 SPEAKERS.

restricted movements between the house and the shelter – a truncated existence.'[1]

The idea and the dimensions of the corrugated iron wall stands in the tradition with the barn door used by Marcel Duchamp to conceal his final large work, the illusionistic diorama *Étant donnés: 1 la chute d'eau: 2 le gaz d' éclairage ...* (1946–66), which was installed at Philadelphia Museum of Art. Here too, the viewer can only look inside through a pair of spy-holes: in the forefront of an idyllic landscape lay a life-sized nude woman, who, as Herbert Molderings wrote, 'offered her genitals to the gaze of the art lovers'. Molderings interpreted Duchamp's work as a cryptic self-portrait of the artist. 'The work is like a testimony of Duchamp's understanding of the artist in modern bourgeois society: the artist not as the hooker of the bourgeoisie, but as the engineer of a peep-show staged for them, and whose only remaining satisfaction is that of at least being untouchable for the hoard of viewers.'[2]

Hatoum linked into this concept of the artist in her work: in *Matters of Gravity* she withdrew her own body from the viewers, with whom she had communicated in all sorts of ways in other performances; after that she would only encounter them indirectly: in her last performance *Pull* (1995) as an electromagnetic image (though with real hair), as the originator of her installations and objects, and in the reality of *Corps étranger* or *Deep Throat*, where she reproduced, digitally, the actual inside of her body, which she would offer 'to the gaze of the art lovers.' fig. pp. 46-

Notes

1 Programme statement by Mona Hatoum for her performance at 'National Reviews of Live Art', Riverside Studios, London, 8 to 11 October 1987.

2 Herbert Molderings, *Marcel Duchamp: Parawissenschaft, das Ephemere und der Skeptizismus,* Düsseldorf 1997, p. 74 (transl. Pauline Cumbers).

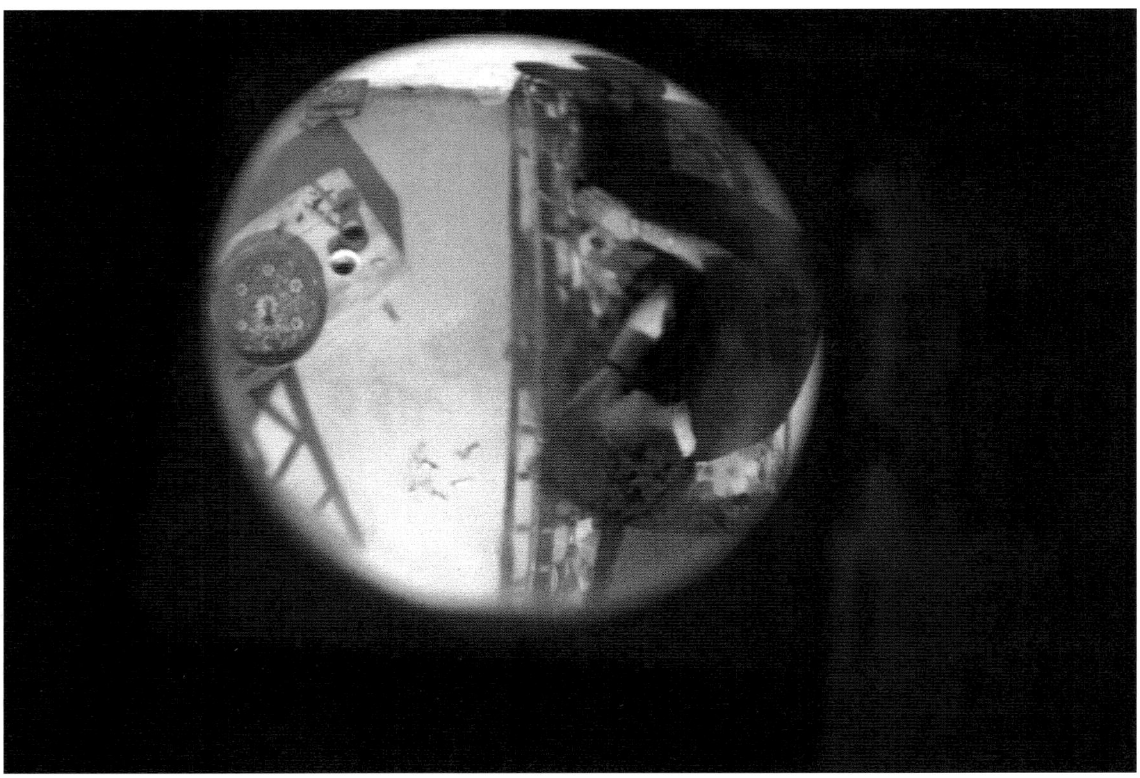

Matters of Gravity · 1987

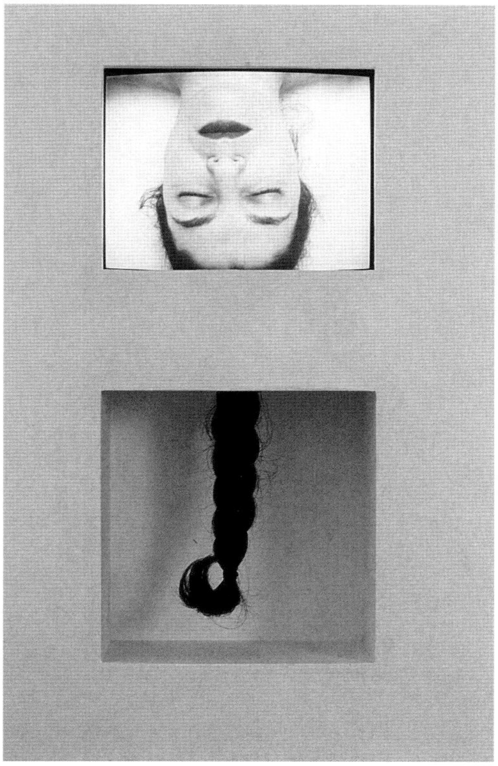

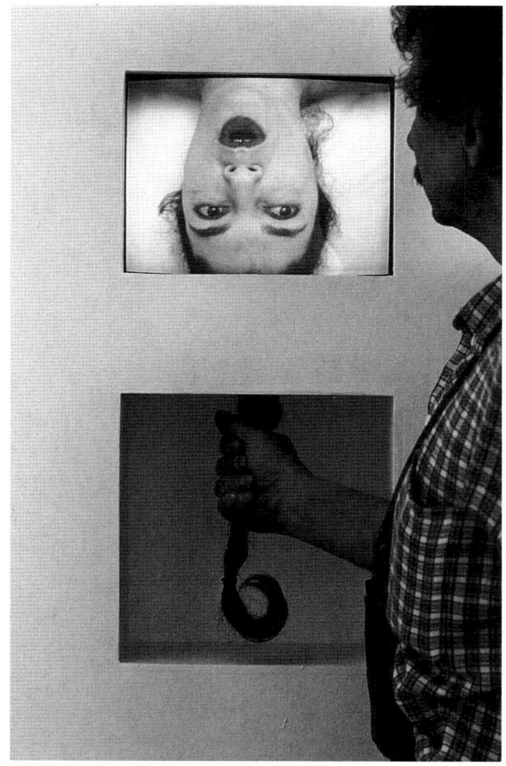

26
Pull · 1995

Live work with live video camera, monitor and hair braid
Performed at 'Körper Formen', Künstlerwerkstatt, Munich, 5 to 7 May 1995
Duration: 2 hours

In a small white space the face of the performer can be seen on a monitor, upside down and apparently sleeping. A plait of real hair hangs below the monitor. When a person touches the hair or pulls at it, she opens her eyes and reacts. This is a live performance where the performer lies on a bed directly behind the monitor with a closed-circuit camera above her head and a hair extension attached to her own hair. As soon as people touch the hair braid, she feels it and reacts by opening her eyes and sometimes registering pain on her face.

Lit.: Archer, Brett, de Zegher 1997, pp. 71, 74.

Seven years after her last performance, Hatoum, in *Pull*, again took up the interplay already characteristic of her first actions, between the physically perceived experience and the electronically mediated image. Through this game with reality *Pull* also became a pointer to social, perhaps even gender-specific behaviour. 'At a certain moment, the spectacle suddenly ceases to be a spectacle. Him or her! The response calls forth one's intimate psychology and Hatoum noticed that, on the whole, men yanked the hair without compunction, whereas women were more gentle, and even reluctant, presumably through self-identification.'[1]

Like the two preceding spaces created by the artist, *Pull* is also an installation which relies on her presence, although strictly speaking, her person can be substituted by another performer. Subsequently this work exists as a set of instructions and is today in a private collection.

Note
1 Guy Brett, in Archer, Brett, de Zegher 1997, p. 74.

A New Installation for the Hamburger Kunsthalle Dome

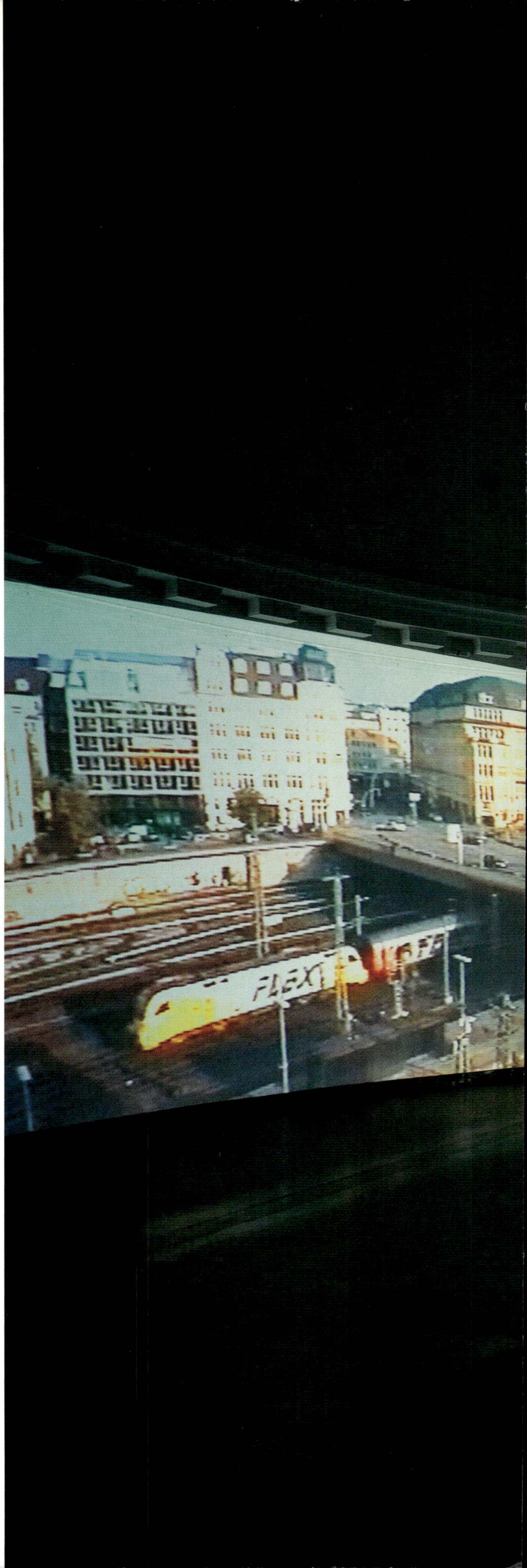

Lookout · 2004
Site-specific installation
Photo of work in progress

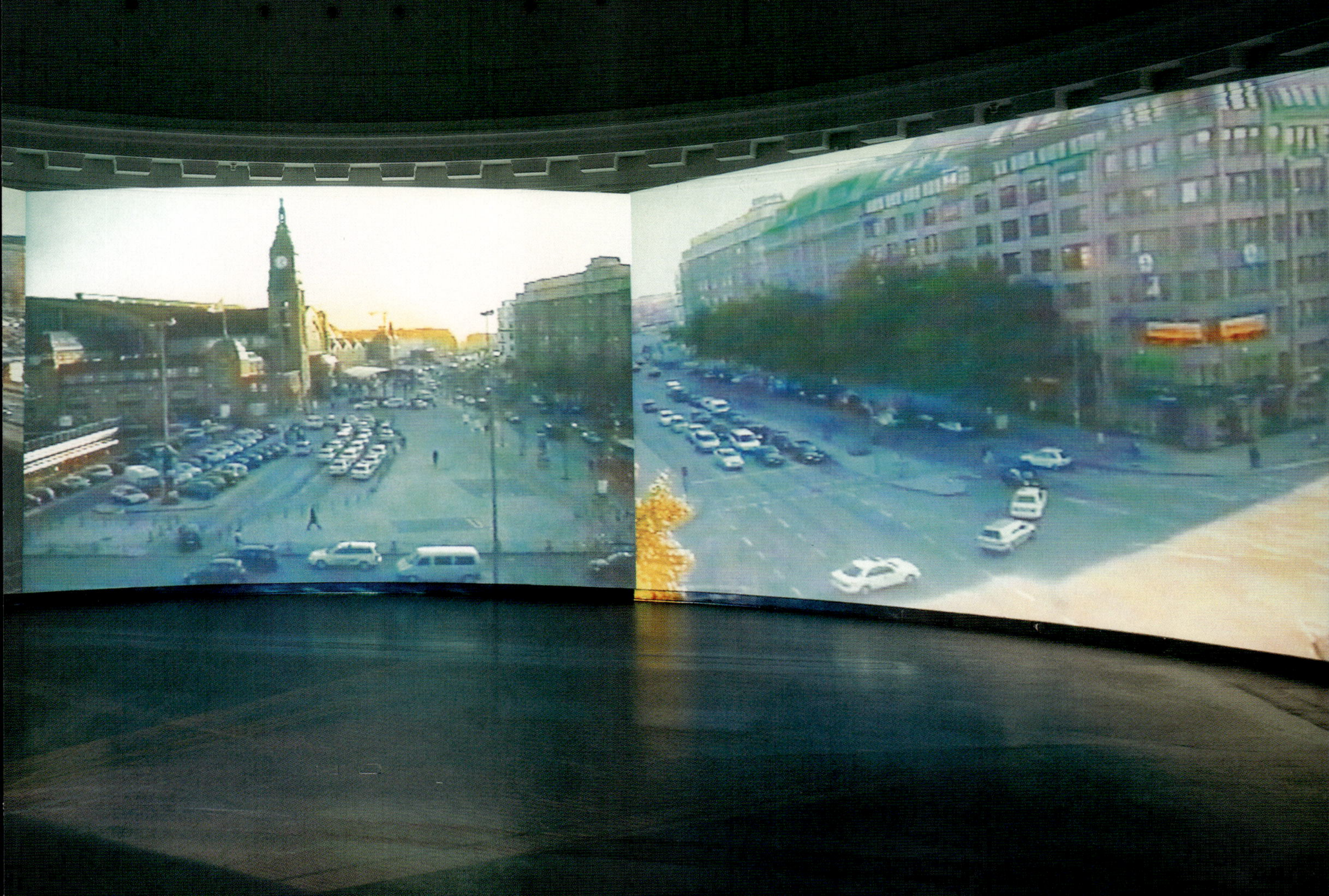

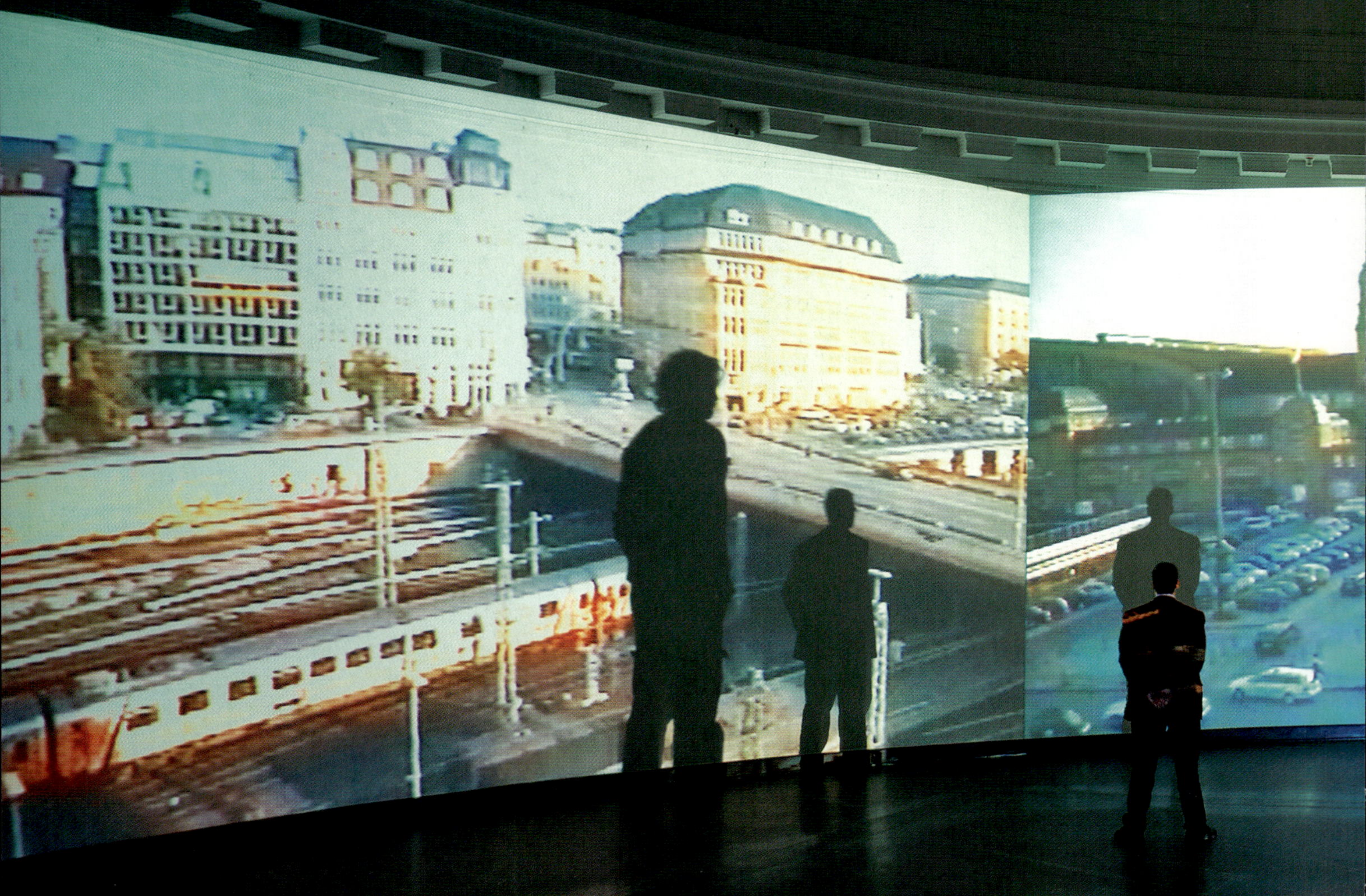

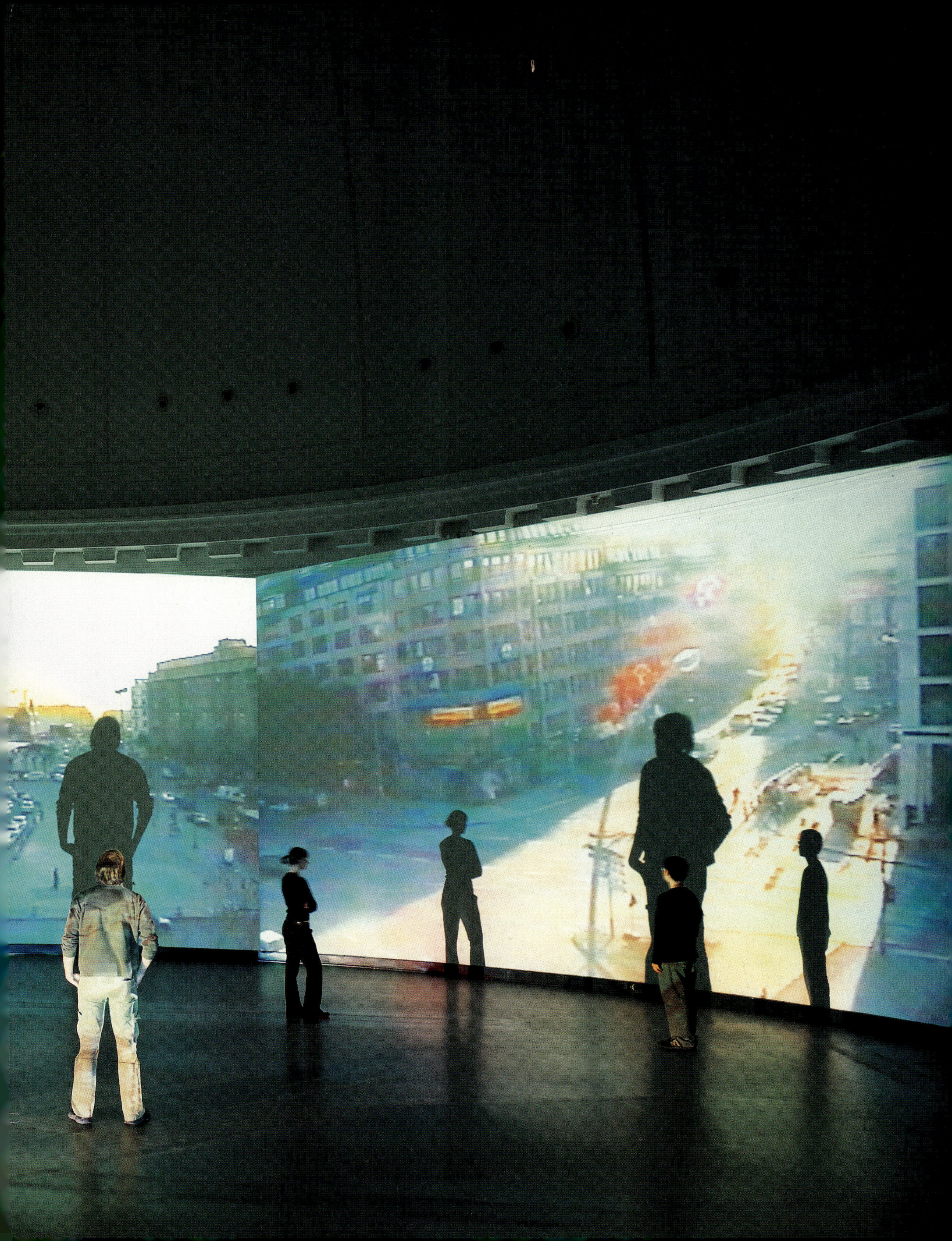

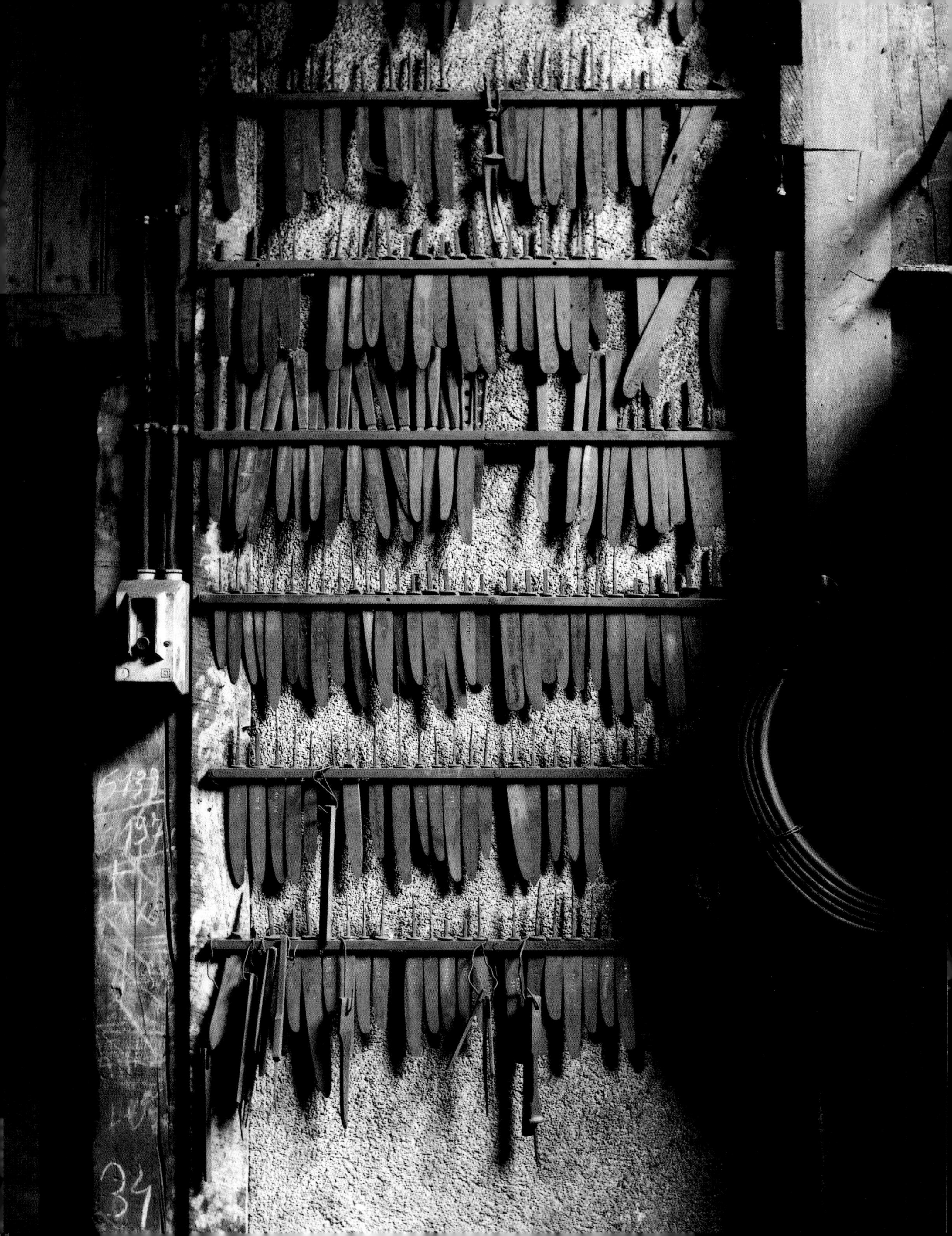

List of Works Exhibited and Reproduced

A Bunch of Carrots (New York) 2001
C-print, 28 x 35.5 cm
Courtesy Jay Jopling/White Cube, London
[H, B]

Baid Ghanam [sheep's testicle] (Jerusalem) · 1996
C-print, 17 x 26 cm
Exhibition copy, courtesy of the artist
p. 64 [H, B]

Balançoires en fer · 1999
Mild steel, 206 x 137 x 50 cm
Installation: Le Creux de l'Enfer, Thiers, France
Artist's proof, courtesy of the artist
pp. 54–55 [H, B, S]

Birds of a Feather II (Newlyn) · 1997
C–print, 25 x 37.7 cm
Courtesy Jay Jopling/White Cube, London
[H, B]

Blood Drawing · 2003
Handmade paper, blood, 31.5 x 25.5 cm
Courtesy Alexander and Bonin, New York
p. 53 [H, B, S]

Cage-à-deux · 2002
Mild steel, painted MDF, 201.5 x 315 x 199.5 cm
Courtesy Jay Jopling / White Cube, London
pp. 26–27 [H, B, S]

Carcasses (Baalbeck) · 1998
C–print, 30.5 x 21 cm
Exhibition copy, courtesy of the artist
p. 65 [H, B]

Chain · 1999
Leather gloves, nylon thread, wood, steel, 100.3 x 25.4 cm variable height
Installation: Le Creux de l'Enfer, Thiers, France
Private Collection, Turin, courtesy Alexander and Bonin, New York
pp. 58–59 [H, B, S]

Changing Parts · 1984
B/w video, sound, 24 min.
A Western Front Video Production, Vancouver, courtesy of the artist
p. 14 [H, B, S]

Corps étranger · 1994
Video installation, with cylindrical wooden structure, video projector, video player, amplifier, four speakers
350 x 300 x 300 cm
Musée national d'art moderne, Centre George Pompidou, Paris
Exhibition copy, courtesy Jay Jopling/White Cube, London
pp. 46–47 [H, B]

Deep Throat · 1996
Table, tablecloths, chair, glass, plate, fork, knife, monitor, DVD, DVD-player
75 x 85 x 128 cm, 5:15 min. loop
F. und W. Stiftung für zeitgenössische Kunst in der Hamburger Kunsthalle
pp. 48–49 [H]

Divan Bed · 1996
Steel tread plate, 60 x 192 x 77 cm
Sammlung Goetz
p. 25 [H, B, S]

Don't smile, you're on camera! · 1980
B/w video, sound, 11:15 min.
Courtesy of the artist
pp. 80, 84 [H, B, S]

Doormat II · 2000–01
Stainless steel and nickel-plated pins, glue, canvas, 2.5 x 71 x 40.5 cm
Exhibition copy, courtesy of the artist
p. 30 [H, B, S]

Drowning Sorrows · 2001
Glass bottles, 10 cm x 250 cm diameter
Artist's proof, courtesy of the artist; Alexander and Bonin, New York & Jay Jopling/White Cube, London
p. 57 [H, B, S]

Every Door a Wall · 2003
Inkjet print on voile, 200 x 277 cm
Exhibition copy, courtesy of the artist
p. 41 [H, B]

Exodus · 2001
Cardboard, metal, human hair, wax, two parts 49.6 cm x 75.5 cm x 80 cm
Private Collection, Stockholm
[S]

Eyes Skinned · 1988
Colour video, sound, 4:04 min
A Western Front Video Production, Vancouver, courtesy of the artist
[H, B, S]

Garfish (Bequia) · 1996
C–print, 33 x 49.3 cm
Courtesy Jay Jopling/White Cube, London
p. 64 [H, B]

Grater Divide · 2002
Mild steel, 204 x 3.5 cm variable width
Artist's proof, courtesy of the artist & Jay Jopling/White Cube, London
pp. 28–29 [H, B, S]

Hair Drawing · 2003
Handmade paper, human hair, 25.5 x 31.5 cm
Courtesy Alexander and Bonin, New York
p. 53 [H, B, S]

Hair Drawing · 2003
Handmade paper, human hair, 34.5 x 41.5 cm
Courtesy Alexander and Bonin, New York
[H, B, S]

Hand Made Paper · 2003
Handmade paper, 61 x 51.5 cm
Courtesy Alexander and Bonin, New York
p. 52 [H, B, S]

Hearing Voices (why me?) · 1994
Four etched glass panels, each 28 x 33 cm
Collection Magasin 3 Stockholm Konsthall
[S]

Home · 1999
Wood, galvanized steel, stainless steel, electric wire, computerised dimmer unit, amplifier, speakers, 77 x 198 x 73.5 cm
Courtesy Moderna Museet, Stockholm. Gift year 2000 by The Friends of Moderna Museet
[S]

Homebound · 2000
Kitchen utensils, furniture, electric wire, light bulbs, computerised dimmer unit, amplifier, speakers, variable dimensions
Installation: Documenta 11, Kassel
Courtesy Jay Jopling/White Cube, London & Alexander and Bonin, New York
pp. 20–21[H, B]

Horizon · 1998
Plastic, aluminium strip, paint, 6.5 x 1.5 cm, variable length
Courtesy Jay Jopling/White Cube, London
pp. 62–63 [H, B]
Courtesy Jan Widlund, Stockholm
[S]

How to turn your ordinary kitchen utensils into modern electrical appliances · 1996
Proposal for Hans-Ulrich Obrist's *Do it* for the Reykjavik Municipal Art Museum's exhibition catalogue
Inkjet and pencil on paper, 29.5 x 21 cm
Collection of the artist, London
p. 144 [H, B, S]

Incommunicado · 1993
Mild steel, wire, 127 x 49.5 x 95.5 cm
Artist's proof, courtesy of the artist
p. 6 [H, B, S]

∞ (Infinity) · 1991–2001
Bronze, 61 x 34.5 x 34.5 cm
Courtesy Alexander and Bonin, New York
p. 60 [H, B]

Jardin public · 1993
Painted wrought iron, wax, pubic hair, 82.4 x 39.5 x 49 cm
Collection of the artist, London
p. 74 [H, B, S]

Keffieh · 1993–1999
Human hair on cotton fabric, 120 x 120 cm
Exhibition copy, courtesy of the artist
pp. 36–37 [H, B, S]

Kroush (tripe) · 1996
C-print, 19.5 x 29 cm
Courtesy Jay Jopling/White Cube, London
[H, B]

La grande broyeuse (Mouli Julienne x 21) 2000
Mild steel, 425 x 325 x 560 cm, discs: each 6.3 x 210 cm diameter
Installation: Tate Britain, London
Private Collection, Korea, courtesy Jay Jopling/White Cube
p. 24

Le creux de l'enfer · 2000
Silver gelatin print, 40.5 x 51 cm
Courtesy Jay Jopling/White Cube, London
p. 134 [H, B]

Light Sentence · 1992
Wire mesh lockers, slow-moving motorized light bulb, 198 x 185 x 490 cm
Fonds National d'Art Contemporain (FNAC) – Musée national d'art moderne, Centre George Pompidou, Paris
pp. 16–17 [H, B]

Lookout · 2004
Site-specific video installation for the Hamburger Kunsthalle dome
3 CCTV surveillance cameras, 3 video projectors, 3 microphones, 3 amplifiers, 6 speakers, 5 x 28 m (projection)
Courtesy of the artist
pp. 130/131, 132/133 (Photo of work in progress) [H]

Marbles Carpet · 1995
Glass marbles, variable dimensions
Installation: The British School at Rome
Collezione Prada
p. 56 [H, B, S]

Measures of Distance · 1988
Colour video, sound, 15 min.
A Western Front Video Production, Vancouver, courtesy of the artist
p. 45 [H, B, S]

No Way · 1996
Stainless steel, 6 x 41 x 13 cm
Artist's proof, courtesy of the artist
p. 22 [H, B, S]

No Way III · 1996
Stainless steel, 10 x 25 x 29 cm
Artist's proof, courtesy of the artist
p. 22 [H, B, S]

Over My Dead Body · 1988
Billboard, ink on paper, 204 x 304 cm
p. 8, 11

Over My Dead Body · 1988–2002
Inkjet on PVC with grommets, 204.5 x 305 cm
Artist's proof, courtesy of the artist
[H, B]

Performance Still · 1985–1995
B/w photograph, mounted on aluminium, 76.5 x 108 cm
Sammlung Goetz
p. 82 [H, B, S]

+ and – 1994
Wood, stainless steel, electric motor, sand, 8 x 30 x 30 cm
Collection of the artist, London
[S]

+ and – 1994–2004
Steel, aluminium, sand, electric motor, 25 cm x 420 cm diameter
Courtesy Jay Jopling / White Cube, London
pp. 4–5, 139 [H, B]

Present Tense · 1996
Soap, glass beads, 4.5 x 299 x 241 cm
Installation: Anadiel Gallery, Jerusalem
Courtesy of the artist & Jay Jopling/White Cube, London
pp. 68–69 [H, B, S]

Quarters · 1996
Mild steel, four units, each: 275.5 x 80.8 x 183 cm, overall installation: 275.5 x · 517 x 517 cm
Sammlung Olbricht
pp. 18–19 [H, B]
Collection Magasin 3 Stockholm Konsthall
[S]

Recollection · 1995
Hair balls, strands of hair hung from the ceiling, wooden loom with woven hair, table, variable dimensions
Installation: Béguinage St. Elizabeth, Kortrijk, Belgium
Collection, De Vleeshal, Middelburg, the Netherlands
p. 73

Roadworks · 1985
Colour video, sound, 6:45 min.
Courtesy of the artist
[H, B, S]

Rous Ghanam [sheep heads] (Jerusalem) 1996
C–print, 17 x 26 cm
Courtesy Jay Jopling/White Cube, London
[H, B]

Routes II · 2002
Pen and ink on five printed maps, variable dimensions
The Judith Rothschild Foundation
p. 38

Routes (A.P.) · 2003
Pen and ink on printed maps, variable dimensions
Artist's proof, courtesy of the artist
[H, B, S]

Self-erasing drawing · 1979
Wood, sand, metal, electric motor, 9.5 x 28 x 28 cm
Collection of the artist, London
p. 32

Set in Stone · 2002
Engraved marble, hemp, oak shelf, 24 x 65 x 20 cm
Edition Schellmann, Munich
Artist's proof, courtesy of the artist
[H, B, S]

Skin, nail and hair · 2003
Handmade paper, human hair, skin, nails, 29.5 x 23.5 cm
Courtesy Alexander and Bonin, New York
p. 53 [H, B, S]

Sissan (chicks) · 1996
C–print, 19.5 x 29 cm
Courtesy Jay Jopling/White Cube, London
[H, B]

So much I want to say · 1983
B/w video, sound, 5 min
A Western Front Video Production, Vancouver, courtesy of the artist
p. 1 [H, B, S]

T 4 2 · 1993–98
Fine stoneware, 5.4 x 24.45 x 13.97 cm
Courtesy of Jay Jopling/White Cube, London & Alexander and Bonin, New York
[H, B, S]

Testimony · 1995–2002
Video installation, diameter 50 cm, 2:37 min. loop
Courtesy Jay Jopling/White Cube, London
p. 42 [H, B, S]

The Light at the End · 1989
Angle iron frame, six electric heating elements, 166 x 162.5 x 5 cm
Installation: The Showroom, London
Collection Arts Council England, London
p. 15

Traffic · 2002
Compressed card, plastic, metal, beeswax, human hair, 48 x 65 x 68 cm
Courtesy Alexander and Bonin, New York
p. 39

Traffic · 2002
Compressed card, plastic, metal, beeswax, human hair, 41 x 65 x 68 cm
Artist's proof, courtesy of the artist
[H, B]

Umbilicus · 2003
Metal, plastic, nylon thread, 46 x 162 x 33 cm
Installation: MACO – Museo de Arte Contemporáneo de Oaxaca, Mexico
Courtesy Alexander and Bonin, New York [H, B, S]
pp. 50–51

Untitled (brain) · 2003
Handmade paper, 25.5 x 31.5 cm
Courtesy Alexander and Bonin, New York
[H, B, S]

Untitled (chinese colander) · 1996
Japanese wax paper, 40.6 x 51 cm
Collection of the artist, London
[H, B, S]

Untitled (crutches) · 1991–2001
Rubber, variable dimensions
Artist's proof, courtesy of the artist & Jay Jopling/White Cube, London
p. 33 [H, B, S]

Untitled (flat colander) · 1996
Japanese wax paper, 40.6 x 53.3 cm
Collection of the artist, London
[H, B, S]

Untitled (grater) · 1996
Japanese wax paper, 27 x 40 cm
Collection of the artist, London
p. 23 [H, B, S]

Untitled (graters) · 1999
Silver gelatin print, 40.5 x 51 cm
Exhibition copy, courtesy of the artist
p. 141 [H, B]

Untitled (grey hair grid with knots) · 2001
Human grey hair, hair spray, tracing paper, 35 x 27 cm
Courtesy of the artist
p. 35 [H, B, S]

Untitled (hair grid with knots) · 2001
Human hair, hair spray, tracing paper, 35 x 27 cm
Courtesy of the artist
p. 34 [H, B]

Untitled (hair grid with knots 2) · 2001
Human hair, hair spray, tracing paper, 35 x 27 cm
Collection Magasin 3 Stockholm Konsthall
[S]

Untitled (large Shaker colander) · 1996
Japanese wax paper, 54.6 x 68.6 cm
Collection of the artist, London
p. 23 [H, B, S]

Untitled (milk strainer) · 1996
Japanese wax paper, 27.3 x 40 cm
Collection of the artist, London
[H, B, S]

Untitled (passoire à queue) · 1999
Japanese wax paper, 43.5 x 54.5 cm
Collection of the artist, London
[H, B, S]

Untitled (rape cylindrique) · 1999
Japanese wax paper, 40.5 x 54.5 cm
Collection of the artist, London
[H, B, S]

Untitled (passoire de J-L) · 1999
Japanese wax paper, 43.5 x 50 cm
Collection of the artist, London
[H, B, S]

Untitled (wheelchair) · 1998
Stainless steel, rubber, 97 x 50 x 84 cm
Sammlung Olbricht
p. 31 [H, B]

Untitled (wheelchair II) · 1999
Stainless steel, rubber, 94.5 x 48.5 x 63.5 cm
Artist's proof, courtesy of the artist
[S]

Van Gogh's Back · 1995
C-print, 50 x 38 cm
Exhibition copy, courtesy of the artist
p. 79 [H, B, S]

Vicious Circle · 1999
Glass bottles, 8 cm x 176 cm diameter
Installation: Mass MoCA, North Adams, USA
Exhibition copy, courtesy of the artist
p. 61 [H, B]
Artist's proof, Collection Magasin 3 Stockholm Konsthall
[S]

You are still here · 1994
Etched mirrored glass, metal fixtures, 38 x 29.2 x 0.5 cm
Artist's proof, courtesy of the artist
p. 12 [H, B, S]

Sketchbook Drawings and Studies

Don't smile, you're on camera! · 1980 (sketchbook drawing)
Ink, pencil on paper, 29.6 x 21 cm
Courtesy of the artist
p. 83 [H, B, S]

Matters of Gravity · 1987 (sketchbook drawing)
Pencil, ink, pen, correction fluid on paper, 29.6 x 20.8 cm
Courtesy of the artist
p. 127 [H, B, S]

Position: Suspended · 1986 (sketchbook drawing)
Ink, pencil, correction fluid, 29.5 x 19.5 cm
Courtesy of the artist
p. 116 [H, B, S]

The Negotiating Table · 1983 (study)
Mixed media on cardboard, 29.6 x 40 cm
Courtesy of the artist
p. 102 (top) [H, B, S]

The Negotiating Table · 1983 (study)
Mixed media on paper, 31.6 x 45 cm
Courtesy of the artist
p. 102 (bottom) [H, B, S]

The Negotiating Table · 1983 (study)
Mixed media on paper, 32 x 44.8 cm
Courtesy of the artist [H, B, S]
p. 103 (top)

The Negotiating Table · 1983 (study)
Mixed media on paper, 33 x 44.8 cm
Courtesy of the artist
p. 103 (bottom) [H, B, S]

Under Siege · 1982 (sketchbook drawing)
Ink, gouache, pencil, pen, correction fluid, adhesive tape, photo collage, 27.4 x 42.3 cm
Courtesy of the artist
pp. 94–95 [H, B, S]

Unemployed · 1986 (proposal)
Typewriter ink, gouache, 29.6 x 19.4 cm
Courtesy of the artist
p. 121 [H, B, S]

H = exhibited at the Hamburger Kunsthalle
B = exhibited at the Kunstmuseum Bonn
S = exhibited at the Magasin 3 Stockholm Konsthall

Biography

1952
Born in Beirut, Lebanon
1970-72
Beirut University College, Beirut
1975–79
The Byam Shaw School of Art, London
1979–81
The Slade School of Art, London
1986–94
Visiting lecturer at Central Saint Martins College of Art and Design, London
1989–92
Senior Research Fellow in Fine Art at Cardiff Institute of Higher Education, Cardiff
1992–97
Part-time teaching post at Jan van Eyck Akademie, Maastricht
1994–95
Guest Professor at L'Ecole Nationale Supérieure des Beaux-arts, Paris
1997
Awarded Honorary Fellowship of the Dartington College of Arts, Devon, England
1998
Awarded title of Visiting Professor by Chelsea College of Art and Design and Central Saint Martins College of Art and Design, London
2000
Awarded the George Maciunas Prize, Wiesbaden
2003–04
DAAD scholarship, Deutscher Akademischer Austauschdienst, Berlin
2004
Awarded the Sonning Prize, University of Copenhagen

Lives and works in London since 1975

Solo Exhibitions (Selection since 1989)

1989
The Light at the End, The Showroom, London
The Light at the End, Oboro Gallery, Montreal

1992
Dissected Space, Chapter, Cardiff

1993
Recent Work, Arnolfini, Bristol

1994
Mona Hatoum, Galerie René Blouin, Montreal
Mona Hatoum, Musée national d'art moderne, Centre Georges Pompidou, Paris

1995
Mona Hatoum, The British School at Rome, Rome

1996
Mona Hatoum, The Fabric Workshop and Museum, Philadelphia
Mona Hatoum, Anadiel Gallery, Jerusalem
Current Disturbance, Capp Street Project, San Francisco
Quarters, Via Farini, Milan
Mona Hatoum, De Appel, Amsterdam

1997
Mona Hatoum, Museum of Contemporary Art, Chicago and The New Museum of Contemporary Art, New York

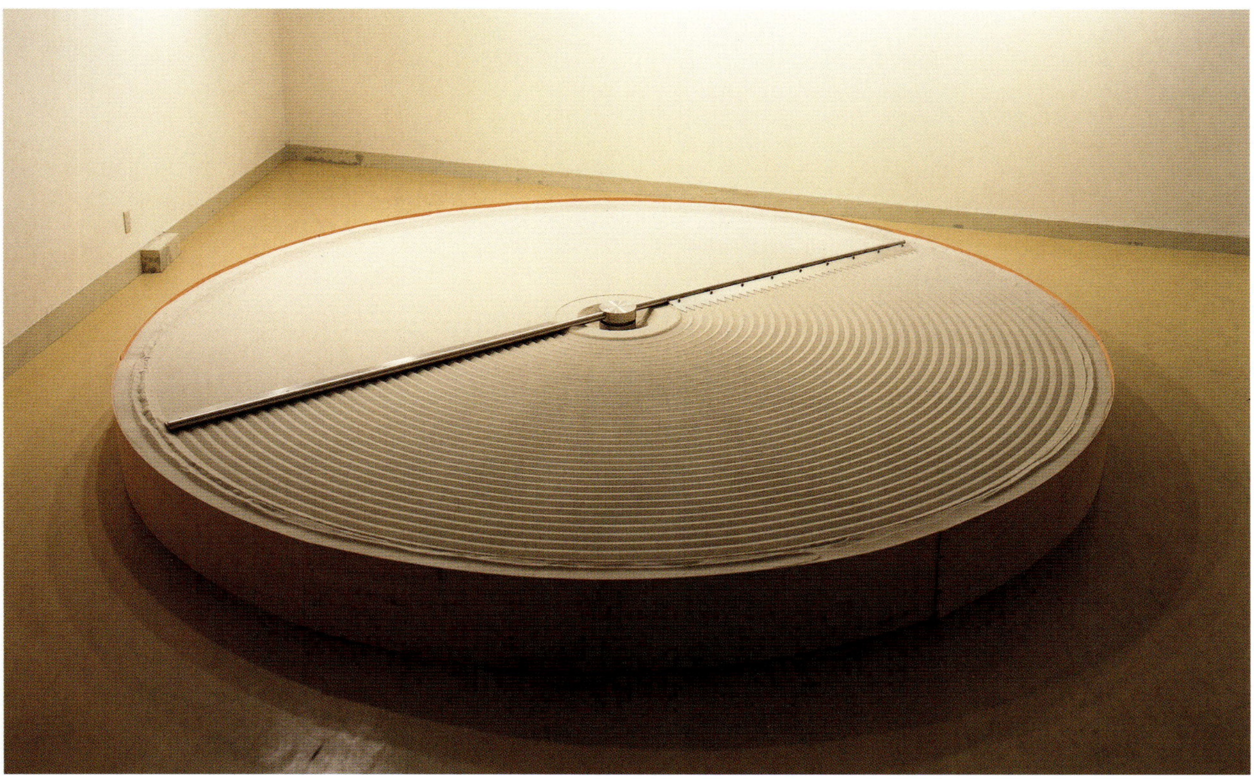

1998
Mona Hatoum, Museum of Modern Art, Oxford and the Scottish National Gallery of Modern Art, Edinburgh
Mona Hatoum, Kunsthalle Basel, Basel

1999
Mona Hatoum, Castello di Rivoli, Museo d'Arte Contemporanea, Turin
Mona Hatoum, ArtPace Foundation for Contemporary Art, San Antonio, Texas
Mona Hatoum, Le Creux de l'Enfer, Centre d'art contemporain, Thiers, France

2000
Mona Hatoum, Le Collège, Frac Champagne–Ardenne, Reims and MUHKA – Museum van Hedendaagse Kunst Antwerpen, Antwerp
Mona Hatoum: The Entire World as a Foreign Land, Duveen Galleries, Tate Britain, London
Images from Elsewhere, fig-1, London
Mona Hatoum, SITE Santa Fe, Santa Fe, New Mexico

2001
Domestic Disturbance, MASS MoCA, North Adams, Massachusetts
Mona Hatoum, Sala Mendoza, Caracas

2002
Mona Hatoum, Laboratorio Arte Alameda, Mexico City
Huis Clos, CASA – Centro de Arte de Salamanca, Spain; (permanent installation)
Mona Hatoum, CASA – Centro de Arte de Salamanca and Centro Galego de Arte Contemporanea, Santiago de Compostela, Spain

2003
Mona Hatoum, MACO – Museo de Arte Contemporáneo de Oaxaca, Oaxaca and Ex–Convento de Conkal, Yukatan, Mexico
Mona Hatoum: Photo and Video Works, Uppsala Konstmuseum, Uppsala, Sweden

2004
Mona Hatoum – A Major Survey, Hamburger Kunsthalle, Hamburg; Kunstmuseum Bonn and Magasin 3 Stockholm Konsthall, Stockholm

Group Exhibitions (Selection since 1989)

1989
The Other Story, Hayward Gallery, London, Wolverhampton Art Gallery, Wolverhampton, Manchester City Art Gallery and Cornerhouse, Manchester

1990
The British Art Show, McLellan Galleries, Glasgow, Leeds City Art Gallery and Hayward Gallery, London
TSWA Four Cities Project, New Art for Newcastle, Newcastle upon Tyne

1991
IV Bienal de la Habana, Havana
Interrogating Identity, Grey Art Gallery and Study Center, New York (and U.S. tour)
The Interrupted Life, The New Museum of Contemporary Art, New York

1992
Pour la Suite du Monde, Musée d'Art Contemporain de Montréal, Montreal

1993
Four Rooms, Serpentine Gallery, London
Grazer Combustion, Steirischer Herbst '93 Festival, Graz

1994
Espacios Fragmentados, V Bienal de la Habana, Havana
Sense and Sensibility: Women and Minimalism in the Nineties, Museum of Modern Art, New York
Cocido y Crudo, Museo Nacional Centro de Arte Reina Sofia, Madrid
Heart of Darkness, Museum Kröller Müller, Otterlo, the Netherlands

1995
ARS 95 Helsinki, Museum of Contemporary Art, Helsinki
Identity and Alterity, Venice Biennale, Venice
Rites of Passage, Tate Gallery, London
The Turner Prize 1995 Exhibition, Tate Gallery, London
Orient/ation, 4th International Istanbul Biennial, Istanbul

1996
Inside the Visible, Institute of Contemporary Art, Boston, The National Museum of Women in the Arts, Washington, Whitechapel Art Gallery, London and Art Gallery of Western Australia, Perth (1997)
fremdKörper/corps étranger/Foreign Body, Museum für Gegenwartskunst, Basel
Distemper: Dissonant Themes in the Art of the 1990s, Hirshhorn Museum and Sculpture Garden, Washington D.C.
Inclusion: Exclusion, Steirischer Herbst '96, Graz
Life/Live, La scène artistique au Royaume-Uni en 1996, de nouvelles aventures, Musée d'art Moderne de la Ville de Paris, Paris and Centro Cultural de Belém, Lisbon

1997
De-Genderism: détruire dit-elle/il, Setagaya Art Museum, Tokyo
2nd Gwangju Biennale, Gwangju, South Korea
Sensation: Young British Artists from The Saatchi Collection, Royal Academy of Arts, London, Hamburger Bahnhof, Museum für Gegenwart, Berlin and Brooklyn Museum of Art, New York (1999)
Art from the UK, Sammlung Goetz, Munich

1998
Wounds: Between Democracy and Redemption in Contemporary Art, Moderna Museet, Stockholm
Echolot, Museum Fridericianum Kassel
Real/Life: New British Art, Tochigi Prefectural Museum of Fine Arts, Fukuoka City Art Museum, Fukuoka, Hiroshima City Museum, Hiroshima, Tokyo Museum of Contemporary Art, Tokyo and Ashiya City Museum of Art History, Ashiya (1999)
Spatiotemporal, Magasin 3 Stockholm Konsthall, Stockholm
XXIV Bienal de São Paulo, Fundação Bienal São Paulo
Emotion – Young British and American Artists from the Goetz Collection, Deichtorhallen, Hamburg
7th International Biennale of Cairo 98, Cairo

1999
Looking for a Place, SITE Santa Fe's Third International Biennial, Santa Fe, New Mexico
La Casa, il Corpo, il Cuore, Museum Moderner Kunst Stiftung Ludwig, Vienna and the National Gallery, Prague (2000)
The XXth Century – One Century of Art in Germany, Neue Nationalgalerie, Berlin
Art Worlds in Dialogue – From Gauguin to the Global Present, Museum Ludwig, Cologne

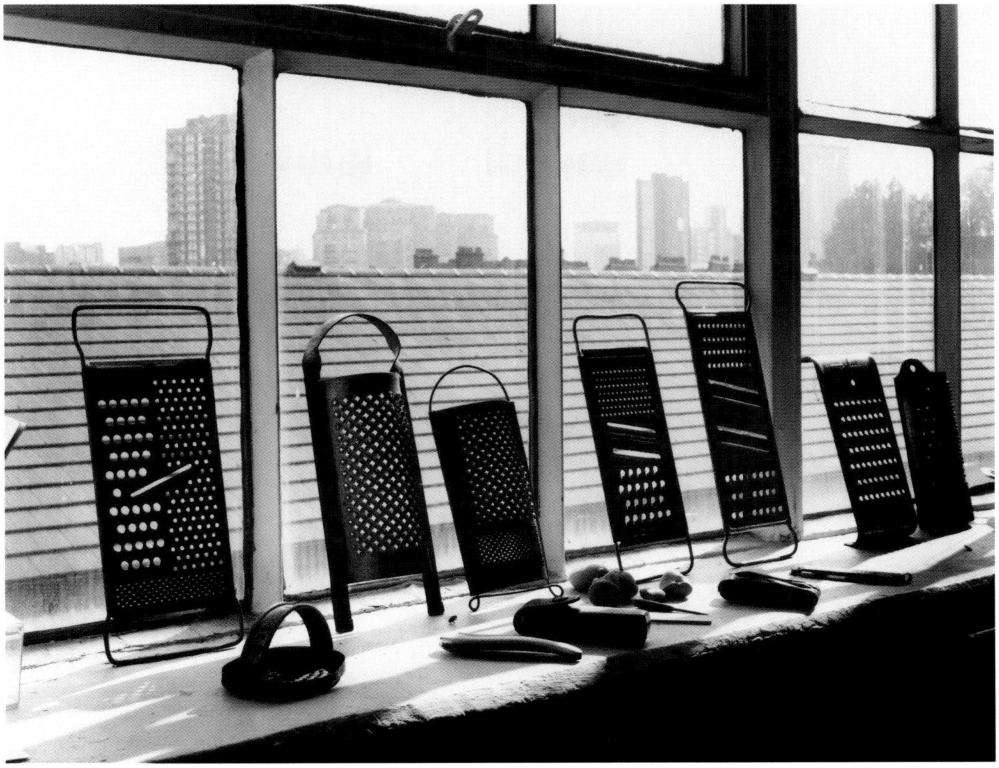

2000
Friends and Neighbours, The 4th EV+A Biennial, Limerick City Gallery of Art, Limerick
Between Cinema and a Hard Place, Tate Modern, London
Orbis Terrarum, Museum Plantin-Moretus, Antwerp
Vision and Reality, Louisiana Museum of Modern Art, Humlebæk, Denmark
No es solò lo que ves. Pervirtiendo el minimalismo, Museo Nacional Centro de Arte Reina Sofia, Madrid

2001
El Instante Eterno/The Eternal Instant: Art and Spirituality at the Change of the Millennium, Espai d'Art Contemporani de Castelló, Castelló, Spain
Field Day: Sculpture from Britain, Taipei Fine Arts Museum, Taiwan
Passage Works from the Collection No. 1, Magasin 3 Stockholm Konsthall, Stockholm
El Mundo Nuevo/The New World, Bienal de Valencia, Valencia, Spain

2002
Documenta 11, Kassel
Another World: Twelve Bedroom Stories, Kunstmuseum Luzern
40 Jahre: Fluxus und die Folgen, Kunstsommer Wiesbaden 2002, Wiesbaden
Comer o no comer/To eat or not to eat, CASA – Centro de Arte de Salamanca, Spain

2003
M_ARS – Art and War, Neue Galerie am Landesmuseum Joanneum, Graz
Il Racconto del filo: Cucito e Ricamo nell' arte contemporanea, MART – Museo di Trento e Rovereto, Trent
(c) EUROPE EXISTS, MMCA – Macedonian Museum of Contemporary Art, Thessaloniki, Greece
Migration, Kunstmuseum Liechtenstein, Vaduz

2004
Made in Mexico/Hecho en Mexico, ICA, Boston
Beyond East and West: Seven Transnational Artists, Krannert Art Museum, University of Illinois at Urbana-Champaign; Hood Museum of Art, Dartmouth College, Dartmouth, Mass.; and Williams College Museum of Art (2005)
Turning Points: 20th Century British Sculpture, Tehran Museum of Contemporary Art, Iran
Trans-cultures, EMST – National Museum of Contemporary Art, Athens

Untitled (graters) · 1999

Solo Exhibitions – Catalogues

Dissected Space, Chapter, Cardiff 1992
Mona Hatoum, Arnolfini, Bristol 1993
Mona Hatoum, Centre Georges Pompidou, Paris 1994
Mona Hatoum, The British School at Rome, Rome 1995
Quarters, Viafarini, Milano 1996
Current Disturbance, Capp Street Project, San Francisco 1996
Mona Hatoum, De Appel, Amsterdam 1996
Mona Hatoum, Museum of Contemporary Art, Chicago, The New Museum of Contemporary Art, New York 1997–98
Mona Hatoum, Kunsthalle Basel, Basel 1998
Mona Hatoum, Castello di Rivoli, Museo d'Arte Contemporanea, Turin 1999
Mona Hatoum: The Entire World as a Foreign Land, Tate Gallery, London 2000
Mona Hatoum, Le Creux de l'Enfer, Centre d'art contemporain, Thiers, Le Collège Éditions, Frac Champagne-Ardenne, Reims, MUHKA – Museum van Hedendaagse Kunst, Antwerp 2000
Mona Hatoum: Domestic Disturbance, MASS MoCA, North Adams; Mass., SITE Santa Fe, New Mexico 2000–01
Mona Hatoum, Sala Mendoza, Caracas, Venezuela 2001
Mona Hatoum, Laboratorio Arte Alameda, Mexico City 2002
Mona Hatoum, CASA – Centro de Arte de Salamanca, Centro Galego de Arte Contemporanea, Santiago de Compostela 2002
Mona Hatoum, MACO – Museo de Arte Contemporáneo de Oaxaca, Oaxaca, Mexico 2003

Selected Bibliography

Janine Antoni, 'Mona Hatoum', *Bomb 63,* Spring 1998, pp. 54–61.
Michael Archer, 'Mona Hatoum: Mario Flecha', *Artforum,* December 1992, pp. 107–108.
Michael Archer, Guy Brett and Catherine de Zegher, *Mona Hatoum,* Contemporary Artists Series, London 1997.
David Barro, 'La ambivalenia perturbadora de Mona Hatoum', *Lapiz* 185, October 2002, pp. 34–43.
Guy Brett, 'Mona Hatoum at the Showroom', *Art in America,* November 1989, pp. 205–206.
Louisa Buck, 'Pass the electric fork, please', *The Art Newspaper* 126, June 2002, p. 36.
Dan Cameron, 'Mona Hatoum', *Artforum,* April 1993, p. 92.
Sara Diamond, 'An interview with Mona Hatoum', *Fuse* 10, no. 5, April 1987, pp. 46–52.
Angela Dimitrakaki, 'Mona Hatoum: A Shock of a Different Kind', *Third Text* 43, summer 1998, pp. 92–95.
Doris von Drathen, 'Fremdheit als Weltsicht', in *Künstler – Kritisches Lexikon der Gegenwartskunst* 51, no. 18, fall 2000.
Catherine Elwes, 'Notes from a Video Performance by Mona Hatoum, Film Co-op 11 July 1980', *Undercut,* London, March–April 1981, pp. 28–29.
Catherine Francblin, 'Mona Hatoum – Sous Tension', *Beaux Arts,* May 2000, pp. 54–59.
Michelle Grabner, 'Positive and Negative', *Frieze* 38, January/February 1998, pp. 70–73.
Paula Harper, 'Visceral Geometry', *Art in America,* September 1998, pp. 106–111.
Nico Israel, 'Mona Hatoum: New Museum of Contemporary Art', *Artforum,* April 1998, p. 114.
Janet A. Kaplan, 'The Quiet in the Land: Everyday Life, Contemporary Art, and the Shakers: A Conversation', *Art Journal,* summer 1998, pp. 5–27.
Lynn MacRitchie, 'Uneasy Rooms', *Art in America,* October 1993, pp. 60–63.
Judith Marth, 'Von der Performance zur Installation am Beispiel Mona Hatoums', dissertation, Hamburg 2003 (typescript).
Silke Müller, 'Mona Hatoum: Geschichte ist ein gieriges Monster', *art,* October 2000, pp. 16–29.
Richard Noble, 'Mona Hatoum: A Living Between', *Parachute* 108, 2002, pp. 178–192.
Alix Ohlin, 'Home and Away: The Strange Surrealism of Mona Hatoum', *Art Papers Magazine,* May/June 2002, pp. 16–21.
Desa Philippi, 'Mona Hatoum. The witness beside herself', *Parachute* 58, April/June 1990, pp. 10–15.
Frances Richard, 'Mona Hatoum', Artforum, January 2000, p. 114.
Claudia Spinelli, 'Ich strebe eine ganzheitliche Erfahrung an – ein Gespräch mit Mona Hatoum', *Das Kunst-Bulletin* 9, September 1996, pp. 16–23.

Photo credits

Guy Brett: pp. 111-112
Lesley Butler: pp. 105, 106 (bottom)
Mimmo Capone: p. 56
Courtesy Chantal Crousel/Kleinefenn: p. 36
Steve Collins, Projects UK Archives: p. 117
Joël Damase: pp. 54–55, 58–59
Iain Dickens: cover, pp. 28/29
Silke Eberspächer, Munich: p. 129
Fotostudio Eshof: p. 73
Arthur Evans: p. 61
Patrick Gilbert (photo), Stephen White (reproduction): p. 82
Hugo Glendinning: pp. 26–27, 34–35, 37
Arturo González de Alba: pp. 39, 42
Mona Hatoum: pp. 11, 18, 32, 64 (top), 68, 68/69, 124 (bottom)
Mona Hatoum / Western Front Video Productions: pp. 1, 14, 45
Mona Hatoum (photo), Christophe Brandt (reproduction): p. 79
Mona Hatoum (photo), Ernst Moritz (reproduction): p. 64 (bottom)
Mona Hatoum (photo), Stephen White (reproduction): p. 65, 141
Christoph Irrgang: pp. 130/131, 132/133
Hirohashi Isao: pp. 4/5, 139
Dan Marmorstein: p. 106 (top)
J. McPherson: p. 93
Eric Metcalfe: p. 104
Philippe Migeat: pp. 16/17, 46–47
Robin Morley: p. 107
Orcutt & Van Der Putten: pp. 23, 60
Carlos Germán Rojas: p. 57
Philipp Schönborn: pp. 48/49
Dieter Schwerdtle: pp. 20–21
Oren Slor: pp. 30, 38
Marcela Taboada: pp. 41, 50–53
Elke Walford: pp. 94/95, 102–103
Stephen White: pp. 12, 33
Paul Whitlock: pp. 126, 128
Edward Woodman: pp. 6, 8, 15, 18/19, 22, 24–25, 31, 62/63, 74, 124 (top)
Corry Wyngaarden: pp. 109, 110

All other images: archive of the artist

Imprint

This book is published in conjunction with the exhibition *Mona Hatoum*

Hamburger Kunsthalle
March 26 – May 31, 2004
Kunstmuseum Bonn
June 17 – August 29, 2004
Magasin 3 Stockholm Konsthall
October 9 – December 18, 2004

Edited by Christoph Heinrich

Hamburger Kunsthalle

Director: Uwe M. Schneede

Exhibition and catalogue: Christoph Heinrich

Junior curator and assistant editor: Nina Zimmer

Proofreaders: Tas Skorupa, Daniel Tsai

Intern: Fiona McGovern

Translations: Pauline Cumbers, Ishbel Flett, Frank Perry, Daniel Tsai

Video technician: Tobias Boner

Registrar: Meike Gerber

Director of specialised services: Anne Barz

Public relations: Martina Gschwilm, Ida Kaufmann, Anuschka Lichtenhahn, Jan Metzler

Conservation: Barbara Sommermeyer, Gerlinde Römer

Set-up: Gunther Kolck

Hamburger Kunsthalle
Glockengiesserwall
20095 Hamburg
Germany
Tel. +49-40-428 131-200
Fax +49-40-428 54-3409
info@hamburger-kunsthalle.de
www.hamburger-kunsthalle.de
Hours: Tuesday–Sunday, 10 a.m. – 6 p.m., Thursday 10 a.m. – 9 p.m.

Kunstmuseum Bonn

Director: Dieter Ronte

Exhibition and catalogue: Volker Adolphs

Set-up: Ernst Nieselt

Technical Assistance: Eberhard Wagner

Registrar: Barbara Weber

Conservation: Gerda Kaltenbruner

Kunstmuseum Bonn
Friedrich-Ebert-Allee 2
53113 Bonn
Germany
Tel. +49-228-77 62 60
Fax +49-228-77 62 20
kunstmuseum@bonn.de
www.kunstmuseum-bonn.de
Hours: Tuesday–Sunday, 10 a.m. – 6 p.m.; Wednesday 10 a.m. – 9 p.m.

Magasin 3 Stockholm Konsthall

Director: David Neuman

Exhibition: Richard Julin (Senior Curator) and Elisabeth Millqvist (Curator)

Exhibition Coordinator: Tove Schalin

Technical Coordinators: Thomas Nordin, Peter Westman

Board of directors, Magasin 3 Stockholm Konsthall: Robert Weil, David Neuman, Amy Simon

Magasin 3 Stockholm Konsthall
Frihamnen
115 56 Stockholm
Sweden
Tel. +46-8-545 680-40
Fax +46-8-545 680-41
art@magasin3.com
www.magasin3.com
Hours: Thursday, 12 noon – 7 p.m., Friday–Sunday, 12 noon – 5 p.m.

Graphic design: Michael Sauer, Hamburg

Lithos: Pallino Media Integration, Ostfildern-Ruit; Beyer Hamburg

Printed by Dr. Cantz'sche Druckerei, Ostfildern-Ruit

Published by
Hatje Cantz Verlag
Senefelderstrasse 12
D-73760 Ostfildern-Ruit
Germany
Tel. +49-711-44 05-0
Fax +49-711-44 05-220
www.hatjecantz.com

Hatje Cantz books are available internationally at selected bookstores and from the following distribution partners:
USA/North America – D.A.P., Distributed Art Publishers, New York, www.artbook.com
France – Interart, Paris, interart.paris@wanadoo.fr
UK – Art Books International, London, sales@art-bks.com
Belgium – Exhibitions International, Leuven, www.exhibitionsinternational.be
Australia – Towerbooks, French Forest (Sydney), towerbks@zipworld.com.au
For Asia, Japan, South America, and Africa, as well as for general questions, please contact Hatje Cantz directly at sales@hatjecantz.de, or visit our homepage www.hatjecantz.com for further information.

ISBN 3-7757-1444-8 (English)
ISBN 3-7757-1443-X (German)

Printed in Germany

Cover:
Grater Divide · 2002 (detail)

Page 1:
So much I want to say · 1983

Page 4/5
+ and – 1994–2004 (detail)

The exhibition was sponsored by:

British Council

Kunststiftung NRW

ZEIT-Stiftung Ebelin und Gerd Bucerius

die tageszeitung, taz nord

Videotronic Nord

and the Berlin Artists-in-Residence Program/DAAD

HOW TO TURN YOUR ORDINARY KITCHEN UTENSILS INTO MODERN ELECTRICAL APPLIANCES

extract from ***Surviving in the 90 s*** by Mona Hatoum

Easy to follow step by step instructions:

- Take your favourite steel colander.
- Take a 2 meter length of dual electrical wire for a light bulb.
- Separate the cords of the electrical wire for a length of about 50 cm down the middle part.
- Cut one of the cords at centre point and connect one end of the cut cord to one handle of your steel colander. Connect the other end to the opposite handle. (see diagram)
- Fit an electrical plug to one end of the wire and a light fitting and bulb to the other end of the wire. The purpose of the light bulb is to indicate when your appliance is on.
- Plug in and enjoy!

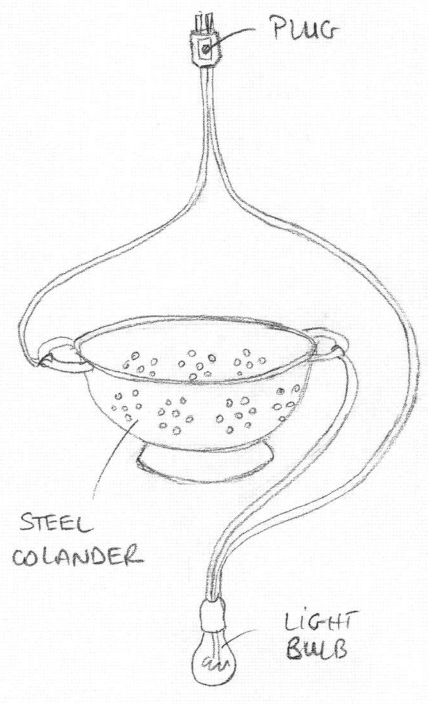

NOT RECOMMENDED:
for anyone who hasn't got a clue!

RECOMMENDED:
for euthanasia enthusiasts.

Next week: hints from ***How to Cook Yourself*** cookbook by Gerry Collins

How to turn your ordinary kitchen utensils into modern electrical appliances · 1996